Indian Fiction in English
Recent Criticism

Indian Fiction in English Recent Criticism

Edited by

Chhote Lal Khatri

ADHYAYAN

ADHYAYAN PUBLISHERS & DISTRIBUTORS
New Delhi-110002

Published by
ADHYAYAN PUBLISHERS & DISTRIBUTORS
4378/4B, 105, J.M.D. House, Murari Lal Street
Ansari Road, Darya Ganj, New Delhi - 110002
Ph.: 011-23263018, 011-23277156, Fax: 23280028
Email: adhyayanpublishers@yahoo.com

Indian Fiction in English: Recent Criticism

Edition 2010
ISBN 978-81-8435-120-0

Printed in India

Published by Harish Chandra Yadav for Adhyayan Publishers & Distributors, Delhi. Laser Typesetting at V. M. Graphics and Printed at Tarun Offset Printers, Delhi

Dedication to

Indian Publishers

Who

Dare

Care

&

Share.

Preface

Indian novelists writing in English have been continuing to make their mark in the global market of novels. With Kiran Desai and Aravind Adiga winning Man Booker Prize in 2006 and 2009 respectively and Chetan Bhagat adding a new dimension to Indian fiction market by manipulating his managerial skills in the making of the novel be it the racy and pulp style, identification with the concerns of the gen-next or the reader friendly price.

Indian novel in English, having got solid socio-political and philosophical basis in the novels of the trio- R. K. Narayan, Raja Rao and Mulk Raj Anand, witnessed a phenomenal growth in the 1980's with the magic realism of Salman Rushdie whose *Midnight Children,* (1981) an international success led to the development of a new idiom and genre of novel. He created a generation of young Indian novelists working abroad who eagerly followed his footstep. They include novelists like Vikram Seth and Shashi Tharoor. The theme of alienation, exile, rootlessness and cultural conflict occupied the centre-stage.

Contemporary to them but a distinct voice is heard in Amitav Ghosh who in the words of A.K. Ramanujan 'evokes things Indian with an inwardness that is lit and darkened by an intimacy with "Elsewhere". He is one of those few contemporary Indian novelists who were praised by C.D. Narasimhaiah.

The contemporary scene of Indian novel in English is

peculiarly dominated by the female writers who are feminist in their own distinct ways. But the struggle for female identity is common in them. Rama Mehta is not a feminist the way it is perceived in the West. But the strong resistance of her protagonist Geeta in her maiden debut *Inside the Haveli* makes her a feminist in the Indian context. Kamala Markandaya, Shashi Deshpande, Anita Desai, Kiran Desai, Jhabvala, Nayantara Sahgal, Suchitra Bhattacharya, Sudha Murty, Namita Gokhale, Shobha De, Arundhati Roy and others have brought about a feminist resurgence in such a big way that even their male counterparts seem to echo the concerns of the women; and it occupies a prominent place in the discourse of literature today.

Despite the fact that Indian novelists have to travel a long way to capture the changing contemporary socio-political and cultural realities in India and the world and to tread in different modes of narrative like humour, children, science, tribal, fantasy, etc., it has proved to be 'the most popular vehicle for the transmission of Indian ideas to the wider English speaking world': (William: *Indo-Anglian Literature*: 109)

Its relevance has got a further impetus and the corpus of fiction got richer with the growing recognisation of fiction in translation. Shivasankara Pillai's Malayalam novel *Chemmeena* in this anthology is a sample to this trend.

These novelists and their works certainly deserve a serious research and evaluation as representative of the post-modern age in cultural terms. The present anthology on Indian fiction in English comprising twenty two papers is primarily focussed on the post 1980's novelists besides giving space to R.K. Narayan, M.R. Anand, Manohar Malgonkar and Kamala Markandaya. It aims at making it an in-depth study of the work/works of eighteen novelists who have the credit of ushering in new trends in the scope and art of the novel keeping pace with the world at large.

I take this opportunity to express my gratitude to the scholars who kindly contributed their scholarly papers to this volume. Finally I am thankful to the publisher Shri Harish

Chandra Yadav for bringing it out so promptly and elegantly. This tribute to Harish Chandra Yadav is a tribute to all Indian publishers who have virtually revolutionized the Indian book market and have at least given scope to creativity and critical talent. Hence, I dedicate this book to Indian publishers.

Chhote Lal Khatri

Contents

1

Traditionalism in R.K. Narayan's Novels

Dr. Shyam Bihari Tiwari

> "The impact of life, the material and substance of our thoughts are the same everywhere, in any state, traditionally India in the *Ramayana,* the *Mahabharata* and the Puranas. The values remain the same in every village town or city." — R.K. Narayan

Unlike M.R. Anand, R.K. Narayan upholds the old traditional values of life prescribed by the ancient Indian culture and embodied in Indian epics, 'Shashtras', 'Puranas', myths and mythologies. Naturally he gives the philosophy of traditionalism which permeates all of his novels. It is the fountain head from which his other philosophical concepts, such as, orthodoxy, superstition and the role of fate in life flow as its inseparable channels.

He presents his concept of traditionalism through the middle-class life of Malgudi, an imaginary small town in South India, which forms the background to all his novels.

> "'Malgudi', says Iyengar, is Narayan's 'Casterbridge', but the inhabitants of Malgudi—although they may have their recognizable local trappings—are essentially

> human, and hence, have their kinship with all humanity. In this sense, 'Malgudi' is everywhere." (Iyengar, p. 360)

Narayan's novels show that success and happiness in life lie in resignation to and acceptance of the *shastra* - approved traditional values. Human life is suggested as a (journey in quest of self-identity or emancipation from the miseries of life. But influenced by man's modernism, ego and *karma* and governed by fate and chance, human life moves in a zig-zag way and at last comes to the same state from which it starts but with man's self-realization of his puny stature and the truths of life in the tradition-bound social set-up. In the novels of Narayan "there is generally a flight," observes Iyengar, an uprooting, a disturbance of order - followed by a return, a renewal, a restoration of normalcy." (Ibid., p. 385) Any deviation from traditional norms results in disruption of regular, normal life. Chandran in *The Bachelor of Arts,* Savitri in *The Dark Room* and Mali in *The Vendor of Sweets* run away in protest against their family traditions, suffer from a lot of troubles and later on come back or are brought back willingly or unwillingly for a life better or worse.

The traditional world of Malgudi does not sanction romantic love, as it has its own custom of arranged marriage which is settled by parents after negotiation and horoscope-matching. Chandran in *The Bachelor of Arts* falls in love with Malathi at first sight and is determined to marry her. But their parents stop marriage negotiation when the horoscopes of Chandran and Malathi do not match. Later on Chandran has to marry Susila, a girl of his parents' choice. Sriram in the novel, *Waiting for the Mahatma* loves Bharati and wants to marry her but the latter gives her consent for this only after obtaining approval from Gandhiji who is her godfather, *guru* and guardian. Bharati acts as an ideal for modern girls by following Indian values and traditions. The marriages between Chandran and Susila and between Sriram and Bharati are supposed to give happiness in life. Unlike Chandran's parents, Margayya in *The Financial Expert* regards horoscope-matching only as a formality in the settlement of the marriage of his Balu with Brinda, the only daughter of a rich man. He says to the astrologer, "Well, probably I shall be able to add a couple of rupees to your usual charges. . . and if alliance concludes successfully, well, of course a lace *dhoti* and all honours for the *pundit*" (*The Financial Expert, p.* 107). At last the horoscopes are anyhow matched. Though Balu and Brinda are married, the consequent events show that their married life is not so happy as it was expected. Brinda has to suffer much on account of Balu's indecent way of life.

Malgudi has its own set sexual ethics according to which sex-aberration or perversion with any motive is bound to end in frustration and misery. Man and woman living together as husband and wife without getting married are regarded as sinners. Hence it is sacrilegious to violate the sanctity of sex.

In the novel, *The Dark Room,* Ramani, a branch manager of Englandia Insurance Company falls in love with Shantabai, the probationary insurance assistant who has deserted her husband. His immoral relation with her terribly upsets his normal family life. Shantabai who tries to thrive on her love with crazy Ramani fails to fulfil insurance business. She is at last forced to leave Malgudi in frustration. Ravi and Sampath in *Mr Sampath* establish immoral relation with Shanti Devi, the actress. Ravi goes mad in frustration and is sent to the police lock-up. Shanti leaves Sampath for good. Also Sampath is forced to leave Malgudi in order to escape the notice of his creditors, Somu and others. When Marco, the husband of Rosie in *The Guide,* comes to know about Rosie's immoral, illicit relation with Raju, he grows angry and leaves her saying: "You are a woman who will go to bed with anyone who flatters your antics . . . I don't want you here." (134) After separation from her husband she lives with Raju as his wife under the assumed name, Nalini without marrying him. Raju's mother who is an orthodox woman is dead against her son's way of life with Rosie. She tells Raju about Rosie: "Why can't she go to her husband and fall at his feet? You know living with a husband is no joke as these modern girls imagine" (*The Guide,* p. 137). She does not want Rosie to stay in her house. But Raju has no regard for his mother's sentiments. Hence she leaves the house for ever. In course of time, Raju's romantic love for Rosie (Nalini) changes into love for money that he gets through her dancing. He exploits her in a variety of ways. Not only this, he possesses Rosie's box of jewellery by forging her signature for which he is arrested and jailed. Rosie (Nalini) severs her relation with Raju at last. Thus romantic love between Rosie and Raju not only causes miseries to them but also ruins their families. Like Raju Mali, the only son of Jagan in *The Vendor of Sweets* lives with Grace, his half-Korean, half-American girl friend without marrying her. This is against the wishes of his father as also against the social and ethical tradition. His son's living in sin terribly offends his moral sense. But their romantic love does not continue for long. Mali is arrested and jailed on the charge of prohibition and thereafter Grace plans to go back to her country. Disillusioned with his life and in desperation against his son's conduct and character, Jagan leaves his home for ever. Raman, the painter of signboards in *The Painter of Signs* is in romantic love with Daisy, an officer of a Family Planning Centre. They do enjoy privacy like husband and wife. Raman intends to marry her, but his orthodox aunt questions: "What is her caste, what is her history? She ran away from home! Don't you know all that?" (p. 154) Thus she opposes Raman's marriage with Daisy because the latter's identity is quite unknown. When she finds Raman adamant, she leaves her house like Raju's mother and goes on a pilgrimage. Daisy first accepts the marriage proposal, though on some unconventional conditions, but later on she changes her mood and leaves Raman saying: "Married life is not for me. . .I can't live except alone" (*The Painters of Signs,* pp. 178-9). She goes away from Malgudi in order to do social work. Both Raman and Daisy thus, remain unmarried throughout their lives. Raman has no one in his family to look after him.

It is, thus, obvious that the people of Malgudi have their roots in traditional family systems and moral codes of conduct against which they cannot revolt for freedom. Their revolts are bound to bring about despair and frustration which amount to their ultimate defeat. In Narayan's novels traditionalism dominates and overpowers modernity whenever there is a clash between them. "Narayan seems to point out, overtly and obliquely, Says Shantha Krishnaswamy, "the value of a heritage, of a past. What the Shashtras have prescribed is good for everybody" (Krishnaswami, p. 96) for a peaceful, harmonious and happy life.

Most of Narayan's woman characters excepting only a few are typically Indian housewives. They are meek, docile, submissive and orthodox having traditional views of virtue and family life. They seem to think that their virtues lie in their perfection in the roles allotted to them in their male-dominated families. As they are fully aware of the fact that the happiness in family life depends on the mutual understanding of husband and wife, they merge their individualities in their husbands'. They avoid quarrelling with them just to preserve the peace of the family life. They appear to be resigned to their fate, but they are the depositories of social and family traditions. Chandran's mother, Susila, Janamma, Ambika and Meenakshi to name a few are to all appearances happy. Janamma, though a minor character in *The Dark Room* gives a clue to the happy married life in a traditional family. She tells Savitri : "As for me, I have never opposed my husband or argued with him at any time in my life. I might have occasionally suggested an alternative. but nothing more. What he does is right. It's wife's duty to feel so" (*The Dark Room,* p. 59). It appears that she is fully aware of and complacent with her duties and status in her male-dominated family. This is why she has adjusted herself to her family customs so as to lead a normal peaceful life. Though Savitri leaves her family as a token of revolt against the brutality and immoral conduct of her tyrannical husband Ramani, she comes back (or is forced to come back) realizing that she can't remain happy in seclusion of her own home and family. Her unconventional manner of resistance to her husband's conduct and character causes her so much suffering that she feels: "I am like a bamboo pole which cannot stand without a wall to support it" (p. 189).

Indian epics, 'Puranas' and '*Shastras*' are the depositories of ancient values of life and moral codes of conduct. Indian myths and mythologies were enunciated by Indian sages, seers and saints who were divinely inspired and blessed. They are commonly accepted and acceptable even today for a peaceful, happy and prosperous worldly life. These epics and Puranas have been sources of moral teachings to common man and of inspiration to the creative writers. Raja Rao in his novel, *The Cat and Shakespeare* refers to the Shiva Purana to show how God is by His very nature, and without any cause, extremely compassionate and supremely benevolent to all. Savitri in *The Serpent and the Rope* symbolizes Savitri of the *Mahabharata.* She saves the spiritual life of Ramaswamy by reminding him of his pursuit of self-realization and illumination. In *Comrade Kirillov,* Raja Rao shows Kirillov's great reverence for Sankaracharya and his *Nirvana Astaka.* Allusion to the *Ramayana* is found in Anand's novel, *Gouri* though with a very different motive. Narayan shows that the values of life preached in our scriptures are still relevant to human life in the present context. Traditionalism becomes more pronounced in Narayan's frequent allusions to myths, mythologies, Puranas and epics in his novels in order to show the content and continuous conflict between good and evil right from the ancient times in which the evil forces however powerful they may be, are ultimately destroyed by themselves or by some invisible power. Vasu, the taxidermist in the novel, *The Man-Eater of Malgudi* is the symbol of evil. He is, indeed, an embodiment of the 'Asura' as described in the sixteenth chapter of the *Bhagavadgita.* He is ugly, ferocious in appearance, amoral by nature and devoid of the sense of gratitude and sympathy. He possesses super human strength and takes cruel pleasure in inflicting pain to others. The novelist has presented him as a man-eater. He says: "The man-eater is a man, not a tiger, an ego-centered man for whom the objective world is non-existent – a modern *rakshasa*

(*Miscellany*, p. 50). He has an insatiable appetite for killing both dangerous and domestic creatures. This is against the ancient Indian philosophy of *ahimsa parmo dharmah*. Not only this, he exploits the people of Malgudi in general and Nataraj, the printer in particular. He silences all with threats. Nataraj, the symbol of Good is too weak and timid to do anything against Vasu. Even then there is a smouldering conflict between the two though Nataraj is always on the defensive. He fails to understand how to face Vasu and get rid of him. But Shastri, the Sanskrit scholar refers to the epics and Puranas to show his faith in inevitable downfall of the evil. He says that Ravana in the *Ramayana* had "enormous yogic and physical power and a boon from the Gods that he could never be vanquished . . . still he came to a sad end" (*The Man-Eater of Malgudi,* p. 96) In the *Markandeya Purana* Mahishasura, had acquired a boon of immortality and invincibility but was killed by Goddess Durga at last.

> Then there was Bhasmasura who acquired a special boon that everything he touched should be scorched. . . . He made humanity suffer. God Vishnu was incarnated as a dancer of great beauty, named Mohini with whom the *asura* became infatuated. She promised to yield to him only if he imitated all the gestures and movements of her own dancing. At one point in the dance Mohini placed her palms on her head, and the demon followed this gesture in complete forgetfulness and was reduced to ashes that very second. (pp. 96-97)

God incarnates Himself from time to time for the redemption of pious souls, for diffusing the light of religion, for the suppression of Evil through the destruction of Evil doers and for infusing love and piety among the people through manifestation of His divine sports on the earth. Vasu plans to kill Kumar, the temple elephant. But he is found dead, the next morning, from concussion in a mysterious way. Vasu's mistress Rangi solves the mystery of his death. According to her, Vasu himself was responsible for his death.

While trying to kill a mosquito settled on his forehead, he slapped it with all his might and killed himself Shastri's remark is that Vasu's fist was meant to batter thick panels of teak and iron. He never hit anyone, in spite of any provocation, because "he had to conserve all that might for his own destruction" (p. 242). Vasu is the modern counterpart of demon Bhasmasura. Both of them are killed at last by the strange powers of their own hands for their unethical, immoral and anti-traditional conduct and character. The novelist seems to show here that even in the modern age there are Bhasmasuras like Vasu heading towards self-destruction for their evil deeds. Shastri says philosophically:

> Every demon carries within him, unknown to himself, a tiny seed of self-destruction, that goes up in thin air at the most unexpected moment. Otherwise what is to happen to humanity? (p. 242)

Allusion to the ancient myth of Ganga-Shantanu mentioned in the *Mahabharata* is found in the novel, *The Painter of Signs* to present similar context but with a slight difference in the ways and motives of characters. Raman, the painter of signs proposes to marry Daisy, an officer of the Family Planning Centre. But Daisy accepts his marriage proposal on two conditions (as against one laid down by Ganga in the epic):

> One that they should have no children, and two, if by mischance one was born, she would give the child away and keep herself free to pursue her social work. . . . If you want to marry me, you must leave me to my own plans even when I am a wife. On any day you question why or how, I will leave you. (pp. 158-59)

Raman like King Shantanu promises neither to interfere with her duties nor to question her activities. In addition to other concepts the novelist intends to place the selfless duty to humanity above worldly pleasures. Thus it is found that through the allusions to the epics and Puranas the novelist juxtaposes antiquity and contemporaneity to show, as M.K. Naik observes, how "the basic imperatives of the human conditions remain the same, in spite of differences in time, place, milieu and even the plane of existence" (Naik, p. 88). Though it amounts to the conservatism of people's thought it undoubtedly shows their devotion to the ancient Indian culture and tradition.

Religion is deep-rooted in Indian life. Indian writers view it from different angles according to their tastes and temperaments. M.R. Anand does not believe in traditional religion and the concepts associated with it such as orthodoxy, superstition and fatalism which in his opinion are the hindrances in the way of human progress. Even then the peasant community in his novel, *The Village* has deep-seated faith in the age-old philosophy of *karma*. Krishna's mother in *Seven Summers* shows her faith in all religions. She yields to all kinds of superstitious beliefs. There are numerous examples to show that his minor characters have faith in religion, orthodoxy and fate. Though the novelist makes them objects of ridicule, he seems to admit that religion, orthodoxy and fatalism are the integral parts of Indian life. R.K. Narayan and Raja Rao, who believe in Indian religion, scriptures and culture and old values of life show in their novels that religion and its constituent parts can't be separated from life. Even though they cause conservatism of thought and some kind of inertness, they give a sort of systematic, normal life in Indian social set-up. Chandran's mother in *The Bachelor of Arts* is conservative and orthodox in all matters. She performs *puja* every morning, with full faith in the protective power of God as also the people of Kanthapura in Raja Rao's novel, *Kanthapura* have faith in their goddess Kenchamma. There are plenty of examples in Narayan's novels to show the religiosity of characters. Superstition, orthodoxy, fatalism, belief in the theory of *Karma* and life after death are implied in Indian religion. Swaminathan, though a child has inherent superstitious belief in the benevolence of God and in His power to turn the impossible into possible. Also Margayya in *The Financial Expert* worships goddess Lakshmi for becoming rich overnight and for this he undergoes a penance for forty days.

When Savitri in *The Dark Room* steps down the river, her conscience pricks because she has talked back to her husband and disobeyed him for which she may be punished by Yama in the *Other World*. She thinks:

> In Yama's world the cauldron must be ready for me for the sin of talking back to a husband and disobeying him. (p. 121)

Malathi's father D.W. Krishan Iyer in *The Bachelor of Arts* says that the marriage between Malathi and Chandran is not possible because their horoscopes do not tally. In his letter to Chandran's father he writes:

> . . . I have known from experience that the marriage of couples ill-matched in the stars often leads to misfortune and even tragedy. (*The Bachelor of Arts*, p. 86)

Velan and other villagers in *The Guide* are of the view that a saint is capable of curing a man of any disease as he has supernatural power for this. They also believe that Raju the saint (or pseudo saint) can do miraculous deed for saving the village from draught and famine.

Ravi's mother in *Mr. Sampath* is highly superstitious. When Ravi goes mad because of his failure and frustration in love for Shanti, she thinks that he is possessed by some ghost. She believes that exorcising can surely restore him to his normal state.

The old priest of the village temple of the Goddess in *The Painter of Signs* is a hypocrite. He says that barren women conceive within thirty days after offering prayers to the goddess for three days. The simple, credulous villagers think that he is a *yogi* who knows the past, present and future. Also Raman prays to Goddess in order to get Daisy as his wife. He mutters: "May Daisy be mine without further delay" (p. 77). One of the flowers falls down from the crown of the Goddess. The priest interprets it as an excellent omen which means success. There are several examples in Narayan's novels to show that superstition is inherent in Indian life.

The adherence of the people of Malgudi to the commonly accepted theological or religious doctrines shows their orthodoxy on the one hand and their traditionalism on the other. When Srinivas in *Mr. Sampath* picks up his tooth-brush and unscrews the tooth-paste top, the old man (his house owner) remarks:

> What is the world coming to? Everybody has taken a fancy to their toothbrushes; they are made of pig's tail. Why should we orthodox, pure Aryans go in for these things? Have you ever tried Margosa or banyan twigs? They are the best and they were not fools who wrote about them in the *shastras*. (*Mr. Sampath*, p. 51)

As mentioned earlier, Raju's mother in *The Guide* and Raman's aunt in *The Painter of Signs* are highly orthodox in their ways of life. Like them Jagan in *The Vendor of Sweets* is against his son's immoral life with Grace. He is haunted by the thought that his pious ancestral house has become polluted. This is why he makes desperate attempts to save himself from moral pollution by locking the connecting door to the room of Mali and Grace. Moreover, he is very dogmatic. He uses shoes made out of the hides of animals who have died natural death.

According to Indian religion and philosophy *karma* and fate play important roles in human life. Though these concepts appear to be inter-dependent, it is an established belief that in this *karma bhumi* fate is determined by *karma*. As you sow so shall you reap is a universally accepted proverb. The exponents of the theory of *karma* hold to the view that the present existence of all individual is the effect of the past and its future would be the effect of its present existence.

After wandering for eight months Chandran in *The Bachelor of Arts* comes home and marries Susila the girl of his parents' choice instead of Malathi. Chandran's mother says:

> You can marry only the person whom you are destined to marry and at the appointed time. When the time

> comes let her be the ugliest girl, she will look all right to the destined eye. (p. 158)

She means to say that the marriage and its time is already settled in heaven. It is only performed on the earth. Nobody can go against what is allotted by destiny.

Raju in *The Guide* attempts several possible explanations for the movement of events in his life. What he says with a painful self-awareness shows his faith in pre-ordained fate:

> It is written on the brow of some that they shall not be left alone. I am such one. . . . (p. 49)

Savitri in *The Dark Room* and Rosie in *The Guide* believe in karmic laws according to which everyone has to bear the consequence of his deeds. She thinks that she has led a religious life and she has not deliberately committed any sin. So she will not be punished in the other world. This shows her staunch faith in the theory of *karma*. When Raju in *The Guide* is arrested on charge of forgery, Rosie (Naliny) tells him :

> I felt all along, you were not doing right things. This is "Karma" what can we do? (p. 193)

Joys and sorrows, rewards and punishment are the results of one's deeds done in the past. The *karmas* of human beings influence, control and condition their lives. Every action good or bad has its reaction. This is shown also by the narrator in Raja Rao's novel, *The Chess, Master and His Moves.*

R.K. Narayan stands contrasted against M.R. Anand in his view of life and death. Anand the anti-traditionalist is of the view that there is only one vast universe with man, woman and other living beings. There are no two worlds, heaven above and the earth below. There is no spiritual world separate from the material world. The soul is the body and the body is the soul. But Narayan who believes in ancient religion and philosophy has an altogether different view of life and death. He says:

> Perhaps death may not be the end of everything as it seems – personality may have other structures and

> other planes of existence, and the decay of the physical body through disease and senility may mean nothing more than a change of vehicle. (*My Days*, pp. 146-47)

This shows clearly his faith in the immortality of the soul as well as in life after death. This concept is found in the *Gita* in which Lord Krishna says that as after rejecting worn out clothes a man takes up new ones, likewise after rejecting worn out bodies the embodied one (soul) unites with other new one.

Narayan's faith in life after death is quite obvious in his novel, *The English Teacher* in which Krishna succeeds in establishing spiritual contact with the spirit of his dead wife through occultism. Though she does not present herself physically, he feels her presence and talks to her. He comes to know from her the nature and meaning of life and death. In answer to one of his questions she says: "ours is also a life of aspiration, striving and joy. A considerable portion of our state is taken up in meditation and our greatest ecstasy is feeling the Divine Light flooding us" (*The English Teacher*, p. 158). Her spirit gives a detailed description of the spiritual world and shows how it differs from the material world. Susila's spirit tells Krishna: "When I think of you or you of me I am at yor side" (p. 160). Krishna is fully convinced of the existence of life after death in some form or the other. It appears that Narayan also has a unique communication with the spirit of his dead wife. Though it seems to be very surprising, it has helped him very much. Narayan himself says: "This outlook may be unscientific, but it has helped me survive the death of my wife" (*My Days*, p. 135).

In addition to this, Savitri's fear of torture in the Other World in the novel, *The Dark Room* and other philosophical musings of other characters on life in Narayan's novels confirm their beliefs in life after death. The comments of Srinivas on the derangement of Ravi's mind in *Mr. Sampath*, show his faith in a series of births. When the tiger (Raja) in *A Tiger for Malgudi* describes the sufferings of his imprisoned life in the cage of a circus, the Master comments:

> You probably in a previous life enjoyed putting your fellow beings behind bars. One has to face the reaction of every act, if not in the same life, at least in another life or series of lives. There can be no escape from it. (*A Tiger for Malgudi,* p. 42)

This shows the Master's faith not only in present and previous lives but also in the *karma* which affects, and shapes life in general. There are numerous examples in Narayan's novels to show that the people of Malgudi have firm faith in religion, orthodoxy, superstition, life after death and karmic laws which they have inherited also from their ancestors. In fact, almost all of his novels present as Graham Greene says "a strong framework of social convention with which the author sympathises but which he does not share. . . But the life of Malgudi . . . proceeds in exactly the same way as it has done for centuries" (*The Financial Expert* vii).

"The institution of sanyasa or the renunciation of worldly goods and attachment," says Luxmi Holmstrom, "is an ideal that remains constant in Narayan's novels." (Holmstrom: 72) According to the Hindu religion there are four stages or *Ashramas* of life — *Brahmcharya, Garhasthya, Vanaprastha* and *Samnyasa* (asceticism). It is only after passing through the first three stages that one can enter into *sanyasa* successfully. Sanyasa, as an ideal of ancient Indian life is very difficult if not impossible. The spiritual motive behind *sanyasa* is the attainment of the salvation of soul through meditation on God as well as self-purification by renouncing material goods, worldly relationship and attachment. But it is found that the characters in Narayan's novels choose this state with different motives.

When Chandran in *The Bachelor of Arts* fails to marry Malathi only because their horoscopes do not match, he renounces his home and family and accepts *sanyasa.* But his renunciation or *sanyasa* is in protest against the traditional norms as also in frustration with life. As the novelist says, it is "a revenge on society, circumstances, and perhaps, too on destiny" (p. 108). Thus his remmciation or *sanyasa* lacks the inherent spiritual motive. Moreover he takes to *sanyasa* without passing through the prior stages of life and hence it is premature. This is why he fails as a 'sanyasi'.

Likewise Raju's mother in *The Guide,* Jagan in *The Vendor of Sweets,* Raman's aunt in *The Painter of Signs* leave their houses in opposition to the anti-traditional, unethical ways of life of Raju, Mali and Raman respectively. But they don't appear to renounce the world willingly in order to attain the salvation of soul which is the only spiritual aim of renunciation or *sanyasa.*

But in *A Tiger for Malgudi,* a tiger and his master, after passing through different *ashramas* or stages of life, accept *sanyasa* at last in the usual, conventional manner of ancient Indian *sanyasis* (ascetics). The novelist gives his own concept of a *sanyasi*: "When one is seized with a passion to understand oneself, one has to leave behind all normal life and habitual mode of thought, one becomes an ascetic. . . *sanyasi.* A *sanyasi* is one who renounces everything and undergoes a complete change of personality. (p. 8)

In this novel the tiger realizes that deep within he is not different from human beings. When the people of Malgudi are terror-struck at the sight of the tiger, a hermit tells them: "You need not fear; he has only the appearance of a tiger, but he is not one — inside he is not different from you and of me" (p. 126). Hence, there is nothing surprising that he accepts *sanyasa* later on. He has human understanding of life and its problems. Though he is fifteen, he is over seventy years in human terms. So the hermit advises him to give up his violent nature and start a new life in an altogether different manner. Subdued by the spiritual power of the hermit, the tiger comes out of the room and follows him wherever he goes. He baptizes the tiger as Raja and accepts him as his spiritual disciple while Raja accepts him as his master. He advises Raja to control his desires, and also preaches sermons about God, religion and life. Thus the master initiates him into renunciation and asceticism. The spiritual teachings of the master bring about a complete change in the life of Raja who renounces his wild life. He avoids going to the forest to hunt animals for food and determines to live on sugar-cane and rice only. Whenever the Master sits in meditation on God, Raja sits beside him. He feels lighter at heart and his physical state becomes secondary. He finds this phase of life quite elevating. Thus Raja becomes a real ascetic spending long hours in his quiet corner behind the shrub. He prefers to go without food. In course of time Raja and his master grow too old to do anything. The master realizes that the time for his *Samadhi* is near. As this state is neither suitable nor possible for Raja, the tiger, the master makes arrangements for Raja to do selfless service to humanity in the zoo. Raja does not want to be separated from his master. Even then he accepts his plan though with a heavy heart. When the head of the zoo asks Raja to enter his cage, the Master says, "Both of us will shed our forms soon and perhaps we could meet again" (p. 152) in heaven. This novel, thus, gives the traditional Indian philosophy of *sanyasa* (asceticism) leading to the salvation of soul from the bondage of body. Also Raja Rao in his novel, *The Cat and Shakespeare* deals with this traditional philosophy of life in a symbolic way.

Thus traditionalism in its varied forms pervades almost all of Narayan's novels. It promotes blind acceptance of the traditional values of life. Though in a sense it amounts to the philosophy of *status quo,* it gives a homogeneous, systematic life. Moreover, Narayan does not appear to support passivity as it is found that his characters are actively engaged in their struggles for existence. His concept of *sanyasa,* slightly different from the Upanishadic *sanyasa,* is conditioned by selfless duty (*nishkam-karma-yoga*). Religion, no doubt makes people orthodox, superstitious, fatalist, etc., but it gives moral strength to human being in miseries and enables them to take a calm view of life. The theory of *karma* which is supposed to mould human fate makes people virtuous and conscientious by injecting moral scruples in them: "Abhor to that which is evil, cleave to that which is good" (*New Testament*).

Works Cited

A I R Interview on 8 September, 1961 published in Writers Workshop *Miscellany,* No. 8, (1961).

Green, Graham, Introduction to *The Financial Expert,* Mysore: Indian Thought Publications, 1989.

Holmstrom, Lakshmi, *The Novels of R.K. Narayan,* Calcutta: Writers Workshop, 1973.

Iyengar, K.R.S., *Indian Writing in English,* New Delhi: Sterling, 1989.

Krishnaswami, Santha, *The Woman in Indian Fiction in English,* New Delhi: Ashish Publishing House, 1984.

Narayan, R.K., *The Financial Expert,* Mysore: Indian Thought Publications, 1989.

Narayan R.K., *The Guide,* Mysore: Indian Thought Publications, 1985.

Narayan, R.K., *The Painter of Signs,* Mysore: Indian Thought Publications, 1986.

Narayan, R.K., *The Dark Room,* Mysore: Indian Thought Publications, 1988.

Narayan, R.K., *The Man-Eater of Malgudi,* Mysore: Indian Thought Publications, 1988.

Naik, M.K., *The Ironic Vision,* New Delhi: Sterling Publishers, 1983.

Narayan, R.K., *The Bachelor of Arts,* Mysore: Indian Thought Publications, 1987.

Narayan, R.K., *Mr. Sampath,* Mysore: Indian Thought Publications, 1986.

Narayan, R.K., *My Days: A Memoir,* Mysore: Indian Thought Publications, 1975.

Narayan, R.K., *The English Teacher,* Mysore: Indian Thought Publications, 1989.

Narayan, R.K., *A Tiger for Malgudi,* London: Penguin Books, 1983.

2

Psychological Suffering in R.K. Narayan's *The Dark Room*

Amandeep Rana

Indian English novel has achieved a significant position in the works of Mulk Raj Anand, R. K. Narayan and Raja Rao. Along with the other two, Narayan is regarded as the founding father of Indian fiction in English. The novel, for these three novelists, is a source of political awakening, social consciousness and spiritual quest. Though all of this 'trio' are basically concerned with Indian life, yet there is a significant difference between their innate attitudes. Anand's romantic cult leans heavily towards the downtrodden. Raja Rao shows interest in the spiritual aspects of life. It is in the novels of Narayan that the middle class Indian life finds an authentic expression. His fiction is remarkable for capturing with ironic humour the human weaknesses of ordinary men and women of his fictitious locale, Malgudi. He is a meticulous recorder of the ironies of life, "a modern story-writer, a realistic fiction writer in English" (*My Days,* p. 102).

Suffering is generally considered as an individual and subjective experience. It is a response to which there are social, physical, psychological and spiritual aspects. During our lifetime, we inevitably have to endure physical suffering such as sickness, injury, tiredness, old age and eventually, death. Psychological suffering, on the other hand, occurs to a person when he fails to fulfil his desires. Every individual has certain desires and almost everyone suffers from a deep feeling of not being enough. When these desires remain unfulfilled, the outcome is psychological suffering. Our desires are reflected by our decisions, and when we make wrong decisions, we suffer psychologically. Psychological suffering is the result of some extraordinary stressful events that shatter our sense of security and make us feel helpless and vulnerable. It may also arise from scolding in public, from asking to do an act which is contradictory to one's beliefs, from not getting the urgently required objects, from inability to care for one's own needs, from inability to participate in hobbies such as children's disruption in play activities, etc. Clash with reality, unpleasant feelings and negative emotions also result in psychological suffering. When our falsehoods clash with reality, we suffer terribly. Psychological suffering may manifest itself in sadness, fear, anger, frustration, depression, hatred and disappointment, etc. Bearing of psychological suffering induces negative behaviour and threatens self-integrity of an individual. The result is a change in relation to feelings of helplessness, value-system, sense of reality and despair. Therefore nobody wants to suffer and everybody looks forward to going to a place where there are no tears, no disappointments, no deaths and, above all, no suffering. This article highlights the theme of psychological suffering in R.K. Narayan's novel *The Dark Room.*

Narayan's *The Dark Room* "examines the marriage relationship in a state of crisis" (Harrex, p. 69), and brings out the psychological suffering of Savitri, the heroine. Marital unhappiness or domestic disharmony is a major cause of psychological suffering. The distasteful domestic situations and incidents result in depression and mental anguish for both, the husband and the wife. In this novel, Narayan has highlighted the miserable condition and helpless lot of Indian housewives in pre-Independence India. At that time, the wives had to depend completely on their husbands, who had all freedom to exercise any sort of cruelty on their wives. This novel draws a "poignant picture of a south Indian middle-class family, in which the wife's life becomes much of a hell, because of the frequent fits of anger, and irritation of her whimsical and obstinate husband, Ramani" (Agnihotri, p. 89).

The novel recounts relationship between husband and wife, what married life has been for Savitri and the kind of person her husband, Ramani is. Ramani represents the male chauvinism established by tradition. Everybody in the house including children, servants and even his wife, live in a state of terror because of his cynical behaviour. He behaves like a dictator and regards his wife merely as a slave. He "is primarily projected through his absolute dictatorship at home and the slavish treatment he gives to his wife" (Dnyate, p. 66). Savitri, on the other hand, is much concerned about all house-members, especially her son, Babu. In the very opening of the novel, Ramani does not bother when Babu feels fever one day and refuses to attend the school. He forces him to get ready for the school, and when Savitri interferes, he commands: "Go and do any work you like in the kitchen but leave the training of a growing boy to me. It is none of a woman's business" (p. 1). Such tyrannical and callous nature of her husband makes her feel sad. She does not understand what to do or what not to do. When "she does not offer any explanation of his bitter criticism of this and that, he is infuriated by her silence and sarcastically observes that she intends to save her energy by being silent" (Sharma, p. 83). Then on the breakfast table, Ramani is not satisfied what he is served with. He scolds his wife shouting that there seems no use of his working hard in the office if he gets such a food to eat. He warns her to prepare the food herself properly if the cook fails to do so. He shouts at her: "I don't know when I shall have a little decent food to eat. I slave all day in the office for this mouthful. No lack of expenses, money for this and money for that . . ." (p. 2).

The condition of the house, in fact, is not normal when

Ramani is at home. He finds fault in almost everything. He chides Savitri and Ranga for not taking care of his dress. His presence in the house means there is no silence at all. The way his old Chevrolet car behaves, every morning when he leaves for his office, symbolizes his grumbling outbursts. Narayan exemplifies: "For a moment Savitri lingered in the doorway to hear the protests and growls of the old Chevrolet as it was taken out of the garage. When the noise of the engine ceased, a calm fell on the house" (p. 4). Similarly, the very sound of his car approaching home is quite enough to get an idea of his mood. Moreover, Ramani neither foretells the arrival of a guest nor does he tolerate any poor show at the dinning table. Any suggestion of giving a prior notice of a guest to his wife makes him furious: "We are not so down-and-out yet as not to afford some extra food without having to issue warning beforehand" (p. 13). Such incidents take place very often and result in a bitter exchange of words between the husband and the wife:

> "But if one should have a lot of food left over everyday?" Savitri had asked once or twice.
> "Throw it into the gutter."
> "Or we can give it to the beggars." Savitri suggested.
> "Certainly. By all means, make it a rule everyday to give some food to the beggars. Remember, if I see any beggar turned away from our door, I shall be very wild." (p. 13)

This is how their domestic life moves on everyday in a routine manner. Savitri feels disillusioned and fails to find any interest in her life. The domestic disharmony and the misunderstanding between her and her husband make her life menial. When she ponders over her relationship with Ramani, she reaches the conclusion that she herself is responsible for her present condition. She realizes that all her suffering would have been averted if she had been asserting and dominating at the early stages of her married life. She thinks:

> "How important she was, she thought; she had not the slightest power to do anything at home . . . she felt she ought to have asserted herself a little more at the beginning of her married life and then all would have been well. There were girls nowadays who took charge of their husbands the moment they were married. . ." (p. 6)

It is, however, true that Ramani is not a villain, but a boss-father and a boss-husband. He "is highly tyrannical and impatient in his attitude towards women and children, and this also accounts for the perpetual clash and tension between him and his spouse" (Sharma, p. 89). Later in the novel, he beats Babu for switching off the lights. Babu is completely unaware of his guilt. His innocence makes Savitri upset and she, at once, gets angry with her husband. "The mother in Narayan's novels has unlike the father, a hidden source of power to remain silent, to suffer and protect her children, to rise to their defence if need arises. It is with the mother that the child feels safe" (Shirwadkar, p. 81). Savitri knows that Babu has no fault at all. She suffers terrible mental anguish. She is "conscious of her identity, self-respect and rights as an individual. But she has adapted herself to the role of a selfless mother and uncomplainingly suffers the tyrannical behaviour of her arrogant, eccentric and self-opinionated husband" (Ramana, p. 52-53). The result is:

> "Savitri rose, went to the dark room next to the store, and threw herself on the floor. Later the cook tracked her down there and requested her to take her food, but she refused. The children came to her one by one and tried to coax her. She turned her face to the wall and shut her eyes." (p. 49)

Savitri is full of grief, and thus, retreats into a dark room after realizing that "her own will and desire have no meaning outside the parameters of her husband's will and authority" (Goyal 8). It underlines and symbolizes her psychological torment, restlessness and helpless lot. The image of the dark room follows her like a shadow wherever she goes. The darkness of the dark room is the externalization of her psychological torment. It symbolizes the possessiveness and oppressiveness of the male smugness that the Indian middle-class women cannot overcome. Savitri, thus, is "the representative of thousands of Savitris of India who suffer mental tortures at the hands of their husbands" (Mohod, p. 77). The frequent quarrels between Ramani and Savitri cause a lot of anxiety and mental torture to their children. Ramani always remains in an unpleasant and angry mood and his lack of cheerfulness creates an atmosphere of tension and confusion at home. The children do not have courage to question him at any level and keep themselves busy with their books when he is at home. Sharma points out:

> "The worst sufferers are the children when the parents quarrel. Obviously Kamala, Sumati and Babu are in a miserable plight when Savitri throws herself in the dark room." (p. 91)

William Walsh calls *The Dark Room* an "account of marriage given throughout from the point of view of the wife, in which the image projected is that of the Indian woman as a victim" (p. 43). Apparently content with the part she is supposed to play, Savitri is increasingly oppressed by her loud, assertive and exigent husband. She is bound to the blind tradition and "when she realizes that her search for independence and personal dignity does not lead her anywhere because the dice is heavily loaded against her, she accepts her fate with calm resignation though an inexpressible despair seeps into her soul" (Goyal, p. 9). Her domestic life, however, completely shatters when Ramani is infatuated with Santa Bai, a new employee in his office. Contrary to Savitri, she is an attractive, pretty and educated young woman. Her glamour, her smartness and her physical and mental charms captivate Ramani, and gradually, there develops a love-affair between the two. Sharma opines:

> "A person, whether a man or a woman generally likes and loves just the antithesis of his or her spouse, and this is true of Ramani also. Therefore, he develops

> the habit of visiting Santa Bai every late evening on his way home from the club; it is impossible for him to go home directly without meeting her. Though moody, dictational, and freakish, she, by virtue of her education, possesses the capability of mastering her moods, and this greatly impresses him because Savitri lacks it completely." p. (94-95)

Santa Bai's authoritative and dominating attitude towards Ramani is even more intense than that of Ramani towards his wife. She commands and uses him the way she likes. By and by, she begins to compel him to spend nights with her. This makes Savitri suspicious and anxious about her husband. When she questions him about this, the result is a quarrel between them. It is now obvious that she feels neglected and unhappy when she comes to know about Ramani's extramarital affair with Santa Bai. A sense of inferiority grows in her and thus adds to her psychological suffering. She begins to consider herself less beautiful and less voluptuous than Santa Bai and thus lives in a state of depression and defeatism.

The tyrannical behaviour of her husband and the subsequent marital disharmony not only cause psychological suffering to Savitri, but also result in her revolt against her husband. She bursts out in a fit of suffering: "You are not having me and her at the same time, understand? I go out of this house this minute" (p. 111). When Ramani refuses to change his ways, she shouts at him: "Don't touch me! You are dirty, you are impure. Even if I burn my skin, I can't cleanse myself of the impurity of your touch (p. 112). These lines by her vividly depict the agonized and tormented wife's rage and anger. Her revolt also underlines an overwhelming despotism of the traditional morality. To quote Narayan: "A wife in an orthodox milieu of Indian society was an ideal victim of such circumstances. My novel deals with this philosophy broadly in the background" *(My Days,* p. 119). In desperation, she decides to leave her home, her husband and her family. She does not want to take anything with her believing that woman can possess nothing in this man-dominated world:

> "Things? I don't possess anything in this world. What possession can a woman call her own except her body? Everything else that she has in her is her father's, her husband's, or her son's. So take these too . . ." (p. 113).

According to Sundaram:

> "This novel is neither a tragedy nor a comedy, but a thing that takes place in every society where the double standards are still valid, and the women are economically so helpless that they just have to lump what they do not like" (qtd. in Mishra, p. 104).

Chapter seven of the novel is a long interior monologue by Savitri which brings out her pathetic condition due to the psychological suffering that she experiences. On her way to drown herself in a river, she is in a state of sheer confusion and perplexity. Narayan describes her condition: "Her mind was numb. Otherwise she could not have walked through the town at midnight. Nothing seemed to matter now, not even one's children. They were after all a husband's. . ." (p. 115). She is surprised at her own behaviour of talking back to her husband. She ponders over her plight; "And I must be someone else posing as Savitri because I couldn't have had the courage to talk back to my husband. I have never done it in my life" (p. 116). She is an ideal Indian wife and can never think of indulging in a controversy with her husband. Thus, after her decision of leaving home and all her possessions, she is at once caught in a conflict between her wifely devotion and her new individual existence. Her mind, like that of Hamlet, is in a state of dilemma – to be or not to be. A. Hariprasanna writes in this connection:

> "There is a conflict within her between the traditional values of ideal womanhood where it is a sin even to talk back to one's husband and disobey him, thus, and her new found individuality." (p. 93)

At the time of her departure from her husband's house, Savitri thinks of living under open sky in her future life.

She is completely unaware of the fact that the situation in her new found individual life can be much worse than her previous life at home. This is exactly what happens. Pallan comments: "Central to the novel is the contrast between the two dark rooms – the one in the house implies a limited privacy and the other in the temple implies a final and frightening choice of asserting individuality" (p. 104). Her loneliness in the temple and the stillness in the air make her suffer terribly. The dark river and the dark night prove her to be more menacing than the darkness of the dark room. Her suffering leads her to the realization that she cannot live alone and needs a support. Her sheer mental grief makes her feel pity for women who live without any support. She laments: "What despicable creations of God are we that we can't exist without a support. I am like a bamboo pole which cannot stand without a wall to support it" (p. 189). Goyal compares Savitri to Ibsen's Nora and comments:

> "In several respects, she reminds us of Ibsen's Nora, who revolts against being treated as a doll, first by her father and then by her husband. But while Ibsen's Nora could afford to leave her husband's house, perhaps never to return or be reconciled to a very selfish person, Narayan's Savitri has to return to her husband's home because of an all-pervading fear of loneliness and abject misery." (p. 9)

According to O.P. Mathur: "Savitri's ultimate triumph is achieved after a great deal of suffering, and it is only a pyrrhic victory, for the heroine is doomed to lead a shattered and partial existence even after" (p. 128). At this stage of the novel, however, it is not only Savitri who suffers terribly. Ramani, at the loss of his wife, also loses his mental equilibrium and realizes that he and the children after all require the support of a housewife. But his psychological suffering is not intense and we only witness a slight change in his approach towards his wife and children. Confused and distressed, he curses Savitri for the humiliating and agonizing situation. On the other hand, Savitri's alienation in the temple's dark room and her loss of identity enforce her to retrace her steps. The children are happy to see their mother back home and Ramani also heaves a sigh of relief. For Savitri, however, there is not much joy in reconciliation as Ramani remains the same person. She feels that an essential part of her is dead. She does not submit to Ramani but submits to her familial obligations. It seems that "centuries of tradition have made the Indian woman the most unselfish, the most self-denying, the most patient and the most dutiful woman in the world, whose pride is suffering" (Pallan, p. 111). Thus, the novel ends on a sad and pathetic note.

To sum up, *The Dark Room* is Narayan's study of human relationships in a the light of husband-wife incompatibility. The novel is remarkable for presenting the helpless lot of women in man-dominated world. Narayan is not a writer of woman class, but this novel takes him very dose to feminist writers who write to raise the voice of suffering women who are the victims of their husbands' dominating attitudes in their domestic lives.

Works Cited

Agnihotri, G.N. *Indian Life and Problems in the Novels of Mulk Raj Anand, Raja Rao and R.K. Narayan*, Meerut: Shalabh, 1984.

Dnyate, Ramesh. *The Novels of R.K. Narayan: A Typological Study of Characters*. New Delhi: Prestige, 2000.

Goyal, Bhagwat S., "Thematic Pattern in the Early Novels of R. K. Narayan," *R.K. Narayan: A Critical Spectrum*, Meerut: Shalabh, 1983.

Hariprasanna, A. *The World of Malgudi: A Study of R.K. Narayan's Novels*, New Delhi: Prestige, 1994.

Harrex, S.C., *The Fire and the Offering: The English Language Novels of India 1935-1970*, Calcutta: Writers Workshop, 1978.

Mathur, O.P., "The West Wind Blows Through Malgudi." *Indian Journal of English Studies*, 19 (1979).

Mishra, Bal Ram. *Ironical Comedy of R.K. Narayan*, Jaipur: Book Enclave, 2002.

Mohod, Veena V[andan], *Social Realism in R.K. Narayan's Novels,* Jaipur: Book Enclave, 1997.

Narayan, R.K., *My Days,* London: Chatto & Windles, 1975.

——, *The Dark Room,* Mysore: Indian Thought Publications, 2000.

Pallan, Rajesh K., *Myths and Symbols in Raja Rao and R.K. Narayan.* Jalandhar: ABS, 1994.

Ramana, P.S., *Message in Design: A Study of R.K. Narayan's Fiction,* New Delhi: Harman, 1993.

Sharma, K.K., "The Male 'Pure Artist' as Feminist: R.K. Narayan's The Dark Room as the First Authentic Exposition of Feminist Consciousness in Indian English Fiction," *Points of View,* xv.2 (Winter 2008).

Shirwadkar, Meena, *Image of Women in Indo-Anglian Novel,* New Delhi: Sterling, 1979.

3

Sense of Endurance in the Stories of Mulk Raj Anand

Prabhat Kumar Thakur

The real place of woman in a traditional Indian society is a burning theme in the fiction of Mulk Raj Anand. His stories present a wide range of women characters, who are typical of the social milieu from which they come. The stories not only display the picture of the self-sacrificing, silent and submissive woman, but also offer an in depth study in human psychology. Anand, a novelist, editor and art critic, had contributed to Indian awareness of this need for social change.

In the short stories of Anand, the image of a caged bird has been obviously used to symbolise the confined and helpless woman. The story that best illustrates this symbol is "Lajwanti." "Lajwanti" is the story of a young, motherless rustic girl, whose husband is away at college. She finds herself an easy target of the amorous attentions of her lascivious, pock-marked brother-in-law, Jaswant. Jaswant is already married but his wife is a cow and is not able to protest against her husband's advance towards Lajwanti. Lajwanti has tried her best to evade Jaswant, she even slapped him when he once tried to approach her. But she finds herself in a helpless state, because her mother-in-law connives at

Jassant's doing. In sheer desperation, Lajwanti runs away to her father's house, but is sent back; and in the end, tries unsuccessfully to drown herself in a well. As she is rescued and gains consciousness, she cries out "There is no way for me . . . I am . . . condemned to live" (Naik, p. 166). The caged mainas which she carries with her in her flight is evidently symbolic of her own situation, but the stark realism of her plight is unmistakable.

Lajwanti is shown trudging along to her father's house in Gurgaon, carrying with her the maina bird in a cage. The trapped, docile and dumb bird symbolise, Lajwanti's helplessness. Lajwanti talks to the maina bird but it only fluttered its wings in the cage. Lajwanti's long absence has raised suspicions at home and Jaswant had set out to search for her. When Lajwanti heard Jaswant calling at her to stop at once "she merely ran with the instinct to fly, to get out of his reach (p. 88). The maina bird also fluttered its wings wildly and apprenending danger it shrieked and cried. Jaswant ran after Lajwanti like a wild beast. He caught hold of her and twisted her wrist. She tried to get away from his grip but he over-powered her. She sat dumbly, suppressing even her sobs. A large crowd gathered but none intervened. Luckily an engineer and his wife who were passing by come to Lajwanti's rescue. The engineer's wife heard Lajwanti's story and managed to send back Jaswant. She allowed Lajwanti to proceed to Gurgaon, to her father's house.

When Lajwanti arrived at her father's house, with the caged maina in her hand, she was not welcomed by her father. Her father dared not look at her face, because a daughter coming home without due ceremony was inauspicious. She was offered a mat which was given only to guests, indicating, that now this was not her home. She was like a guest and was supposed to go back to her husband's home. Her father took her back to her in-laws' home. On the way the maina in the cage looked as if it were dead. The bird seemed still and Lajwanti spoke to her in wordless word "My maina tell me what will happen now? My heart flutters, as you often do when you are frightened of the cat coming to eat you. And I do not know if Jaswant will relent and not pursue me any more. But perhaps now that my father has brought me up like her, husband Kirodhar would never know that he (the lover) was the father of Phalini's son." Phalini often dreamt of her lover and for days she had scanned the horizon of the sky above the city towards the north in the direction where he had gone. But he didn't seem to be anywhere in the large breathless space. Again the symbol of the caged bird is used to describe Phalini's helplessness as a sense of endurance. Phalini thought that her lover was "wandering perhaps happy and free, while she was caged here with her child" (p. 47). Phalini's grief is further aggravated with the death of her son. Her piercing shrieks tear the ceiling as she wails over the dead child. Crazed and agonized, Phalini tears her hair, there is no escape from this pathetic state of affairs. Phalini, the caged bird, "slapped her cheeks and beat her palms on her breast crying in a weird low voice "Hai Hai" (p. 42).

In the story "Parrot in the Cage" the sense of endurance in the form of a caged bird is very clear. The story presents Rukmini an old woman who has lost her all in the holocaust of the Partition of India and whose sole companion during the migration from Lahore to Amritsar is a pet parrot. Like the maina in the previous story, the parrot here carries a symbolic suggestion; it perhaps shows how the old woman's deprivation is so total that her nearest and dearer now is not a human being but a bird. The parrot is caged and alone and keeps asking Rukmini "Where are you going?" and "What are you doing?" But Rukmini is not able to give him a satisfactory answer, for she herself doesn't know where she is going and what she wants. She goes to meet the Deputy Commissioner who might rehabilitate her. But the Commissioner is dismayed by showing no concern to her. Rukmini is caught in a street violence and a lathi charge by the police. Fortunately she was saved by someone in the crowd. A gram seller makes her sit under the shade of a nearby tree. The parrot's monologue "Ni to Kithi hai?" continues and seems to air the old woman's feeling of insecurity and displacement. She feels lost and alone and this is expressed by her anonymous, meaningless replies, "Nowhere, son, nothing nothing . . ." (p. 111). Just as the parrot is caged and firmly singing the same old question. Similarly the old woman is alone and there is no way to escape from her miseries and loneliness. The story ends at the pathetic moaning of the old woman "I don't know where I am! I don't know . . ." (p. 114).

"Birth" also presents the sense of endurance. Parvati, a poor peasant woman in an advanced state of pregnancy is compelled to work at breaking stones, owing to the strained circumstances of the family. The birth-pangs start as she is proceeding to her work alone; but, in this hour of trial she refuses to panic. Her father-in-law, kept a respectable distance from her, he was almost lost to view. Parvati had been blamed by her mother-in-law, for bringing decline of the whole family. When Parvati married Ramu and entered the house as a bride, her father-in-law had to mortgage the land. But at the moment, her father-in-law's concern was more for the son's son that Parvati might bear for him, than for her. Parvati, a truly traditional Indian woman, also believed that if she would be able to give the old man a grandson it might compensate him for the slow agony of his ruin through the debt and the draught. Even when the birth pangs become intense, "she stamped the earth, as though to beckon it, as Sita had done asking it to open up, but she steadied a little" (p. 54). She could see her father-in-law like a speck of dust away ahead of her. Her native, rustic ruggedness is reinforced by an inner strength derived from her deep-seated, simple peasant faith in the gods. As she lies writhing on the ground, she sees a vision of Goddess Kali in the sky above. This gives her so much courage that when the child arrives she is even able to manage the necessary midwifery herself. At this moment of crisis, "she was gasping for breath, a helpless grey bird, smothered by the overwhelming forces that rose from her belly" (p. 55). She thinks of Ramu who had rushed off to work, leaving her to bear the pain all alone. She longed to touch a sympathetic hand or limb or anything while the excruciating pain gnawed at her entrails. But soon, like a traditional Indian woman, she cursed herself for thinking ill of her husband, the Lord and Master, whom her parents had married off to and whom they expected her to worship. Once again the picture of a poor woman suspended between life and death is shown smothering like a helpless grey bird. At the end of the story we find Parvati putting the baby boy in her basket and going to break stones again. Her father-in-law shows least concern for Parvati. He picks up the boy from the basket and hopes that perhaps his coming there would turn luck in favour of them.

A different mood characterises "A Village Idyll", a story most appropriately entitled. It gives a delightful picture of youthful love in a rural setting. A lyrical nature description is a remarkable feature of this story. Anand again uses the bird symbol to show the status assigned to Govind and Gauri in a traditional Indian social set up. The lovers meet at the village pond and the lentil fields. Gauri, veiled in sheaths of innocence, smiling dimurely, is impatiently pursued by Govind. "He leapt towards her like a tiger towards a young doe" (p. 62). As the lovers rejoice in the delightful setting, Govind is shown protecting Gauri from Lehna, the son of the village landlord. When Govind sees Lehna at a little distance away "Govind flapped his arms like a protective male bird covering his mate under his wings for Lehna was his rival. Gauri snuggled up to him, like a cooing female bird" (p. 63). The symbols of the tiger, male bird, young doe and cooing female bird are highly suggestive of the characteristics attributed to Govind and Gauri.

In the story the "Tamarind Tree" a young and expectant mother cannot satisfy her longing for the taste of the sharp, sweet tamarind fruit. At her in-law's home, she wss kept veiled under her head cloth. She kept her face covered with the head cloth against possible stare. Her lips had become pale, dried by sighs and muffled breath in which she uttered words in answer to others from behind her head cloth. The picture of the veiled Roopa resembles a stifled bird in a cage. The image of the caged bird is suggestive in this story. Roopa remembers with a heavy heart, her days as a girl, when she jumped, capered, ran and climbed trees. Now as a daughter-in-law her childhood innocence and freedom was abandoned. Even now as a bride she is unhappy that the fear of elders and the weight of conventions and traditions have made it impossible for her to communicate with her husband. She is greatly disappointed to see "that her inner impulses always remained where they were, incommunicable even to her man. She felt she wanted to cry. And she covered her face so as not to be seen in her weakness. She strangled the cry in her belly. "Despite her efforts to obey and please her in-laws she is rebuked by them. In desperation, she rushed to the inner sanctum of the barn and lay down on the bridal bed that had come in her dowry. The traditional Indian woman is again shown suffering in silence, sacrificing her desire, spending her days like a helpless caged bird, with no freedom to spread its wings.

In the "Silver Bangles" on her betrothal by her mother is unjustly accused by the lady of the house, Mrs. Goel, of having stolen the bangles. At the end of the story it becomes clear that Mrs. Goel who is sexually frigid is actually jealous of the attraction, her husband feels for the sweeper girl. Her accusations at Sajani are aimed only to hide her own sense of inferiority against the untouchable beauty. Giving vent to her complex Mrs. Goel, sighs "Oh between me and this bird here, there stands a shadow of despair . . ." (p. 276). Mrs. Goel screams at Sajani, "Go get out and never enter this house again! Thief you have not only stolen the bangels but also my . . . (p. 282). Sajani bears the humiliation in silence and lowers her head "as a dove up dives off the earth to fly across the valley, threatened by a rough wind . . ." (p. 282) and quietly went out of the house.

These tales of pathos present the sense of endurance. Lajwanti, Roopa, Rukmini, Parvati, Sajani and similar women of Mulk Raj Anand represent typically a hopeless status of woman in tradional Indian society. In the book, *The Brides Books of Beauty* Anand gives a very real picture of the low status of women in India. *The Brides Books of Beauty* was published in 1947 but it holds true even today "obviously, woman in India has sometimes been exalted as a goddess, but mostly pampered as a doll or kept down and oppressed . . . the Indian woman merely drifted along and became bound to men, more and more as a slave, less and less as an individual apart . . ."(1947, p. 30).

Anand, the champion of the downtrodden, outcastes, waifs and derelicts, does not fail to picture in his short stories the predicament of woman who is another pitiable prey to the rigid social order. He gives a realistic picture of the inevitable struggle of women against the degradation of the female by the male chauvinists in our country. Anand does not stop merely with the portrayal of human problems. As a responsible artist he suggests various solutions to the different problems carefully refraining from imposition of any kind. As said earlier Anand is certain that the cause of all human misery 'is man's inhumanity to man.' A careful study of Anand stories reveals to us his vision of life, his masterly treatment of social evils and the solutions that he suggests for all problems. Anand is certain that the protest is the preliminary requisite to break down all barriers of evil and pave the path of progress. Anand is more effective when he simply interprets life as it is. This is especially true when he depicts women and children.

Thus Mulk Raj Anand focuses on the woman's predicament and struggle to find an identity for herself. Disappointed by the rigid social pattern, gender bias and her own petty human foibles the woman presents the sense of endurance.

Works Cited

Anand, M.R. and Krishan Hutheesingh, *The Bride's Books of Beauty* (Bombay, 1947).

Naik, M.K. ed., *Selected Short Stories of Mulk Raj Ansnd,* Arnold Heinemann (New Delhi, 1947). (All the subsequent references are given in parentheses)

4

The Plural Self: Shashi Deshpande's *Small Remedies*

Namrata Rathore Mahanta

This paper attempts to study Shashi Deshpande's *Small Remedies* as a representation of the contradictory pluralities that form the images of women in Indian English literature and as an attempt to string together varied selves of womanhood to accept a multi-dimensional reality. The paper begins by tracing the images of the two central characters in the novel – Savitribai and Leela. The multiplicity in these images is accounted for in the memories these characters had left behind with the people in their lives. The role of imagination in translating experience into memory is the crux of the problem. Deshpande creates one image only to replace it with the next. Using the analogy of music, she declares that experience alone cannot authenticate. It is one's own rendition of experience that forms one's "truths". The paper attempts to establish that with *Small Remedies* Shashi Deshpande has broken away from mono-dimensional representation of women as victims/dissidents/achievers against a socio-cultural backdrop and has brought into the arena of Indian English literature unique direct images of plurality within womanhood.

> There are so many selves in us which are called forth by other human beings, selves which are dependent on others for their existence . . . Sometimes I wonder whether there is, in fact, a pristine self in us, which will be revealed only when we are totally isolated from others. Or, whether without others, we are nothing. A blank slate. (p. 170)

Shashi Deshpande's novels are well known for their representations of women as victims/dissidents/achievers, against specific socio-cultural backdrops. With *Small Remedies,* Deshpande has brought into the arena of Indian English literature unique, direct images of plurality within womanhood. At the core of the narrative are two women: Savitribai Indorekar, who is obsessed with music, and Leela, a passionate believer in the communist world-view. Both women start their lives within orthodox, conventional family set-ups but break away from their families to devote themselves to their respective passions in life. Savitribai Indorekar started her adult life as a dutiful daughter-in-law in an orthodox Hindu household. Later, she eloped with her Muslim lover and accompanist Ghulaam Saab, whom she deliberately kept in the background while she scaled great heights of fame and success. Leela devoted herself to the Party. She worked closely with the factory workers of Bombay and later married a Christian widower called Joe.

The personalities of these two women are analysed and presented through Leela's niece Madhu. Madhu sees these women as they are remembered by the various people connected with them and what emerges is a striking plurality of selves. The idea that the two women have of themselves and the idea that their family, friends and admirers have of them is often in sharp contrast.

Madhu, the narrator, is also represented in many ways: the motherless child, the young independent woman working for *City Views,* Som's wife and most importantly, as Aditya's mother. The changes that these multiple roles bring about in Madhu serve to foreground the stories of Savitribai and Leela.

Savitribai's first encounter with Madhu is in a remote town, Neemgaon. Savitribai is accompanied by her daughter Munni, and Ghulaam Saab. Madhu befriends Munni. After her father's death, Madhu leaves Neemgaon and goes to stay with Leela and Joe. Many years later she spots Munni on a bus but Munni refuses to recognise her. Munni had framed a new life for herself, totally rejecting her connections with Savitribai. Accepting Madhu's presence in her life could open up those connections once again, so Munni blocks her with steely silence and non-recognition.

Munni wanted conventional social respectability. So she rejected everything associated with her mother - music, genius, ambition, freedom. She even rejected the name her mother had given her — "Indorekar" — the name Savitribai had adopted as a singer, marking Munni out as her child alone: neither the child of her marriage, nor the child of her lover. But Munni's quest for self led her away from Savitribai:

> For Munni, the self that she saw as her own lay in the future, it was towards that self that she moved with deliberation . . . an ordinary looking woman with an ordinary family life and a name so ordinary that it covers pages in the telephone directory. (p. 120)

However, in Savitribai's death Munni had that identity thrust upon her: "Shailaja Joshi the only daughter of Savitribai Indorekar" — this newspaper notification of her mother's death gave her back the identity she had resisted all her life.

Madhu goes to Bhavanipur to meet Savitribai and to write her biography. There she comes to know how Savitribai successfully obscured Ghulaam Saab and Munni from her life once she was established in the world of music:

> She clings fiercely instead to her respectability, the respectability she claimed in her second birth as a singer, when, after a gap of two years, she reappeared in public view, wearing at that first public performance the mangalsutra of the married woman . . . her lover

and . . . her daughter, no longer part of her life. (p. 167)

Madhu is shown turning over each of these numerous images associated with Savitribai. She is to write her biography and does not know how to accommodate all these facets. The publishers want a story of heroism, Savitribai wants it to be a record of her brilliant career with no space devoted to her life before she become an established singer. Madhu deliberates over what the truth is. She finds that the truth of all these images cannot be denied. It is memory and the mind that excludes one from the other in order to spare itself the pain associated with it.

This pattern is repeated in Leela's story. She too had many facets to the life she lived. Leela who was Vithal's wife, Leela who worked to bring up her two young brothers-in-law after Vithal's death, Leela who married Joe, Leela to whose care Madhu's father entrusted her in his will, and Leela who was the rebel of the family. Madhu goes over various aspects of the lives of Savitribai and Leela as she grapples with the question of the rendition of truth.

This quest is not only of purely academic concern for Madhu. It is a part of a healing process for her. She has lost her only son and the security of the relationship she shared with her husband Som. She relates a nightmare to Som and with it pours out another incident, a sexual encounter which occurred when she was over-wrought with grief because of her father's death. Som cannot handle it and it breaks into a maddening quarrel. Her son Aditya comes in and is sent away. Dumbfounded and shocked, Aditya leaves the house and is consequently killed in a bomb blast. The guilt and her exclusion from the experience of death does not allow her to reconcile with her loss. She compares Aditya's death to Leela's. Madhu remembers that she was by Leela's side as she moved towards death and hence could cope with its terror and pain. Aditya's death was sudden, she was not with him to share his pain. Describing the times she shared with Leela on her deathbed, Madhu records her lack of fear and pain:

> When finally I wipe my tears, and hers as well, we are both relieved. And lighter. We've crossed the hurdle of fear – the fear of death, of parting, of loss, we've accepted all these things. We are together after this, sharing the experience of her dying. I can come to terms with her death, because I am part of it. I know now that it helps. (pp. 232-33)

Madhu's own life and the lives of Savitribai and Leela each demand a resolution. Savitribai's biography demands it. Hari wants to know Leela as Madhu knew her. He has the picture of a fireband communist in his mind but the picture of Leela that Madhu has in her mind is entirely different. Chandru wants to know what is wrong between Som and her and she cannot give an answer because she realizes that such answers cannot be in black or white.

There is always a haze of grey where memory constructs different shades. This emphasis on blurred outlines and shades of grey is replicated in the example of Hasina, who is Munni's daughter and the granddaughter of Ghulaam Saab. In the last year of his life Ghulaam Saab spoke to Hasina of Savitribai, they listened to her records and cassettes together as a part of Hasina's training. Hasina recounts to Madhu the pain Ghulaam Saab suffered when Munni left him for her 'father', Savitribai's first husband who was in Pune. Hasina is not bothered by questions that sprout in Madhu's mind. Her idea of her mother Munni is circumscribed by her grandfather's love for her, his grief on loosing her. The information Hasina offers to Madhu about Munni is actually a replay of Ghulaam Saab's recollections. Hasina loved her grandfather so much that to her, his 'truth' was the only 'truth': "I want you to know the truth . . . I want you to know the truth . . . I want you to write the truth . . ." she tells Madhu. Madhu has finally arrived at an understanding of the "truths" one speaks. She realizes that a person's "truth" is constructed by one's own memory:

> Hasina is offering me her truths about her grandfather, but she calls it 'the truth', she wants me to accept

> it as *the truth.* I think of the seven blind men trying to describe the elephant, each one making a different discovery about the animal, each convinced that his knowledge about the elephant is the entire truth. (p. 278)

Thus Madhu concludes that no vision or perspective is perfect and complete, no understanding can be total and final. Through Madhu's dilemmas and the final articulation of her resolution, Shashi Deshpande has raised the question of the plurality of discourse. Since her writings deal with women and their portrayal, it is all the more important that this plurality be acknowledged. There can be no fixed attitudes, no watertight compartments for discourses. Shashi Deshpande challenges this kind of classification. No feminist, marxist or psychological perspective can attempt to discover the truth. Each view has to be seen in the light of the other so that there emerges a unified whole. The task of the writer is to create a whole out of the available fragments:

> The tail, the trunk, the ears, the legs – yes, I have to put them together, I have to create an elephant out of these disparate bits. (p. 278)

There has been an overriding academic effort in the past years to classify Shashi Deshpande into the category of feminist writing. With this book Deshpande not only defies any such classification but puts a question mark on this practice of compartmentalization of discourse.

Works Cited

Deshpande, Shashi, *Small Remedies,* New Delhi: Viking-Penguin Books, 2000.

5

V.S. Naipaul: The Agony of Isolation

Sadhana Chaturvedi
Miss Veena Shukla

In a universe that is suddenly deprived of illusion and of light, man feels a stranger. His is an irremediable exile. (Camus, p. 86)

Love of home and the anguish of exile have been among the basic human emotions in civilized societies. The ethos of the Western world has been dominated by the Biblical myth of the banishment of Adam and Eve from their first abode of bliss. It is a powerful symbol of the feeling of exclusion, of exile, from some perfect home that seems to be deeply embedded in the human psyche and finds expression in the literature and mythology of many societies. Significantly, Adam and Eve as the first exiles place at the very heart of Western man's cultural history the feeling of alienation that is seen to be a twentieth-century perception of man as an exile in an alien universe. In our own country the lament for the lost "Ram Rajya" or for a "Satyuga" can be seen as a parallel to the Lost Paradise motif. The same feeling is expressed by Eugene Ionesco in an essay on Kafka: "Cut-off from his religious, metaphysical and transcendental roots, man is lost . . ." The uprooted, dispossessed colonial, as well as the individual as an exile in an alien universe Naipual's fiction speaks directly to both, one shadowed in the other.

Exile and home are two faces of the same coin—the full meaning of one can be grasped properly only in relation to the other. Home is not simply where one lives. It is one's identity—national, cultural, spiritual. Home is where one belongs to—it is the soil that has nurtured one's body and spirit. It is the language one speaks and the food one eats; it is the trees and the flowers and the animals and insects and the rivers and the mountains that have also been there; it is the rituals and the do's and don'ts, the joys and the sorrows and all the sights, smells and sounds that lap one's childhood and form part of one's growing consciousness. Home is security. Exile, the loss of home, first reveals to secure the meaning of what is lost. Exile is literally an uprooting and often as withering in its effect on the mind and spirit which is deprived of the sustenance it has drawn from native soil. Home is above all that ambience in which one's childhood has flowered and matured into youth.

This, needless to say, is an idealized concept of home and as an ideal it is seldom fully realized. Not uncommonly a sense of emotional alienation even in one's own country can lead to a desire for escape and this has often forced people into physical exile—artists and political idealists in particular. Such alienation, however, is usually a reaction against a particular social or political set-up and often leads to an even stronger attachment to the unfulfilled ideal, usually finding an outlet in expressions of love for the land and the language. The situation in South Africa is perhaps a case in point. In his story "In a Free State" Naipaul talking of the capital of an African state says: "Everyone in it was far from home." In the same connection Gerald Moore writes in *The Chosen Tongue*:

> If there is one characteristic that all South African writers, of whatever class or colour, have in common, it is a kind of struggling, semi-articulate patriotism;

> a common feeling . . . that South Africa, if only it could be otherwise, is incomparably the finest country in the world to live in. (Moore, pp. xv-xvi)

In India, Africa and South-East Asia colonial education alienated men from their own culture and traditions and made them exiles in their own lands. Industrialization and urbanization also caused the people who have been rooted in their villages to move towards the city in search of jobs and property. The anonymity of city life imposed on the villager as bleak an experience of exclusion as any exile can ever feel in an alien land. Homelessness seems to be the condition of the modern man.

In our century, the exile, far from being a solitary an exotic figure has become the type of modern man. It is to this worldwide crisis of homelessness that Naipaul's work is a sensitive response—taking into its sweep both the causes and consequences of the situation. He has no comforting message, only the bleak knowledge that in today's rapidly changing world the yearning for permanence can never be more than an unfulfilled ache—"everyone is far from home."

It is true that separation enforces the meaning of home more acutely on the exile. However, as Naipaul realized early on, the exile, cut off from the people he writes about, cannot go on indefinitely producing novels about them. C.L.R. James, a west Indian writer, has stated the problem clearly:

> The majority of us (writers in exile) keep on talking about the only subject which really explodes in our hearts—our native land. But as it becomes more and more of a dream its contours fade, and when our people at home read what we have written about them, they cannot recognize themselves any more. (James, p. 24)

The writer who is far from his country stands both to gain and to lose by his enforced distance from his subject-be it his home society or his host society. The situation of the west Indian writers, almost all of whom have been forced to leave their native places, illustrates in an acute form the dilemma of the writer.

V. S. Naipaul is the product of a distinctive combination of circumstances. A brahmin Hindu born in Trinidad, he is an Indian by ancestry, a Trinidadian by nativity and British by residence as well as intellectual training and inclination. Most of Naipaul's writing issues from a desire to understand his own position in the world. The unique combination of circumstances which related him to three societies and yet left him with a deep sense of homelessness, undeniably play a predominant part in shaping his sensibility and determining his writer career. He has said: "When I speak about being exile or a refugee, I'm not just using a metaphor" (Webb, et al., p. 34) He was born into exile, separated from his racial and cultural roots. He was driven into another exile from the land of his birth. A third dispossession awaited him in England. He was really and truly "lost". And then he set out to discover himself and his world through his work. The truth in the case of Naipaul's exile did not begin when he left Trinidad in 1950; it began six years earlier, when as a boy of twelve he became conscious of a discontent so deep that he felt impelled to record in his school book a vow to leave Trinidad within five years.

Naipaul's rejection of the West Indies is not due to his Western bias alone. To a large extent, even his Indian heritage, however incapable of providing him with a sense of identity, obstructed the way to a full commitment to Trinidad and the West Indies. Similarly, the west Indian and east Indian components of his personality make him a perpetual outsider in England. After thirty years of residence in England he says: "Living here has been a kind of castration really (Naipaul *Newsweek,* p. 38).

Naipaul's admiration for culture, has always been clear-eyed about his own fundamental distance from it: "London is my metropolitan centre; it is my commercial centre; and yet I know that it is a kind of limbo and that I am a refugee in the sense that I am always peripheral. One's concerns are not the concerns of local people" (Naipaul, C.P.N., p. 41).

He did have a special concern for Indian and thought of it as partly his country. But a confrontation with the reality of Indian showed him how much he had been made by Trinidad and England. Thus Naipaul remains an utterly deracinated man, truly homeless, an absolute exile.

In his novels he has charted the course of his self-discovery from a search for identity to the complete desolation of a realization of permanent exile and exile makes for total self-awareness. In Naipaul it has meant a clear-eyed assessment of his position as a writer. It made him aware that he was using a form, and a language forged by one kind of society to depict a completely different society. He realized that he would have to seek his own literary tradition. The isolation of exile led also to an intense political awareness, to the perception "how much one's concerns in the world are founded on one's political assumptions about the world" (Ibid, p. 40). As an exile himself, the subject engaged him deeply in a personal way. At the same time, as an outsider in all societies he had the necessary balancing detachment. The impetus behind his work has been a kind of compulsion to understand his own situation; it is through his writing that he arrives at a vision of modern homelessness as a product of historical forces; to an acceptance of his own homelessness as final; and to a perception that his own plight was not singular but typical of the post-colonial world. Naipaul's perception of and anguish at his own displacement and rootlessness is central to his creative talent. It has been the stimulus as well as the subject of his work.

Naipaul in his writings begins with an insistent return to the home territory in his early works—these novels are a meticulous reconstruction of the background and the birth place he had rejected. In his later work he moves on "half-made societies that seemed doomed to remain half-made" and to questions about the meaning of history and civilization.

Works Cited

Camus, A., *The Myth of Sisyphus,* cited in *The Glossary of Literary Terms,* ed. M.H. Abrams.

James, C.L.R. cited by Sylvia Wynter in "Reflections on West Indian Writing and Criticism", *Jamaica Journal,* 2 No .4 (December 1968).

Naipaul, V.S. (interviewed by Edward Behr), *Newsweek,* 18 August 1980.

Naipaul, V.S. (interviewed by Ian Hamilton), *Critical Perspectives on V.S. Naipaul,* ed. R.D. Hamner.

Webb, Peter, Edward Behr, and Robert Kirkland, "The Master of the Novel", *Newsweek,* 18 August 1980, cited in subsequent references as *Newsweek.*

6

From Bride to Boredom: A Study of Jhabvala's *Esmond in India*

P.K. Singh

Ruth Prawer Jhabvala is a major novelist writing in English today. However, her position is unique. She is not only different from Indo-Anglian novelists like R.K. Narayan. Anita Desai and Kamala Markandaya, but also from Anglo-Indian novelists like Rudyard Kipling, E.M. Forster and Paul Scott because of her cultural segregation. She has been an expatriate right from an early age. She is a Pole by parentage, a German by birth, an English woman by education and an Indian by marriage. At the age of 24 years amid the prime of her youth in the year 1951, Ruth Prawer left Britain for India as the lovely bride of C.H. Jhabvala, a young and youthful architect, stayed here for the next 25 years and made possible the publishing of her early short stories in *The New Yorker, Cosmopolitan, The Cornhill Magazine* and *Encounter*. She has said, looking back, that "as a writer I consider myself exceedingly fortunate to have come here when I did and the way I did" (Agrawal, p. 36). Her description of this first encounter with India suggests that writing and living blended for her into an intense joy of discovery :

> It came about instinctively. I was enraptured. I felt I understood India so well. I loved everything. (Jhabvala NYT, p. 5)

For almost the first 10 years in India she was in love with everything she saw there:

> "The smells and sights and sounds of India – the mango and jasmine on hot nights – the rich special food – the vast sky – the sight of dawn and dusk – the birds flying about – the ruins – the music."(Jhabvala Blackwood, p. 8)

Her early impressions then were full of the sensuous beauty she saw all around her in the country she described as a "paradise on earth. (Moorhead, p. 16) And just as on her arrival in Britain she had begun to write exclusively about England and the English, so now she writes exclusively about India and Indians. Within two years of her arrival in India Jhabvala had completed her first Indian novel *To Whom She Will.* After its publication Jhabvala was hailed as a talented new novelist and she was compared with Jane Austen, and was seen to be breaking away the established style of Indian English fiction.

In 1960 Jhabvala returned to England for the first time. The trip had a profound effect on her attitude towards India: "I saw people eating in London, everyone had clothes, and everything in me began to curdle about India" (NYT op. cit., p. 31). It appears that since her first trip back to England, Jhabvala like many of her characters, has been strapped to a wheel that takes her through the stages she believes all Europeans who visit India go through. She explains these stages in her much-quoted essay *Myself in India,* the introduction to her third collection of stories, *An Experience of India:*

> There is a cycle that Europeans – by Europeans I mean all Westerners, including Americans – tend to pass through. It goes like this: first stage, tremendous enthusiasm; everything Indian is marvelous; second

> stage, everything Indian not so marvelous; third stage, everything Indian abominable. For some people it ends there, for others the cycle renews it and goes on. I have been through it so many times that now I think of myself as strapped to a wheel that goes round and round and sometimes I'm up and sometimes I'm down. (Jhabvala, p. 9)

Her changed attitude is clearly reflected in her fifth novel, *Get Ready for Battle,* in which she confronts the terrible atmosphere of poverty and disease in India. The problems and frustrations experienced by her Western characters reflect her own growing sense of dissatisfaction with her adopted country. In *Myself in India* she candidly describes her life of loneliness and boredom in India:

> So I am back again alone in my room with the blinds drawn and the conditioner on. Sometimes, when I think of life, it seems to have contracted to air - this one point and to be concentrated in this one room, and it is always a very hot, very hot afternoon when the air-conditioner has failed. I cannot describe the oppression of such afternoons. It is a physical oppression - heat pressing down on me and pressing in the walls and the ceiling and congealing together with time, which has stood still and will never move again. And it is not only these two - heat and time - that are laying their weight on me but behind them, or held within them, there is something more, which I can only describe as the whole of India. (p. 14)

From the above passage it is evident that R.P. Jhabvala has been suffering from a sense of loneliness and boredom in India. Her earlier impression of India as a paradise has gone away, and now she has become aware of the heat and dust of India. Her earlier experience of a newly-wedded bride has also gone and now she suffers from the continuous boredom in India. At the end she decides to go and settle in the U.S.A. in order to get rid of this boredom. Thus her journey from a bride to boredom brings out her thoughts and feelings about her adopted country India.

Jhabvala's third novel *Esmond in India* deals with the conflict between the East and the West; more importantly than any other because of her own dilemma of living in an alien country. The hero of this novel Esmond Stillwood, an Englishman is the male counterpart of the writer R.P. Jhabvala. Whatever Jhabvala feels about India during her stay here, Esmond also feels as a man and the decision of both of them is the same, i.e. to leave India for good.

Gulab, the most important character of the novel is married to Esmond Stillwood, a European residing in India. Mrs. Jhabvala for the first time introduces a foreign character in her novel and it is through him that she brings out the contrast between the East and the West. Esmond in India can be viewed as the expression of the author's inner dilemma: whether to belong or not to India and if one wishes to belong, how to go about it. In *An Experience of India* she states this central problem that bothers the Westerner, especially the sensitive Western writer who lives in India and who aims at concretizing her life in India in her literary work:

> To live in India and be at peace one must to a considerable extent become Indian and adopt Indian attitudes, habits, beliefs, assume, if possible an Indian personality. But how is this possible? And even if it were possible – without cheating oneself – would it be desirable? Should one want to try and become something other than what one is? (Jhabvala, *An Experince of India,* p. 7)

The main characters in this novel try to cope with the experience, the world that is India. Mrs. Jhabvala has externalized her personal predicament, the predicament of transforming her inner life according to the dictates of the outer life. As a matter of fact the theme of the novel is the problem of integration. By presenting a European character, Esmond, Jhabvala has presented her own difficulty in fully integrating herself to her adopted country, India. She makes it apparent for the first that her initial enchantment and excitement about this mystic world, the East, is wearing off. Now she has a deeper insight into this unknown society and is able to make it apparent through these two characters. Both the characters are highly exaggerated and it is the Gulab-Esmond relationship, which is at the heart of the novel and forms the main core of personal and familial tangles in the narrative.

In the novel, Esmond is a European character who is a teacher of art and history. He is greatly attracted towards Indian art and culture. While other Europeans left India after Independence, Esmond continued to live here out of his deep appreciation of Indian culture. He married an Indian woman Gulab and had a son named Ravi from her. Both Esmond and Gulab lived happily for some time and both of them were satisfied with each other. Esmond earned his livelihood by giving tuition of Indian art and culture to the fashionable ladies while Gulab looked after her home and performed the household chores. But soon we get the impression that Gulab and her European husband are not on very amicable terms. It also reveals the fact that Esmond and Gulab are poles apart as far as their habits of sleeping, eating and dressing are concerned. One instantly wonders as to what prompted Esmond to marry a girl like Gulab, so untouched by European influence. Moreover, she remains totally Indian even after being Esmond's wife for five long years. Perhaps here Mrs. Jhabvala is determined to bring out the fact that Indian women can't change, they would remain what they are and Gulab, as it appears, is a true portrayal of Indian women as Jhabvala saw them.

Esmond Stillwood restates the doctrine of Asian inertia and European dynamism. In his initial reaction to India, the East and all that is foreign to him, he avidly studies up on Indian folklore, traditional poetry and history. Perhaps this explains his fascination with and marriage to Gulab who is the very antithesis of all that culture stands for European eyes. In such a marriage there is neither Western rationality nor Eastern spirituality. Esmond prefers to lead his own life, eating his cheese salad. It was very different from Gulab's spicy meal eaten on the floor out of brass bowls. He feels embarrassed taking her out to social gatherings. She is also miserable when forced to meet and mingle with his friends. In the end he leaves her alone and this process of estrangement suits them both: "He found that her absence was far more impressive than her presence."(Jhabvala *Esmond in India,* p. 201). He gives his English friends the false impression of Gulab as a real old fashioned Indian lady, veiled, shy, and sitting in a marble courtyard with the fountain splashing around, her maid singing love lyrics and serving her assiduously. He escapes social scrutiny by cleverly giving evasive or distant replies when questioned about his wife. The initial enchantment of Esmond for India and Indians has gone. He is totally fed up with his wife Gulab and seeks relief in the company of an English woman Betty.

There was no romance about life in India, Esmond knew; only for tourists, he thought bitterly, who clapped their hands in delight over what was, he know, only shabbiness and poverty to a point where the spirit yawned at the boredom and futility of it all. He finds India to be too much to stomach and his decision to leave for England with Betty makes him feel young, free and sprightly. The novelist Ruth Prawer Jhabvala herself came to India as a bride and thus got an opportunity to know and understand Indian culture. Very honestly she tried her best to integrate herself to Indian culture and tradition. Her honeymoon with India continued for some time. But soon despair set in and she felt frustrated with the surroundings of India. She ultimately decides to leave India and settle in the U.S.A. Similarly her European character Esmond is an embodiment of Jhabvala herself as a writer. He suffers from continuous boredom. The enchanting land of India does not appeal to him. Ultimately Esmond decides to leave India. Thus, the novel *Esmond in India* brings out the inner reality of the novelist RP. Jhabvala herself.

Works Cited

Agrawal. R., "An Interview with RP. Jhabvala", *Quest,* 1974.

Jhabvala, R.P. *Disinheritance,* a Blackwood Magazine, July 1979.

—— "A Novelist of India Reflects Two Worlds", *New York Times,* 17 July 1973.

——"Introduction: Myself in India", England, Penguin, 1981.

——*An Experience of India.*

——*Esmond in India,* London: George Allen and Unwin Ltd., 1958.

Moorhead, Caroline, "A Solitary Writer's Window on the Heat and Dust", *Times* (London), 20 November 1975.

7

Cultural Conflict in Malgonkar's *Open Season*

Devesh Chand

A critical survey of Malgonkar's novels gives ample evidence of vitality, variety, humanity and artistic integrity. The quality of his mind reveals his laborious accumulation of data which impart to his writing actuality and authenticity. He has observed the world with conscientious care and rigorous discipline of a researcher. At the same time it is evident that Malgonkar's entire literary works provide abundant entertainment. It is the variety of subject matter and setting which, more than anything else shows Malgonkar's mastery as a writer of novels. To quote M.K. Naik, "Unlike Bhattacharya, Manohar Malgonkar is a realist who believes that art has no purpose to serve except pure entertainment"(Naik, p. 216). Thus, Manohar Malgonkar has entertained the reading public by a variety of themes and subject matter. According to Shankar Bhattacharya, "Malgonkar's novels reveal a sound historical sense. History as the theme of creative fiction seems indeed to exercise a special fascination for him"(Bhattacharya, p. 12). Of course, Malgonkar has used historical facts to weave the fabric of his fictional art but his characters lead their independent life.

Writing history is not the purpose of Malgonkar as a fictional writer, rather writing fiction is his primary aim and history plays only a secondary role in his fictional art. Whatever Malgonkar has written, we find the cultural conflict everywhere. It may be the conflict between the Indian and the Western cultures or it may be conflict between the indigenous cultures of India like that of the Hinduism and the Muslim. The paper is an attempt to bring out the cultural conflict in Malgonkar's novel *Open Season.* This has been a very popular novel and a film is also being made on this novel.

In *Open Season,* Jai Kumar, the hero of the novel is scheduled to go to Princeton in America for higher studies in construction engineering. Education in America will make him a great engineer. Foreign degree as his parents think is a symbol of prestige which will bring him fat down and prestigious job. But the events that develop in America make Jai Kumar's parents puzzled and hence a letter from "Remote Control", i.e. village home is sent to Jai Kumar to return home immediately. Though he has fallen in love with an American girl and is also settled on a well-paid job with an American firm, he feels while visiting to his parents, that India at the moment needs the help of trained engineers as the surging tides of the dam nearby his village has posed a great danger to the local people. But the India to which he finally returns is not the traditional India, it is the modern India in the throes of development beckoning her sons and daughters to return and find their fulfilment in purposeful action.

Jai Kumar and his parents represent Hindu culture. His parents are orthodox brahmins. It is but natural for them to be particular about their culture as their son, Jai Kumar is going to a foreign country in a different culture. They are apprehensive of their son being victim to a foreign culture. His parents are strictly vegetarian and devoted to the worship of their gods and goddesses. They abstain from drinking and eating any non-vegetarian food. So long as Jai Kumar is here it is strictly followed but in America far away from here it is a different thing. Drinking, eating non-vegetarian food and even free mixing with women are common there. As Jai Kumar's mother is not ready to lose her religion, caste etc. on account of these things. The parents are extremely glad at the prospect of their son but mother is very apprehensive of some flaws as he will have to live in a different culture. She says:

> ... half the boys, who go to foreign countries to learn, don't come back at all; those who do come back bring their own 'muddams', And they come back with all the bad habits; learn to eat meat, drink liquor. (Malgonkar, p. 8)

Jai Kumar's mother has already come to know that he has started eating eggs forbidden in the family though his father wants to give this much concession because of the cold season in America.

Before visiting to Princeton Jai Kumar goes to see Rachappa, an engineer, whose son Krishnaswami was already at Princeton. Krishnaswami's parents had the same apprehensions about their son and unaware of the changes in their son. They still think that their son is a strict vegetarian, abstaining from drinking and women. But when Jai Kumar happens to go to Princeton, he has lots of problems to face — the first one regarding his food. He cannot live on vegetarian food which is very diffcult to manage and hence remembering his father's statement 'the flesh of animals born in foreign lands not forbidden', an excuse, he immediately turns a non-vegetarian. To his utter surprise he finds that Krishnaswami of whom their parents have very high opinion about the adherence of religion and other instructions is quite a changed man. He is a non-vegetarian, addicted to drinking and making love to an American lady. At last he marries her and settles in America against the wish of his parents. Jai Kumar gets introduced to Krishnaswami and through him to Abe. Gradually Jai Kumar learns the new culture of America somewhat conflicting to his own. He finds a change in Krishnaswami as reported earlier by his parents.

According to their own cultures Abe and Jai Kumar greet each other in conflicting ways. Abe greeted with 'hello' and 'hi' whereas Jai Kumar greeted with bowed head and shaking the proffered hand. Jai Kumar now short named as Jake is introduced to Kate, Abe's girl-friend but he is surprised to learn and see as it clashes with his culture that the girl is equally fond of drinking.

In the next chapter 'At the Golden Rod' we find that despite Jai Kumar's refusal to drinking Krishnaswami offers him drink. This is the first taste of liquor in his life. It is there that Jai Kumar comes to know about Krishnaswami's love affair with an American lady, named Judy whom he has decided to marry and settle there permanently at the C.E.C. Plant, Seattle at fancy monthly salary. The clash of dress has also been mentioned in this novel. Indian women, for instance, wear saris, suited to their culture. Jai Kumar's and Krishnaswami's mother put on particular dresses, i.e., saris according to their own culture. They can't even dream of drinking. But the American lady Kate is seen wearing corduroy jeans too tight for her ample buttocks and canvas ankle boots and her blond yellow hair. Judy is also putting on the tight suits and they all attend clubs with their lovers and drink together. Even old ladies in America pose to look young in smart dresses.

In the chapter 'The Last Thursday of November' of this novel we happen to see the whole of America rejoicing thanks giving Day that relates to the harvest festival and the affluence of America. Jai Kumar finds this function closely akin to the basic tenets of Hindu philosophy. Kate, her father Harding, Sammy, Abe and all other enjoy this ceremony. In the meantime it is reported that Abe is going to India with the Peace Corps to serve the poor Indian villages. Jai Kumar is surprised to think that Indians are rushing to America for fat job and Americans on the other hand are deserting their luxurious lives just to serve the poor and the illiterates.

After the departure of Abe for India, Kate and Jai Kumar come close with each other and start loving. Jai Kumar is prospering day by day and manages to buy Rambler Car.

While visiting to Kate's house he falls a victim to the conspiracy of Bert and Nancy, notorious kidnappers and murderers who have come to kidnap Kate and extort money. After g reat suffering and skilled machination, Jai Kumar gets them arrested by the Ring Police. Kate is naturally attracted towards Jai Kumar more and more who has saved her life. When Jai Kumar's father comes to know about his courage and heroism highlighted in the newspaper (just for a girl as he thinks), his decision not to return to India makes the parents puzzled. His parents are shocked to learn that it happened all on account of an American girl and that in the dreadful night. Sabnis, Jai Kumar's father is very much concerned with this development as he knows the affairs of Krishnaswami who has already settled in America with his foreign wife. Life in America is very risky. Americans carry guns with them. If one is out late in New York's Central Part, one will be beaten senseless and robbed of. So Jai Kumar's father writes a letter to him with some instructions to come back to India immediately after the course is over. Actually Sabnis does not want to lose his culture and his son.

As time passes Jai Kumar is offered a fancy job at Schlemmer Corporation. With some fear and curiosity Jai Kumar wants to know from Brecht who offers him this job about the job prospect. Jai Kumar has already in his mind the instruction of his father. Even Brecht accepts that the family ties here in America and in India are different. In India it is much stronger than anywhere else. But material prosperity is possible only here and not in India. As a matter of fact Jai Kumar is charmed to see the difference of standard of living in the two countries. When Jai Kumar receives a letter from his father, he becomes totally perplexed. The envelop contains the return journey Air India ticket. Jai Kumar has, in course of time, become much more acquainted with the American way of life. His father's letter makes him perturbed so far he had been in dilemma - whether to stay in America or to return to his native place. Now he decides to take on the Schlemmer job. India holds no promise for his qualification and bent of mind. America has become his land, the land of prosperity and opportunity.

Earlier we have seen the development of love affairs between Jai Kumar and Kate. Jai Kumar has decided to stay in America while Kate is scheduled to go to India to complete her thesis for Master degree. But so far Jai Kumar had not clearly expressed his feeling to Kate. So in his own native language he tells her about his love and to repeat the same:

> Main, tumse prem karta hun. (p. 93)

He proposes his marriage to her but conflicting views of the two come on the surface:

> But don't be absurd! You don't want to acquire just a . . . just a dependent, do you, by marrying me? I want to help too, all I can, and besides . . . I too want to pursue my career. That's what I have trained for, all my life. (p. 95)

The novelist describes Jai Kumar's state of mind in these lines:

> He felt weak. This too was part of the pattern, the pattern of America, whereas his thought processes were still conditioned by his Indian upbringing. Here wives were not merely wives; they were women first, independent, the equal of men; they had to think of their own careers, careers which could not be subordinated to the demands of domesticity. (p. 95)

Jai Kumar has seen Kate off. He feels her separation very much. Accidentally he comes across a lady - an Indian lady whom he later knows as Neela Rawat - falling victim to a foreigner photographer who wants her to write something on the piece of paper. He cautions her in Hindi: "Aap phas jaogee, kuchh likhana nahin" (p. 101). Later on he offers to show her the Metropolitan city. In course of watching and talking, Neela Rawat finds Jai Kumar a changed man, not acting according to his own culture.

The contrast of culture is clearly shown in the character of Kate and Neela Rawat - the former wishing for independent career and the latter depending on the choice of her future husband. The conversation between Neela Rawat and Jai Kumar makes the viewpoint clear:

> "Un-hun," she shook her head. "I'm not working girl."
>
> "What do you mean to do?"
>
> "Do? What other girls do. Get married, look after a house, raise a family. . . ."
>
> "But wouldn't you want to pursue a career of your own?"
>
> "Career! What does a woman want a career for? Careers are only for manly women; those who can't find husbands."
>
> "That is the difference, between here and there. Here, a girl like you would want to remain independent... Go on working at her job even after she was married."(p. 112)

Through the above passage the novelist brings out the difference between the Indian culture and that of the West where women want to lead their independent life pursuing their own career like men. Family is not their priority. The encounter of Jai Kumar with the Indian woman Neela Rawat opens his eyes who were dreaming to marry the American woman Kate and settle in America. He now changes his mind and feels himself attracted to Neela who can understand his emotion in a better way. Ultimately he decides to come back to India and serve his motherland.

Jai Kumar goes to see Rachappa only to break the shocking news to the family how Krishnaswami is known as Sammy and is likely to beget a child from an American wife. He also finds that no change has been done in the construction work of the dam which is posing danger to the locality. Rachappa keeping in view the past record of rains thinks that it is all O.K. with the dam while Jai Kumar is apprehensive of the danger. Rachappa does not want to be accused; hence he denounces Indian engineers settling abroad. This pinches the conscience of Jai Kumar. The cultural conflict forces Jai Kumar to change his decision. He now decides to settle in India and serve his motherland. As an engineer he has much to contribute to the development of his country. So far as his personal life is concerned, he decides to forget his American beloved Kate and marry an Indian woman Neela Rawat. Thus in *Open Season* we have plenty of examples of conflicting cultures exemplified by different characters.

Works Cited

Bhattacharya, Shanker, *Manohar Malgonkar: A Study of His Mind & Art*. New Delhi, Creative Books.

Malgonkar, Manohar, *Open Season,* Orient Paperback.

Naik, M.K. *A History of Indian English Literature,* New Delhi: Sahitya Akademi, 2005.

8

Rama Mehta: An Epitome of Indian Feminism

Tribhuwan Kumar

The new literature, especially by the new woman writers focuses light on a new woman bulging with a new spirit of confidence and a sense of change. This new woman is out to establish her own identity in a male-dominated society.

Rama Mehta appears on the horizon of new literature with the same intent. However, she is different from other women writers. She is one who does not strive for sexual description, nor does she advocate sexual freedom in her fiction. She writes of new woman but within the ambit of Indian Feminism.

Rama Mehta established herself as a writer in the genre of woman writing by writing her one and only novel *Inside the Haveli*. This novel brought her recognition in the form of Sahitya Akademi Award in 1979. Before writing it, she had produced her studies on two important aspects of Indian women indicated by the titles *The Western Educated Hindu Woman* (1970) and *The Divorced Hindu Woman* (1975). In 1976, she wrote an article entitled *From Purdah* to *Modernity*. All these articles served as a prelude to her novel *Inside The Haveli*.

What women writers write is not a presentation of just figment of their imagination, it is rather a presentation of their real life situations. Janet Wolff says thus in her book *Feminine Sentences*–

> What women write or point is clearly related to their experiences. These experiences, in the nineteenth century, early twentieth century and now, have been very different from those of men. Women writers have focused on and they are concerned with "the situation of women in society". (Wolff, p. 3)

The observation of Janet Wolff is largely true about Rama Mehta who is at the cross-roads of feminism. There are interesting parallels between the life history of Rama Metha and the narrative in *Inside the Haveli.* Her own female self-intercedes in the narrative. She was among the first women to be appointed in Indian Foreign Service and was married to Jagat Mehta, a fellow officer, and was forced to resign after her marriage. Thereupon, she took up residence at Udaipur which was her husband's native place. Their residence was known as Jiwan Niwas where she was looked after by two maids called Pari and Dhapu. She gave birth to a daughter and the child was named Vijay. All this echoes the fate of Geeta, the focus of *Inside the Haveli,* who is an educated and vivacious girl. She is married into a very conservative and traditional family of Udaipur and she abruptly finds herself living in *purdah* in her husband Ajay's ancestral *haveli,* Jiwan Niwas.

The plot of the novel centres around Geeta's struggle to maintain the modern values that she had imbibed and lived by in her parental home. It is a chronicle of her struggle to hold on to her identity in claustrophobic surroundings.

Professor Malashri Lal has pointed out in *The Law of the Threshold* that Rama Mehta was passionately concerned about two things – the effect of tradition and the effect of change on Indian woman. Both these concerns took concrete shape in the form of the novel *Inside the Haveli.* She herself had a deep and lasting respect for Hindu traditions and Indian values and yet she was modern enough to realize that change is necessary.

Inside the Haveli is a documentation of life in the women's quarters in feudal aristocratic Rajasthan. The novel insightfully depicts the day-to-day routine of a Hindu family of Udaipur. The author has captured the essence of this conservative community by her perceptive observations and delightful details of their living. Set in the *haveli* of a traditional Indian extended family the novel depicts a young bride's growth from the marginal status of a daughter-in-law to the supreme position of the mistress of the household. The novel is not just a portrayal of an orthodox society in which women must justify their presence by upholding the conventions of their ancestors, it also articulates the emerging consciousness of the 'modern' Indian woman caught in the cross-fire of internalized traditional roles and the sighting of new ones, her pains and joys resulting from this transfiguration and her flight from orthodoxy to modernity.

At the centre of the narrative stands Surajmal's *haveli,* Jiwan Niwas a stately but a decrepit structure. Tradition and respect for culture, fondness for rules and regulations which bind society together is an amalgamating feature of this *heveli.* The women in the *haveli* are secluded from the mainstream of social life enclosed by the powerful barrier of the *purdah.* Like the women in the *purdah,* the *haveli* too is "well-enclosed" and there is no way "one can look into the courtyards: the windows are so high that none can look through them".

The *purdah* is a constant element of everyday life in the *haveli*. Geeta, the protagonist of novel who is brought up and educated in the free and uninhibited environment of Bombay is constrained to unlearn many things as a bride in order to conform to the altogether different world of Udaipur. She is inducted into the world of *purdah* culture the moment she puts her foot on the railway platform of Udaipur:

> She was immediately encircled by women singing, but their faces were covered. One of them came forward, pulled her sari over her face and exclaimed in horror where do you come from that you show

> your face to the world?" (Mehta, *Inside the Haveli*, p. 17)

Pari, the senior maid-servant who has almost as much authority as Geeta's mother-in-law twice repeats the same injunction even before Geeta has stepped into the *haveli*. "In Udaipur we keep *purdah*", she informs Geeta, "Strange eyes must not see your beautiful face". And little later again she reminds Geeta, "Don't ever forget that your head must always remain covered." (p. 18)

Very soon does Geeta discover that behind the *purdah* is its extremely restrictive life style which is stifling and self-denying. She feels that women were like shadows who "followed their instruction with meticulous care". (p. 21)

In the *haveli* there is a maid - Lakshmi who serves as the other self of Geeta. They resemble, particularly, in their sense of dissatisfaction with the suffocating traditions and the constricting atmosphere of the *haveli*. But unlike Geeta who could not openly voice her discontent and defiance against the hypocrisy and rigidity of the old customs, Lakshmi is full of complaints about her marriage to Ganga Ram, a servant in the *haveli*. Lakshmi moves about in the *haveli* with her face uncovered in spite of repeated reminder that she is no longer a child but a married woman. Pained by the unjust accusation of her husband, later on, she leaves not only him, but also their daughter, Sita as she cannot accept the conventional right of a husband to treat his wife the way he likes. Thus defying the encrusted conventions of patriarchal dominance and the security of the confining walls of the *haveli*, Lakshmi steps out of her enclosed domestic space towards the domain of freedom, never to return.

Geeta also wants to revolt against the norms and rituals imposed by the feudal system. Quite early in the novel, she seriously considers leaving the *haveli* and even her husband. In a retort to Ajay, she says, ". . . I don't even see any point in being here. I may as well go and stay with my parents. You won't miss me. . ." (p. 54). But Geeta does not leave the *haveli*. Eight years after her marriage, Geeta who is by now a mother of three children is more adjusted to the mores of the *haveli* than at the beginning. However, she continues to chafe at her existence, though privately:- "There were many times when she felt the crushing weight of the walls that shut off the outside world" (p. 88). When she questions the orthodoxy of the *haveli,* she is admonished by Dhapu:

> There you go again attacking the *havelis.* Whether you like us or not, it is here that you have to live and the sooner you understand us, the better. (p. 91)

Looking for freedom and some space, Geeta creates a new space for herself in the *haveli.* Contrary to the dark rooms of the *haveli,* Geeta makes her room "comfortable and cheerful" by wall hangings and paintings.

Geeta asserts her individuality when she decides to send Sita, the daughter of the servants, Ganga Ram and Lakshmi to school, even though she is opposed by Pari, the senior maid, on the grounds that "Udaipur and its customs" do not allow girls to go out of the *haveli* for they "must be protected from the outside world" (p. 98).

In the *haveli,* education for girls and women is not perceived as essential for their development. In fact, there was real fear that education would tarnish a girl's reputation, hamper her chances of marriage and make her unfit for a married life. Not only an educated girl is perceived as unlikely to make a docile and obedient daughter-in-law, but there is also a suspicion that she would be incompetent to do the simplest of domestic chores. Rama Mehta in *The Western Educated Hindu Woman* points out that families feared that educated women would threaten the harmony of family life by developing personal ambitions and goals. The only role envisaged for girls in the *haveli* was that of a wife and a mother.

Geeta is filled with a sense of outrage at the rigid society in which women must live uneducated and unenlightened. She is conscious of the reality that education alone could free women from their circumscribed mental world and win for them their social and intellectual freedom. She realizes that education alone can open the minds of young women which could lead them to independence and self-worth. She obtains the permission of her father-in-law who is to some extent open-minded to send Sita to School. Thus, Geeta brings about a change and this change is metaphorically communicated in the novel:

> Geeta had opened the tiny windows in her room to let in the fresh air and the rays of the morning sun. (p. 105)

This pattern is repeated in Geeta's second venture when she begins to hold classes for the poor children and the illiterate women of the *havelis*. By turning the *haveli* into a school, Geeta subtly changes her immediate environment and the people concerned.

Although Geeta gets accustomed to the *haveli* culture, she does not respond to the rigidity with which women hold on to the old and archaic customs. She could never become one with those women. The tension between her and the other women remains. A rather diffcult situation occurs for her just before the novel concludes. It concerns the proposal of marriage for her adolescent daughter Vijay from one of the richest families of Udaipur. She is reluctant to see her daughter married so young and without completing her education. It is to her credit that though she is urged to give her consent to the proposal so that her father-in-law could die in peace, she does not make a compromise or get emotionally blackmailed. Thus, she shows resistance, not rebellion against the customs.

Rama Mehta, the author herself, though supported 'modern' outlook as does her young heroine Geeta, she was not a votary of the Western concept of individualism which appeared to her destructive. She favoured change, but a change that would not destroy the very fabric of society. She pointed out in her article that those countries which wanted change were undergoing change but still continued to "maintain their way of life" and that change was based on the foundation of their culture". This belief is amply reflected in the character of Geeta. Geeta as a representative of modernity has a deep and lasting influence for the timeless traditions of *haveli* through a slow process of "contact, change and transformation". She does not attempt to bring a radical transfiguration on those around her as that would have an unsettling and devastating effect on society. She firmly believes in integration with her surroundings first and then begins a slow process of transformation.

Rama Mehta tries her best to pose a balance between tradition and modernity keeping in mind Indian feminism. K.R. Srinivasa Iyengar writes:

> "The balance between repose and movement (in *Inside the Haveli*) is well- sustained, there is romance, but no cheap sex, there is tension but no violence, and there is a feeling for the values and the verities". (Iyengar, p. 753)

Works Cited

Iyengar, K.R. Srinivasa, *Indian Writing in English,* (New Delhi: Sterling Publishers Private Limited, 2002).

Mehta, Rama. *Inside the Haveli,* New Delhi: Penguin Books, 1977. Subsequent references are from this edition page no. given in the parenthesis.

Wolff, Janet. *Feminine Sentences: Essays on Women and Culture,* Cambridge: Polity Press, 1990.

9

The Youth in *Three Mistakes of My Life*

Smita Ajgaonkar Nayak

Chetan Bhagat, a well-known novelist has created a firm place in the minds of the modern readers. He has portrayed young, dynamic and modern Indian youth trying hard to become successful in their lives. He comments upon the ethos in modern life. The issues that we feel our own are reflected into his writing. Urban milieu is his main concern. His characters represent middle class. Chetan Bhagat has developed his own style of story telling. The story seems real life story and it unravels the minds of the contemporary youth especially when we refer to *Three Mistakes of My Life (2008).* It is very much contemporary India, easily relatable and identifiable by the urban youth. In his simple and lucid language and relating it with existing facts, Chetan has definitely made an excellent effort to make his readers stick to the book till the end. It has a simple plot with three average youths Govind, Ish and Omi who try to establish themselves in entrepreneurship.

The book depicts Gujrat and Gujrati youth representing not only a particular region but making a youth represent a whole country and its enthusiastic folk. Chetan depicts how the mind of the modern youth is affected by some of problems of the country and contemporary issues. *Three Mistakes of My Life* deals with the young Indians and the trials and tribulations in their life. Unlike his earlier two novels *Five Point Someone* and *One Night @ the call Centre. Three Mistakes* covers the big canvass of life c three young men and it does not limit itself to the elite class in India or the IT persons like those working in the call centres.

Bhagat has developed a peculiar style just like in his earlier novels. He receives an email from a certain Ahmedabad based businessman who was just going to commit suicide at the beginning of the novel because of his unsuccessful attempt to cope up with the problems of his life, in his own words 'mistakes of his life.' This young man swallows one sleeping pill whenever he uses a full stop. The author Chetan Bhagat tracks him down to a hospital in Ahmedabad. Govind tells him his story and that is nothing but the story-line of the book.

Modern young generation and its reactions to the political, social and personal issues are the main concern of the novelist. Youth is the important section of the society who is supposed to build the nation. Chetan Bhagat, while delivering inaugural speech at Symbiosis, Pune says,

> Life is one of those races in nursery school, where you have to run with a marble in a spoon kept in your mouth. If the marble falls, there is no point in coming first.[1]

Govind, Ish and Omi are three best friends and are the central characters in the novel who represent developing part of Ahmedabad and have different passions in their lives namely, business, cricket and religion. Business, Cricket and religion are three crucial factors which play a significant role in Indian scenario. The idea of starting some business together becomes successful. The cricket shop started by these three friends is running very well. The novelist has included many of the issues that Gujarat and ultimately India had faced like severe earthquake in Bhuj on 26 January, 2001, Godhra mishap of 27th February 2002 and the grim condition thereafter with communal riots as its consequence. What exactly is the reaction of young generation is caught by the author exceptionally well. Human emotions are showed very realistically. Truly, *Three Mistakes* is a real insight into 21st century experiences of Indian Youth. He has proved himself to be the writer of the masses. The three passions of three friends are actually the passions of Indian youth.

The novel has some indirect comments on religion. Govind and Ish are not keen on the issue of religion like Omi and his Mama are. Omi is interested in religion only because of his family background. Mama sees him as a prospective national leader. Promoting Hinduism or the politics revolving round Hinduism is the main part of Gujarat politics. The novel clearly depicts how the religion-based political events can act and affect the lives of common man especially the youth.

Indian youth's love and craze for cricket is commented on through Ish who doesn't get any support from his family. Despite this discouraging atmosphere at home he dares to coach the students in the city. Cricket is also part of their business because their shop sells cricket material. Ish supports Ali's talents in cricket 'hitting sixes' even in the dire situation. He is extremely concerned with Ali's cricket career. The three guys try to follow their passions and face success and failure in life. Average youth has nothing to do with race, religion and politics. Ish's support to Ali is regardless of all this.

The events like sudden discovery of a boy with exceptional talent in cricket and his trip to Goa and Sidney seem somewhat filmy and dramatic and also have the connotation of the movie like story. However these things add to the charm of the novel and make it more entertaining. Govind and Omi also support Ali along with Ish. Individual traits like hard work, sense of responsibility, talent and clear insight into life are really seen in the youth of *Three Mistakes*.

Govind is just another youth who loves mathematics and has good talent in business. He renders financial help to his mom by teaching mathematics.

The novel also has a subtle relation between Govind and Vidya, Ish's sister. Their romance is a wonderful part of the novel and adds to the beauty of it. Vidya is a bold young lady representing the womanfolk of her age. She has her own identity and she's very keen in asserting her own feelings and opinions. She advocates a strong recognition of right for women to make their own choice in their lives. Though Govind is her tutor in mathematics, she is quite enthusiastic and takes initiative in their romance. She represents the clan of today's modern girls who do not mind enjoying sex coming out of the shell of conservatism. This shows nothing but how women are changing these days. Fair sex has changed itself and has become more dominant and bold. Girls are not 'chotiwali' college going girls these days, but they are stylish modern girls with bobbed hair and wearing midi skirts. This change is not only in their outfits or grooming but it shows the change in their attitude, way of their thinking, the change in their whole personality and ultimately it shows their search for self-identity, space to breathe. Despite being a very talented young man Govind is hesitant and shy in this relationship because she's his friend's sister and he is her tutor. There's a great pressure on Govind's mind and he can't forget the trust that the family of Ish has in him and his friendship with Ish. Finally, love overtakes them both. Due to the guilt consciousness in his mind about the relation he considers it as one among other three severe mistakes of his life. It is quite obvious to the reader that falling in love is not at all a mistake.

The title of the novel has association with Govind's life. These three mistakes are Govind's mistakes. He has to suffer because of them and is frustrated in life. After brooding over Govind's character, it seems that he is like J. Alfred Prufrock, measuring life with coffee spoons. His first mistake is the investment in the mall which unfortunately collapses in the earthquake of 26 January. He thinks this first mistake of his life to be a very serious mistake. The pressure of debts and shattered dreams makes him fall sick. Vidya helps him to recover. He feels that making love to and to indulge in intimate relationship with Vidya is the second mistake of his life and the third mistake is the delay of a moment to save the kid Ali from violent Mama's trident and the cost of his own life. Finally he manages to save Ali's life. He feels very sad and realizes that he has lost his both dear friends. Omi is dead and Ish goes away taking Ali with him, because of his second and third mistakes. He is frustrated and tends to commit suicide. He is a very sensitive man with a pure mind. The novelist tracks him down to the hospital and saves his life and reconciles the friends after three years' gap.

Govind, Ish and Omi are such young men who are whipped with political acts like Godhra mishap and communal riots after that. This is quite clear that young generation is against religion-based politics and wants to think globally. Govind is shattered with natural calamity i.e. earthquake and its consequences losing the money invested in mall and also the moral tensions like relationship. He gets frustrated by all this and tends to think that these are going to remain the unresolved questions of his life and considers that suicide is the only way out of all this.

Chetan himself has said in the Symbiosis speech "I have told you three things—reasonable goals, balance and not taking it too seriously that will nurture the spark. However, there are four storms in life that will threaten to completely put out the flame. These must be guarded against. These are disappointment, frustration, unfairness and loneliness of purpose." Young India is learning its lessons and becoming mature. Though it is disconcerted, the young generation has a ray of hope in the novel. By keeping the storyline simple and easily relatable and identifiable by the urban youth Chetan makes *Three Mistakes of My Life* the most readable novel.

The real life events like the Gujarat earthquakes, India-Australia cricket series and Gujarat riots are cleverly woven into the story which makes it more relevant to our regular life. We realize that the characters in the novel discreetly become part of our own life. Its witty style and easy language captivate our mind.

Works Cited

Bhagat, Chetan. *Three Mistakes of My Life*. New Delhi: Rupa & Co, 2008.

Speech delivered by Chatan Bhagat at Symbiosis B.B.A. Inaugural Program on 23 July 2008. Published in *The Times of India* Dated 24 July 2008.

10

Alienated Women in the Fiction of Suchitra Bhattacharya

Alka Saxena

Suchitra Bhattacharya is a distinguished writer of recent times. Born in 1950, in Bhagalpur, Bihar, she started writing from her childhood. After her graduation from Calcutta University and marriage, she came into prominence in the mid-1980s with the publication of her novel *Kacher Dewal* (Glass Wall). She is one of the major women writers of Bengal. She has written over 24 novels and a number of memorable short stories, which have been published in prominent Bengali literary magazines. Her works have been translated into several Indian languages and also in English.

Bhattacharya's writings focus on contemporary issues, especially those encountered by the urban middle class. Exploitation and suffering of women irrespective of their social and economic identities finds a distinct voice in her writings. The purpose of the present paper is to examine the alienated women characters that have been repressed in a male dominated world. In *I Am Madhabi,* a collection of short stories, she shows the dilemma of repressed and alienated women who find their loneliness inevitable in a patriarchal society. Bhattacharya explores human relationships, specially women's issues, their status as depicted in mythology as well as in contemporary modern society. She explores the battle of the sexes which has been raging since ancient times till today.

Let us begin by examining the title story *I am Madhabi*. In this story, Suchitra recreates the myth of Madhabi. She shows her concern for the repressed voice of Madhabi, the dutiful daughter of King Yayati. Since ages, myths have played a great significance in moulding the perception of the common man. Myths have had an immense impact on the consciousness of the masses and continue to affect them even today.

In order to understand the story it is important to recount the mythological tale associated with it. The myth is concerned with Galab, a pupil of Rishi Vishvamitra, that, after the conclusion of his studies he implored Vishvamitra to tell him what he should offer as *guru-dakshina* The already content guru got annoyed at his pupils' insistence. Vishvamitra asked him to bring eight hundred white horses, each having one black ear. Only six hundred such horses were to be found in the whole of the Aryavarta. These were owned by three different kings.

A perplexed Galab sought help from Garuda, who took him to King Yayati of Pratishthan. The king known for his magnanimity was unable to provide the horses but gave his daughter Madhabi in the service of Galab. Galab's dilemma was resolved with Madhabi's help. She had been blessed with two boons, one the ability to regain virginity and the other of giving birth to chivalrous kings. Taking advantage of these boons Galab loaned her to the three different kings in exchange for two hundred horses from each of them. Madhabi provided three male heirs to the three kings but Galab still fell short of two hundred horses. Notwithstanding her triple marriage and maternity, Madhabi still remained a virgin. Galab presented her and the horses to Vishvamitra. The sage accepted Madhabi and had a son named Ashtaka. Vishvamitra retired to the woods and Madhabi was returned to Galab. Galab too retired to the woods and gave back Madhabi to her father.

King Yayati was greatly worried now because he had a married yet unmarried daughter at home. As a responsible father it was his duty to get her married. He finally decided to hold a *svaymvara* so that Madhabi could choose her husband. According to the myth Madhabi rejected the suitors and did not perform the *svaymvara*.

Suchitra has narrated this story through Madhabi who shares her dilemma and recounts how she was used by the men in her life. It can be read as a feminist text. In the course of the story all have benifitted except Madhabi. Her physical exploitation was not a matter of concern to either her father, Galab or the three kings or even a sage like Vishvamitra. It seems that the sole aim of Madhabi's life was to provide her body for the fulfilment of Galab's commitment. By giving away Madhabi, her father maintained his status of being known as a gracious king. Galab's commitment to his *guru* was accomplished. The three kings got *chakravarti* sons and even Vishvamitra's lust was satisfied. Madhabi was the only loser. At the sage's hermitage too, she was just a female body. "Like the three kings, the great sage too clawed at my flesh." She reflects on her physical exploitation, "A princess or whatever I might be, every fibre of my body knew that a woman would not have an independent identity"(p. 94).

The story opens with Madhabi who introduces herself as the daughter of King Yayati and when it comes to give her mother's name she is somewhat perplexed. She feels that it is not necessary to give the name of her mother because, "Mother is the name given to a womb. A receptacle for babies. The. mighty King Yayati fathered me. And this is my only identity"(p. 87); In the course of her life Madhabi too becomes a mechanism whose sole purpose is to provide the different kings with *chakravarti* heirs. She is valued only because she can be physically exploited to satiate the sensual desires of lusting men.

King Yayati expresses his inability in arranging for the eight hundred horses but he promised Galab that the problem could be resolved by giving his daughter to him. A woman of flesh and blood is made into a commodity in a male-dominated society. Her father displays her attributes that she is exquisitely beautiful and has an amiable disposition, therefore Galab would have no complaints from her. Taking advantages of these attributes Galab further trades Madhabi for a breed of rare horses. Madhabi enters wedlock and maternity but at the core of her heart she is lonely and alienated. She has no one with whom she can share her sorrows and tribulations. She hardly gets time to reflect and assess her course of life. She undergoes all the humiliation first because she feels that she belongs to Galab and it is her duty to keep him happy and give no cause for complaint. It is only when she is returned to her father that she reflects on the events of her life. Till now the focus was on Madhabi' s physical attributes. On the eve of the *svayamvara*, Madhabi uses her intellect. She asserts her identity and individuality by rejecting the *svayamyvara* ceremony.

From being a dutiful daughter to being a useful commodity Madhabi retaliates against her physical exploitation and realizes that 'I am Madhabi'. She chooses her way to her freedom on the day of her *svayamvara* when she would have been ceremoniously and legally passed on from the custody of her father to the custody of her husband. She does not want to be tied down to men all her life be it her father, husband or son. A more determined and free Madhabi reflects, "after my father's death, will I seek shelter from my brothers? They too are men. Shall I wait until my sons grow up and come to take their mother? By that time they too will be men! Is there no other way? No other way at all?"(p. 99).

Through this story Suchitra has given voice to the anguish of Madhabi. Having been betrayed in love, she discards the falsity of marriage and the so-called concept of love. She rejects the very institution of marriage. Earlier she was the victim of a male ideology that subjugates women. But now she asserts, she protests and chooses to live life on her own terms. She manages to find her space and interacts with herself. She is no more alienated – at least from her own self. For Madhabi it has been a process of self-discovery, of freedom and self-expression.

As compared to *I am Madhabi,* Postmortem is a story of contemporary times. In this story Suchitra has poignantly portrayed the anguish of Anasuya, an alienated housewife. She had been married to Samarendra and the couple have had a married life of well over forty years. They have four children and grandchildren as well. Anasuya is a lonely woman in the midst of her large family. The news of the death of her childhood friend Niharda takesher back memory lane and suddenly all the events of her life till now resurface in her mind. She is so acutely overcome with grief at her non-existent status in the family and also by the death of Niharda, that she attempts to end her life. She consumes an overdose of sleeping pills and is admitted to the hospital in a critical stage. Her husband and her children can't see any apparent reason for her suicidal attempt. Samarendra comes cross a notebook which Anasuya had used as her personal diary. Samarendra was not aware of the fact that Anasuya had been making personal notes in the diary. On reading the inner thoughts of Ansuya he suddenly felt that his wife who had been so familiar for so many years was now turning into a mystery. "He had not imagined in his wildest dream that Anasuya could possibly have any thoughts of her own that she would want to keep secret from him"(p. 27).

Ansuya was a timid, powerless woman, who lacked the courage to voice her feelings. She had been conditioned through scriptures, since her childhood days that' "a woman is a subject all her life", who has to depend on a man at every stage of her life. She had been taught that a woman is not entitled to have a mind of her own and even if she has one, she does not have the right to express it. Traditionally the sole reason for her existence is to give birth to babies. In her forty-five year old marriage, Anasuya had apparently got everything one could think of, but somewhere it hurts her to think that "I have sons and daughters. I have wealth. Yet I think that I have nothing of what I really wanted"(p. 28).

In school, her teacher had recognized her talent and flair for writing. Nobody at home had taken her studies seriously. They had fulfilled their duty by marrying her off to Samarendra an eligible groom. After marriage she had merely become a shadow of her husband. She was a dutiful daughter-in-law, mother and wife and nothing beyond this. Samarendra's pride and power withheld him from showing his concern for his wife. Under his enormous ego Anasuya was a non-entity. She was scared of him and looked upon her husband as her master.

Strict parenting had made her a coward. Niharda was the only person who had tried to instill courage in her. He had opened the outside world to her. During the Independence struggle many women had stepped out of the four walls of the house. Niharda inspired her by pointing out that the time for the awakening of women had come and she should also seek inspiration from women activists. But Anasuya could not voice her feelings. She could not protest or defy her father's decision to get her married to Samarendra.

As a mother of two daughters Anasuya always wished that they should not be victims of humiliating customs. But these things were beyond her control. In her children's life too, she finds traces of the familiar man-woman relationship that expects women to serve and obey their masters. She regrets on seeing that her educated and modern thinking sons did not respect their wives as human beings. She is further hurt to see that their wives, who are educated and modern, did not protest against this behaviour.

A disillusioned and alienated Anasuya concludes that "this life has been a total failure. What do I do in this life? Was I a good mother? At the end of their childhood, my sons were unreachable. They could not think of their mother as anything more than someone who served them. This was what their environment conditioned them to think contempt for women is a trait of real manhood"(p. 39). Thus, ultimately unable to bear this contempt she decides to end her life.

Anasuya's notebook is a touching account of her innermost feelings and secret desires. Her silent thoughts find expression in her writing. Her family members are not aware of her pain and sorrow. They feel that she has tried to commit suicide for no reason whatsoever. They cannot explain why she has taken such a drastic step. Samarendra who has gone through the notebook, knows the truth, but he does not have the courage to make it public. He decides to destroy it so that no evidence of Anasuya's alienation would ever remain. He sets the exercise book on fire and is relieved only when it is reduced to ashes.

The story ends with the news that Anasuya is out of danger. Her life has been saved. No doubt Anasuya has got a second life, but the circumstances and the environment of her home suggest that her loneliness would continue. She would once again lead a suppressed and lonely life. From mythological to contemporary times, women usually are represented as lonely souls who find their loneliness unavoidable against the backdrop of patriarchy.

Suchitra Bhattacharya has tried to investigate the women's status in a patriarchal society. She is a perceptive observer of the changing urban milieu and her writing closely examines the crises faced by the contemporary Bengali middle-class women. All the stories in this winning collection focus on the sense of alienation experienced by the women protagonists. These are stories that make us pause and reflect on the lives of ordinary women. The stories of Suchitra Bhattacharya pose questions on women's issues which we cannot ignore.

Works Cited

Bhattacharya, Suchitra. *I am Madhabi,* New Delhi: Katha, 2005. (All subsequent references are given in parenthesis.)

11

Concept of Internationalism in the Novels of Amitav Ghosh

Punita Jha

> Those of us who love novels often read them because of the eloquence with which they communicate a sense of place. Yet the truth is that it is the very loss of a lived representation possible. (Amitav Ghosh, "The March of the Novel through History: the testimony of my Grandfather's Bookcase")

This then is perhaps also the peculiar paradox of reading – and appreciating Amitav Ghosh's novels, that we respond to the eloquence with which they both convey a *'Sense of place'* and a *sense of* (almost immediate) *dislocation* that make such fictional representations possible.

Amitav Ghosh today cheerfully – if humbly – bears numerous mantles of responsibility in the world of the book (case): anthropologist, sociologist, novelist, essayist, travel-writer, teacher, and slips in and out of these veiled categories with admirable aplomb.

The novel, according to Ghosh has been 'vigorously international from the start' born amidst cross-cultural reading habits and imbibing its nutrients from an experimental cross-breeding of ideas and styles.

In the trajectory of history - as well as of historical fictions — we have always been concerned with the 'other'. It is no doubt fitting that in the age of an extravagant embracing of globalization, we may claim to have closed the gap between battling the other and straddling it; certainly, the legacy of post-colonial angst today appears to have settled into a potentially numbing acceptance of bi- or multi-cultural euphoria. Ghosh's imagination is as necessarily diasporic as it is post-colonial, being a product of specific histories of the subcontinent in the twentieth century.

This article opens up a new vista by establishing Amitav Ghosh who is undeniably the most cosmopolitan contemporary Indian novelist in English.

Born in Kolkata, studied in Delhi, Oxford and Egypt, Amitav Ghosh has been publishing essays, articles, novels, travelogues and interviews since 1984 *Circle of Reason, The Shadow Lines, In an Antique Land, The Calcutta Chromosome, The Hungry Tide, Sea of Poppies,* are all unique novels, each novel explores places and histories, not in the usual sense of the word, but in a deeper sense of unchartered voyages and discoveries into imaginary or little known homelands. In all his novels the metaphor of journey is employed in some form. Perhaps Ghosh's own roots have something to do with it.

Crossing of frontiers — especially those of nationality, culture and language has increased all over the world including India. Though this is an old theme Ghosh gives it a new twist; several other modern Indian novelists have explored this theme, not so much in terms of whether the two can meet or not in terms of political and cultural consequence of the historical fact, that they have met, what is more, they have been looked at together for years in a colonized — colonizer relationship.

Amitav Ghosh maps the personal stories of men and women alongside the political histories of the whole of South and South-East Asia in his novels. He unfolds the Asian Saga with a totally Asian perspective. Public events of a turbulent and momentous century are recounted through the eyes of private individuals caught in a multidimensional perspective, mirroring life, bringing out the innate nature of modern human beings who form the society. Ghosh's novels have an irresistable cultural pre-occupation vigorously manifested with humanistic yearnings. Thereby a sense, for a typical quest for one's identity which invariably has cultural. moorings. The question of survival, existence and a sense of longingness to rise in this materialistic world is what Ghosh tries to communicate by making his protagonists move from one country to another with his strong Indian cultural heritage.

Indira Bhatt and Indira Nityanandam in their 'Introduction' to *'Interpretations of the Shadow Lines* comment that history is always present in Ghosh's novels. They further add that" *most of his novels use time in a non-linear, juxtaposing the past and the present* (p. 11)

Ghosh seems at his best when he is describing public events. The fiction he creates is only a pretext for handing down to his readers the treasure of geographical, political, historical and socio-cultural issues, he has so painfully gathered through arduous research. It becomes irrelevant to talk about Indian English, for post-colonial perspective when we see an author at work with such unselfconsciousness.

In the *'Glass Palace'* and *'The Hungry Tide'* Ghosh portrays the cultural complexities through family relationships. Ghosh portrays women as life-givers, sustainers and continuers of the race as well as women in search of an identity. His women characters get rid of their dependency needs, break the pattern of sexuality and sensuality and take their place as whole human being freely and equally among men.

The *Glass Palace* is symbolic at once of the power and fragility of imperialism. Along with the overturned personal destinies of the royal family of Burma, there are the undulations in the personal destinies of humbler folk tracing the board The *Glass Palace* in front of an alley in Yangon that seems to lead to nowhere. This is the crowded, dingy room where she finds her grand-uncle, Dinu, ostensibly holding forth on the history of photography. The Palace has shrunk in size and the glass is opaque for none can see it from the outside, its transparency lost in the secrecy of the new underground political movement that the young have their hearts with. The link between the royal Glass Palace of Mandalay and the dingy studio is established through Dolly and her son Dinu.

Ghosh seems at his best when he is describing public events. Ghosh's autobiographical voice can be heard clearly in this novel when Dinu is talking to her Burmese husband who is also a writer.

> "U Tun Pe, do you know what I find hardest in my writing?"
> "What?"
> 'The movement I have to step off the street into a house.'
> He frowned, Why? Why that?
> 'It is very hard,' she said, "And to you it may seem like a small thing."

But I do believe that it is this moment that marks the difference between classical and modern writing of all things. 'how so?'

> 'You see, I, in classical writing, everything happened outside-on streets, in public squares and battlefields, in palaces and gardens - in place that everyone can imagine. "But that is not how you write says Dinu 'No' she laughed. 'And to this day even though I do it only in my mind, nothing is more difficult for me than this going into a house, introducing violating. Even though it's only in my head, I feel afraid - I feel a kind of terror - and that's when I know I must keep going, step in past the threshold into the house.

He is at his best when talking of issues that bind the individual to the society outside. It is through his novels that he wants to protect the common citizen's life from the triviality of politics. Which has only yielded misrule and tyranny.

The Circle of Reason is a remarkable achievement. It is the intelligence manifested in a brilliant handling of the socio-cultural aspects, which impress us.

Amitav Ghosh's first novel, *The Circle of Reason* is a huge, ambitious novel with a crowd of characters and themes, set in a number of countries India, Yemen, Egypt, and Algeria. Ghosh has chosen to make his literary debut with a long, rambling, picturesque novel, with umpteen characters, and diversions that are sometimes so long and winding that we feel we shall never get back to the main narrative. In the early chapters of *The Circle of Reason* the reader feels confident enough. We appear to be in the hands of a capable, accomplished writer who is creating characters we can believe in, however, eccentric their behaviour, and whose descriptions of place combine exotic colouring with a draughtsman's precision.

The Circle of Reason has received less than it's due accelaim. Ghosh is writing for a largely non-Indian audience about Indian matters. He says, for instance, that it is difficult for anybody who has not been through the sort of debates that Indian socialism indulged in during the 1960s and 1970s to understand one his main themes; that you cannot expect rational solutions to problems while ignoring the history of the people you are practising on Indian socialism, he says, has always been more international, less rooted in its own soil, than European socialism, which perhaps partly accounts for its evident failure to turn India into a socialist country.

In an Antique Land is an astonishing and profoundly exciting book, thrilling and quite compelling. A moral puzzlement over borders informs all of Ghosh's portrayals of entangled worlds; intricate novels, critical travel writing, and *In an Antique Land* part travel memoir, part archival detective story, and part experiment in multi-local ethnography. Its title is drawn ironically from Shelley's "Ozymadias", although the Egyptian past unearthed by Ghosh differs sharply from the sublime antiquities of European Romanticism. *In an Antique Land* reaches back to a 12th century cosmopolitan world linking Arabs, Jews, and South Asians, a world not yet structured by five hundred years of Western economic and cultural expansion, Ghosh recovers for use now, a submerged tradition of contracts between South Asia and Middle East. And this past situates in a sense authorises his own late 20th century ethnography; a series of disturbing encounters with worldly peasants in the Nile Delta. Ghosh's poignant, tragic, sometimes hilarious account connects the time of the crusader and Ibn Battuta with current labour migrations and the Gulf war.

In *The Calcutta Chromosome* Ghosh frolics with breath taking intensity and variety to produce a novel like none other in the Indo-Anglian shelf. This novel is an amazing amalgam of the theory of existentialism with an Indian-cultural perspective. It is through his complex plotting that he tries to highlight the thoughts typical Indian, regional Calcuttan thoughts society and culture of a person outside his homeland.

Indian culture, plot and cultural consciousness are considered the outcome of the long processes of historical accidents, cultural suppressions and geographical dislocations, according to Ghosh are the dominant impression he conveys in the sheer compulsion and authenticity of experience gathered en-route the long phase of history of his or her society, particularly their problematic relationship with the Western world. This is the *'Ethno Cultural'* experience, which he conveys in his next novel *'The Shadow Lines'*.

> War is their (the English) religion. "That's what it takes to make a country. Once that happens people forget they were born this or that... They become a family born of the same pool of blood. That's what you have to achieve for India, don't you see?

These lines from *The Shadow Lines* is a fervent praise of territorial nationalism. The novel starts off with the boy's perceptive and eccentric cousin Tridib, who finds himself sucked into history, his grandmother stuck in an age-old family feud; Tridib and his family in 1939; their English friends whose daughter's love for Tridib can only end in a tragedy. All the while private upheavals are mirrored by public turmoil — *(the Blitz in war-time London),* (civil strife in post-Partition Dhaka, a riot in Calcutta).

This novel beautifully focuses on the meaning of political freedom in the modern world and the force of nationalism/ *the shadow line* we draw between people and nations, which is both an absurd illusion and a source of identifying violence.

'Do you remember? - In *The Shadow Lines* this is the insistent question that brings together the personal and the public. It shapes the narrator's search for connections for the recovery of lost information or repressed experience, or the details of great trauma or joy that have receded into the archives of public or private memory.

It is in this novel that fear is understood as formative and enduring, fear for oneself: It is this that sets apart the thousand million people who inhabit the subcontinent from the rest of the world. Not language, not food, not music- it is the special quality of loneliness that grows out of the fear of the war between oneself and one's image in the mirror! Nationalism, militant and brilliant thoughts of anti-imperialism, is tarnished in its need for defining oppositions within and enemies across the borders. At the origin of India and Pakistan lies the national trauma of Partition, a trauma that freezes fear into silence. *The Shadow Lines* seeks to find a language, a process of mounting, through the narrator Thamma, as she moves from her nationalist certitudes to an awareness that borders confirm identity even though they are meant to affirm difference.

Realities do not go away just because you call them illusions. This is exactly what Ghosh has tried to convey through his novels.

Various books, reviews and articles have appeared in India and abroad on different aspects of his writings, they all confirm that Amitav Ghosh's novels at once communicate the double paradox of 'sense and place' and 'sense and location'. He is a writer of strong historical imagination. He has admitted that his main interest lies in observing the 'world around him' listening to 'other people's stories' and trying to understand them by looking at them from a distance.

Works Cited

Kirpal, Viney (ed.) *The New Novel in English: A Study of the Novels of 1980s,* New Delhi, Allied (1980).

Bhatta, Indian and Indira, Nityanandan (ed.) *The Fiction of Amitav Ghosh,* New Delhi: Creative Books.

Dhawan, R.K. (ed.) *The Novels of Amitav Ghosh,* New Delhi: Prestige Books.

Ghosh Amitabh, 2002, *The Circle of Reason.*New Delhi: Ravi Dayal.

Ghosh Amitabh, 2002, *In an Antique Land,* New Delhi: Ravi Dayal Publisher, New Delhi.

12

Amitav Ghosh's *Sea of Poppies* : A Potent Reflection of Language Variation

Arjun Kumar

Amitav Ghosh's latest novel *Sea of Poppies* is set in an era of agricultural scandal: burgeoning Western demand for profitable but inedible crop is causing starvation and catastrophe in the subaltern world. Thrown in some imperialist cries of war in the name of freedom and things start to sound depressingly familiar – but the year is 1837 and opium, rather than biofuels or animal feed, is the culprit. The Chinese are hooked, the Indians have been coerced into cultivating the stuff, and Britain is the prosperous dealer. Recent Chinese attempt to curb the trades means that "gunboat diplomacy" is on the horizon.

Sea of Poppies opens in a remote village devastated by these circumstances. A young woman, Deeti observes her inert husband yield to addiction, he collapses at the opium-packing factory where glazed workers move "as slow as ant in honey"(Ghosh, p. 24) and even the monkeys are sunk in a "miasma of lethargy" (p. 48). She has a small plot of land, but its poppies will not feed her and nor will the proceeds of their sale. After she is widowed, *sati* seems the most appealing option.

On the coast, near old Kolkata, a *raja* entertains British merchants and seaman aboard his budgerow. There is champagne and chicken and talk of forthcoming Chinese hostilities. But the bonhomie masks a perilous situation for the *raja:* he owes money to a prominent Liverpudlian trader and, with opium profits down, the thumbscrews are tightening. The *raja* is soon framed for fraud and bankrupted; notice of his crime is branded on his forehead; he is exiled and ruined.

Upriver, the Ibis is preparing to set sail for Madagascar, loaded with a cargo of coolies and convicts. Its captain is more interested in smoking than steering, and leaves proceedings to his sadistic first mate. Out at sea, conditions deteriorate as boredom fans the flames of cruelty. The serang has a specially sharpened toenail for kicking sailors and local justice prevails. A mutiny is brewing.

The outline of events is barely skeletal: as in his previous novels, Ghosh juggles a huge cast, weaving in overlapping strands and themes: racial porosity, imperialist hypocrisy, cultural relativism. It is characteristic of his scope to have an entire vessel of protagonists. Moreover, this is merely part one in a perspective trilogy. The Opium Wars have not even started, though it is implied that the Ibis will later be involved in them. There are various tantalizing hints of an auspicious future for the characters. One will find a dynasty, another is starting a religion, all are destined to end up in a shrine.

Sea of Poppies, a historical novel, is also a love legend flowering both on land and water. It is in fact the account of thriving global trade, addictions greed betrayal, caste, race and power. Thoroughly researched, Ghosh meticulously creates the culture of 19th century India in the early grips of foreign occupation and that of seafaring adventurers, pirates and mercenaries. It is set in a time when the East India Company had discovered that among the varied natural resources across the vast expanse of India, the land and climate of the north central Gangetic plains offered one more lucrative opportunity of raising revenues for the British crown which had the additional enticing value of becoming the gateway of China. Under British supervision, the first large scale opium production in India's history began in a region across eastern Uttar Pradesh and in Bihar where farmers were commissioned to devote their entire tract of agricultural land to the growing of poppies for opium. Some quantities of the opium produced in India entered the local markets and it was also utilized for medical purposes in the form of morphine, an effective pain killer and anesthetic. But a large portion of the raw opium was exported to China, the other large Asiatic nation whose wealth and resources the Brits eyed hungrily and whose rulers, fearful of the Europeans intent in Asia, had adamantly barred entry to foreigners. The plan was to make the Chinese so addicted and dependent on opium that out of desperation, the wily mandarins would open the doors of the secretive land to the procurers of the drug. Apart from the complicated shenanigans of opium trafficking, the novel also introduces us to another British export— the first large scale relocation of Indian labourers to Africa, the Caribbeans and the far east as indentured servants, slaves with a new name.

A survival tale of desperation and adventure, *Sea of Poppies* is also very much about language. The novel contains potent language variation. In fact, the author seems to have deliberately set about to create a primer for his readers in Maithili, Bhojpuri and the arcane domestic English of the Indian subcontinent which was to become the common parlance of the British ruling class. The linguistic calisthenics of the dialogues, rather than the dense story line, may prove to be the main stumbling block for many of us. While the foreign tongue of the native characters is dutifully clarified in standard English, Ghosh liberally puts words from Lascar Lingo and Hobson-Jobson without the benefit of translation in the mouths of characters who actually converse in English. Those fluent in Hindi, Urdu and Bengali, will be able to decipher the antiquated mongrel English of those speakers. Others may lose patience after a few tries.

Language with its different varieties is the subject matter of socio-linguistic realizations of socio-cultural meanings which in a sense are both familiar and unfamiliar and the occurrence cultures, languages, societies, social groups, speech communities, dialects, varieties, styles. That is why language variation generally forms a part of socio-linguistic study.

Language can vary, not only from one individual to the next, but also from one sub-section of speech-community to another. People of different age, sex, social classes, occupations or cultural groups in the same community will show variations in their speech. Thus language varies in geographical and social space. Variablity in a social dimension is called sociolectical. Socio-linguists express that a language is code.

And the factors that cause language variation can be summarized in the following manner:

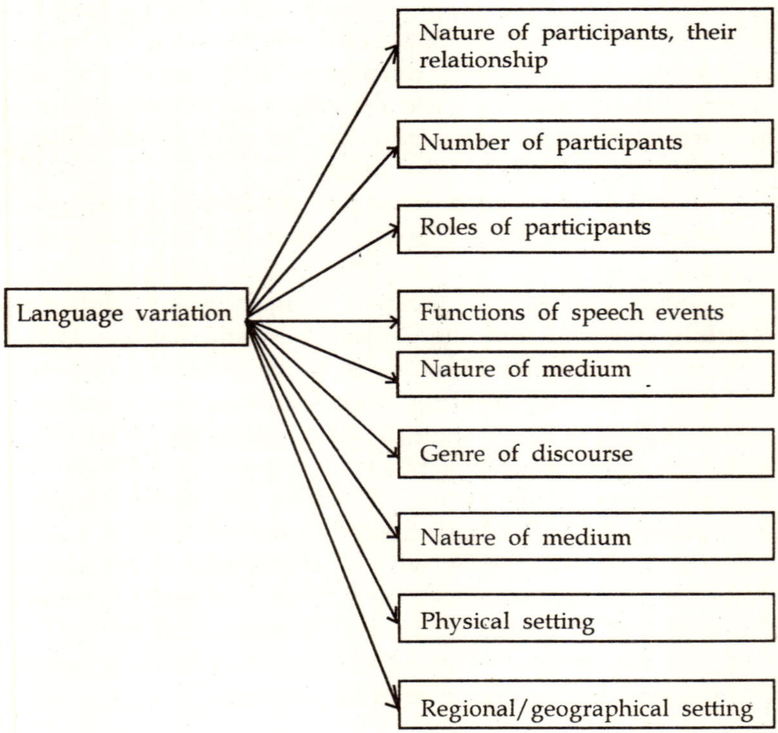

The major varieties that exist within the code are the following:

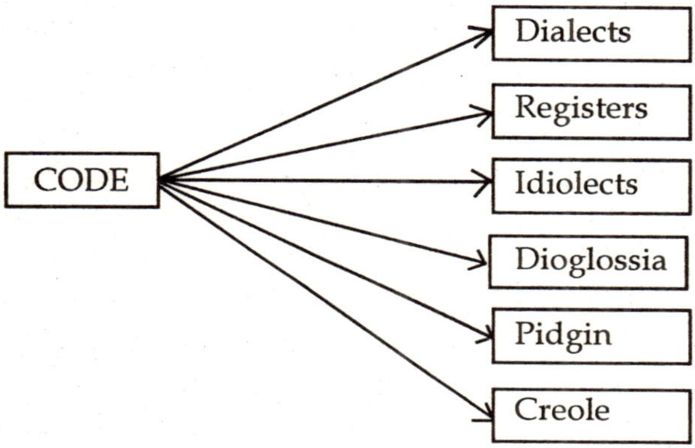

On the Ibis, as one migrant wisely puts it, "On a boat of pilgrims, no one can lose caste and every one is the same. From now on and forever afterwards, we will all be ship-siblings- jahaz-bhais and jahaz-bahens – to each other. There'll no differences between us" (p. 94). Words like "jahaz-bhais" and "jahaz-bahens" are different in pronunciation, grammar and vocabulary from the standard language, which is in itself a socially favoured dialect. So a dialect is a variation of language but not different enough to be classed as a separate language. Take the frequent references to all the tradesmen and people in service. To be sure, there were risaldars, *subedars, silahdars, paiks, barkandaz* and other denominations of Indian paltan, but even Hobson-Jobson (the glossary) throws up its hands on the distinctions.

Sociolect, Isogloss, Registers, Idiolect, Diglossia, Pidgin and Creole which are major classifications in language variation with the colourful characters, another be dazzling aspect of *Sea of Poppies* is the clash and mingling of languages. Bhojpuri, Bengali, Laskari, Hindustani, Anglo-Indian words and phrases and a fantastic spectrum of English including the malapropisms of Baboo Nob Kisan, Burnham's accountant, create a vivid sense of living voices as well as the linguistics resourcefulness of people in disaspora. The "motley tongue" (p. 102) is as much a part of the cultural scene at the lower reaches of the Ganges, and of the multilayered history of the subcontinent, as the collision of people on the subcontinent, as the collision of people on one of the great rivers of the world.

The British unheedingly break-up traditional structures, but dislocation need not be experienced as pure loss. The movement of *Sea of Poppies,* as shown by its three sections, 'Land', 'River' and 'Sea', from fixity to flux, a running together of categories that once seemed absolute. As the novel gathers momentum, having only one identity becomes like having no identity at all. This is reflected in the language of *Sea of Poppies.* The narrative voice has a period of neutrality that can seem wan where it is not enlivened with local terms. "How is this for a CV, for instance? Starting as a serishta at Gillanders, Nob Kissin rose to become successively, a carcoon at the Swinhoe factory, a cranny at Jardine and Matheson, a munshi at Ferguson Bros, and a mootsuddy at Smoult and Sons".(86)

Spoken English on even more of the perfume of the native spices: "There is a paltan of mems who would give their last anna to be your jooties . . . . .there is a lot to be said for men of that age. No badmashee at all hours of the night, for one thing. I can tell you, dear, there is nothing more annoying than to be buckrowed just when you are looking forward to a sip of land anum and a nice long sleep. . . . ."(p. 224) That is a respectable Englishwoman talking, but we hardly know it.

Sometimes, the caricaturally colourful lingo can become rather wearing. Mlle Paulette Lambert, for instance, sounds like Hercule Poirot [he was quite bouleversed], while Nob Kissin sounds like a Peter Sellers Indian [I will do maximum best] and the lascar Serang Ali recalls Charlie Chan [china-side can catch one nice piece wife-o . . . make Malum Zikri too muchi happy inside].

The character whose language is least adulterated is Raja Neel Ratnam Halder, but that is only an aspect of his weak grip on reality. The English with whom he deals mistake an educated reference to chatterton as being to 'Chatterjee'. The Raja has more familiarity with the waves of Windermere and the cobblestones of Canterbury than with his own economic position. He has been lured into the opium business by the hope of huge profits and when there is a downturn in the trade, he becomes insolvent. Even so, he imagines he can ride out the crisis until he is accused of forgery and transported for hard labour.

Ever since Walter Scott published *Waverley* in 1814, readers have turned to historical fiction not just for escape from a straitened and conventional present but also for instruction. Scott gave his readers not merely the bizarre character types and wide open spaces of a fantastic pre-industrial Scotland but antiquities, dialect, language variation, history, geography and lastings of political economy.

There are many varieties of English which can be classified according to the following criteria:

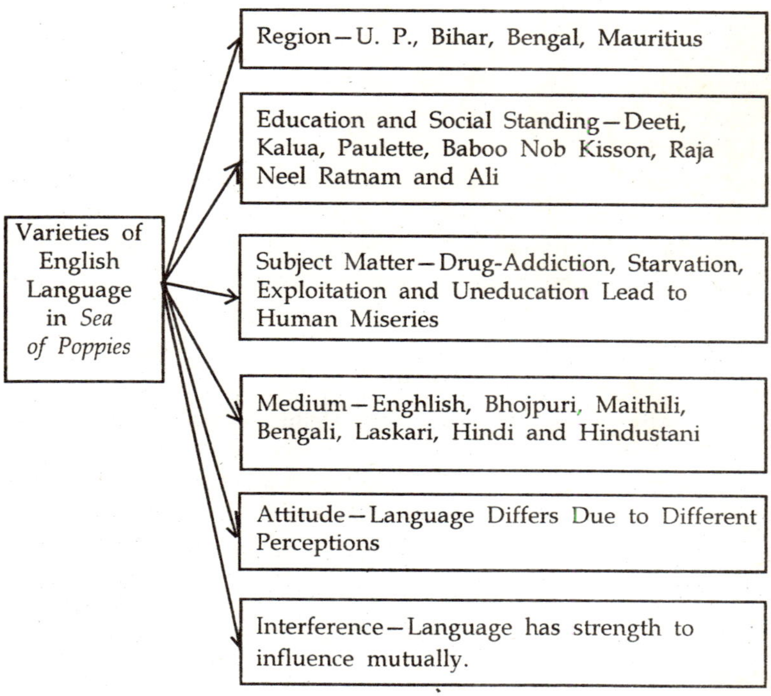

The language of *Sea of Poppies* also takes on an interesting historical dimension. The novel is written in English, but Ghosh calls attention to English's role as a colonizing tongue and does not position it as an assumed norm of the time. Rather, his characters' dialogue reveals English to be as eccentric and confusing a language as Laskar, the sea specific language of the sailors, or culturally based and geographically specific as perhaps Bhojpuri, Maithili and local Indian dialects which adds to language variation. This is nowhere more evident than in the person of Doughty, an Indian-born Englishman, whose unique mixture of languages is both mildly humorous and indicative of the nature of cultural exchange that resulted from colonial commerce.

Indian writers in English of an earlier generation, such as the late R.K. Narayan or V.S. Naipaul, aspired to a pure metropolitan or 'Oxford' English. Ghosh, like Salman Rushdie, introduces words from the Indian languages and from the various creoles, pidgins and slangs that have arisen in India and the Asian seaports since the 18th century. He has combed the colonial-era dictionaries and lexicons for nautical speech, barrack-room slang and all sorts of thieves' and whores' argot. The most important of these sources is Sir Henry Yule's Hobson- Jobson: A Glossary of Colloquial Anglo-Indian Words and Phrases (1886), which is also a particular favourite of Rushdie. Some of us may be perplexed by such sentences as "Jodu had been set to . . . stowing pipas of drinking water, tirkaoing hamars, hauling zanjirs through the hansil-holes" (p. 104).

Works Cited

Ghosh, Amitav,*Sea of Poppies,* New Delhi: Penguine Viking India Pvt. Ltd., 2008. (Subsequent references are from this edition and page number is given in parenthesis.)

13

Sudha Murty's *Mahashweta:* Leukoderma to the Society

Rajendrakumar B. Chaugule

> Like Rohini to Chandra, like Lakshmi to Narayana, am I to him. Just as the creeper depends on a tree, emotionally I depend on him. I cannot live without him, and for his sake, I am ready to renounce everything. Let society say anything it wishes, I do not care . . . (Murty: Mahashweta, p. 6)

These are dialogues delivered by Anupama, the central figure of Sudha Murty's novel *Mahashweta.* Anupama is playing the role of Mahashweta in the play organized as a charity show and the play is based on Banabhatta's Sanskrit novel *Kadambari.* A part of this novel has been translated and dramatized by the protagonist. The essence of the novel is the love between the heroine, Mahashweta and the hero, Pundurika. Pundurika, Mahashweta's beloved, meets with an untimely death and the princess wearing a white sari and garland, undertakes a severe penance in the forest. Her resolve is unshakable, her dear friend Kadambari tries her best to dissuade her, but of no avail. Finally Mahashweta's heart rendering love for Pundarika brings him back to life and the lovers are reunited. But can this happen in the real world?

Anupama is not only beautiful but also a brilliant actress. She is a singer in Hindusthani classical music. She is in a postgraduate class and studies with the help of scholarship. She is a daughter of a poor school teacher Shamanna and has lost her mother in early childhood. She is disliked by her stepmother Sabakka and her two step-sisters Nanda and Vasudha. She stays at the hostel and has come to sell the tickets of the charity show to Dr. Desai. Since school days, Shamanna and Dr. Desai are good friends. There she meets Dr. Anand who falls in love with her. Anupama's beauty is described in the following manner:

> Anand looked up trom his notes, and was stunned to see a young girl of extraordinary beauty standing before him. He had met countless girls over the years, but never had seen anyone startlingly lovely. With her beautiful large eyes, exquisite complexion, and the face framed by long, jet-black hair, she looks like an Apsara . . . When she smiled at Anand, deep dimples appeared in her cheeks. (p. 8)

Dr. Anand goes to see the play in which Anupama is playing the role of Mahashweta and her friend Nirmala the role of Pundarika. Mahashweta is an extremely beautiful princess and the daughter of the king of Gandhara. One day she goes on a picnic with her friend, Kadambari, and meets Pundarika the dazzlingly handsome son of a *rishi*. It is love at first sight for both of them. Anand also has love at first sight for Anupama.

Anand's late father Gopal Rao was a successful contractor and has left a lot of money for Anand. His mother Radhakka is extremely orthodox and narrow-minded. His sister Girija behaves harshly with everybody and nobody has the courage to remonstrate her. Radhakka always finds excuses for her conduct. Their house is aptly named "Lakshmi Nivas". Anand has won a scholarship to go to England for his further studies but his mother does not let him go until his marriage. She is a dominating woman and is always nagging Anand to get married. Anand wants a beautiful bride whereas his mother wants one who could match their status in the community. After his meeting with Anupama, Anand tells his mother that he has chosen the girl he wishes to marry.

Dr. Desai plays a vital role in arranging the marriage. He sends a letter to his friend Shamanna asking for the horoscope of Anupama as horoscopes plays a very significant role in the Indian marriage system. The horoscopes of Anand and Anupama also match. At the beginning Anupama's stepmother is not happy with the proposal of Dr. Anand. The reason behind it is that she wants Anupama to get married with her brother Ranga, though he is elder to Anupama by ten years. Girija, Anand's sister has seen Anupama in the college as she studied in the first year M.A. She tells her mother that though Anupama is poor, she is very good looking and there should not be any wonder if Anand likes her. As there is no plausible argument against the proposal Radhakka has to accept Anupama as her daughter-in-law.

Anupama and Anand get married. Mahashweta gets her Pundarika. With her right foot overturning the measure of rice that was kept on the threshold in order to bring prosperity to her parents-in-law. Anupama enters Lakshmi Nivas. Almost all of Anupama's friends from the hostel are present at the wedding as she is popular with them. Sumitra is constantly by her side. Sumitra is one of the close friends of Anupama.

After marriage, Anupama's life has become a perennial fountain of joy, love and happiness. Anybody would envy her. Without any obstacles she is married into such a distinguished family. But she is worried to some extent because Anand is supposed to leave for England for further studies. So, the next two months they go everywhere together and spend every minute in each other's company. Deepavali is only two months away and Radhakka wants her new daughter-in-law to perform the Lakshmi Puja and then leave for England. Anupama is restless when the time of Anand's departure comes close. Anand consoles her by saying

> What a foolish girl you are! Haven't you heard what they say in a church wedding? 'Till death do us apart . . .' And that is my promise to you. We shall always

> be together. Anu, how can I ever think of anybody other than you?' . . . (p. 38)

By promising Anupama to live together till death Anand leaves for England.

While returning from airport to home, Anupama accidentally opens the purse of Girija and finds a packet of oral contraceptives. It raises certain questions in the mind of Anupama but she calms herself down. She also thinks that she might have misjudged her. She wants to tell Anand about the behaviour of Girija but stops herself. The richness has made Girija arrogant. She does not pay any attention to Anupama. At the same time she is not friendly with her. Girija tells her mother that a tour of her class has been arranged to Belur and Halebidu. But this is a sheer lie. She goes with her boy-friend there. When Anupama comes to know that no tour has been arranged by the college, she does not tell this thing to her mother-in-law. On the contrary Girija is very angry with Anupama when she is advised by her. The things are put before Radhakka in a different way and she is very angry with Anupama.

> No wonder they say you should check out the family background before you bring a girl into your home. She wanted to ruin our reputation! How dare she! I agreed to this alliance only because Anand was so adamant. (p. 45)

The condition of Anupama is being worsened day by day, she is not even sent to her mother's house for Gouri festival.

The day comes for which Anupama is waiting. It is the day of Lakshmi Puja. Because after Laksmi Puja she is to join Anand in England but Anupama does not know that the tragic period of her life is to begin from the auspicious day of Lakshmi Puja. Radhakka asks Anupama to get the hot coals to light the incense for the goddess. On her way back from the kitchen, a red-hot piece of coal falls on Anupama's foot. A couple of days later she notices something very odd. *There is a small white patch on her foot where she has got burnt.*

Anupama decides to go for a check-up and if her suspicions about the patch proved to be true, she will also find out how it can be treated. Anupama has seen many people with leukoderma but has hardly given them a fleeting thought. She cannot talk about her problem to Radhakka and Girija. Without bringing to the notice of these two she visits Dr. Rao' s clinic. There she comes to know that her suspicions have come true. She has vitiligo, in other words leukoderma. Anupama tells the doctor that nobody in her family has got the same kind of disease. Dr. Rao gives her prescription and consults her how to treat the white patch. Anupama feels as though there is a sharp sword hanging over her head. She is haunted by the fear that someone would find out her secret. Anupama's bad patch of life has started already. Her disease is disclosed and Girija, Radhakka, Narayan, the cook and the driver, all come to know about her white patch.

Radhakka thinks that Anupama has the white patch before marriage and she has deceived them by not informing them. Narayan suggests Radhakka that as it is a bad disease, Anupama cannot perform any puja. He adds that it must be the result of a sin from her previous life. Anupama is dumbstick by the treatment given to her. Even her food is sent to her room. A feeling of misery engulfs Anupama.

Anupama receives a letter from Anand. He has written about British theatre, Globe Theatre in London and Shakespeare's birthplace. He is missing Anupama's presence in London. Anupama also misses the presence of Anand.

Radhakka sends a message to Shamanna by a telegram. As a response to telegram Shamanna visits Lakshmi Nivas. Radhakka blames Shamanna as well as Dr. Desai for deceiving her. Anupama is made to leave for her mother's house from Lakshmi Nivas.

Anupama is not welcomed by her stepmother Sabakka. The reasons are many. First, she is her step-daughter. Secondly, Anupama is more beautiful, more intelligent than her own daughters Nanda and Vasudha. Thirdly, she does not want any addition to her family. The income of Shamanna is meager and one more addition is not welcomed. Fourthly, she thinks that the white patches bring bad luck and it is a contagious disease.

Anupma does not want to hide anything from Anand. So she writes a letter to Anand informing him about her disease. She requests Anand to tell his mother that when they got married there was no white patch on the body of Anupama. She also requests him that Anand should make arrangements of her going to London to stay with him. But there is no reply from Anand thinking that the letter might have got lost. Anupama wrote a few more letters, but still there was no reply. Later on she gets the address of Anand from Dr. Desai, but the address is the same to which she has posted the letters. It means that Dr. Anand does not want to write her back.

For Anupama to stay with father and stepmother is painful. More than that the disease she was carrying created problems in the family. Nanda's proposed marriage is broken. This incident indicates how people look at the disease.

Sudha Murty criticizes people's outlook towards the disease. There are many misconceptions in the society regarding vitiligo. Some think that it is contagious; some think that it is hereditary; some think that it is the punishment given by God the previous sins committed by the person. Many people, many ways of thinking. But Anupama's husband is a doctor. He may know more about the disease than a common man. Still his reaction to his wife is just like a common man.

Certain questions are raised in the minds of the readers by Sudha Murty. This disease may attack anyone at any time. If the husband suffers from vitiligo and his wife gives him bad treatment what would society think? If a doctor husband is reluctant to accept the disease of his wife in which there is no fault of hers, then what about a common husband?

Life in village is very hard for Anupama. No one except her father is interested in her welfare and well-being. One more person is worried about her and is ready to support her in every way, i.e., her friend Sumitra. Anupama receives a wedding card from Sumitra. But she does not want to attend the marriage. Sumitra is getting married to Hari Prasad who is a sales engineer in Bombay. After her marriage Sumitra moves to Bombay and from there she writes a letter to Anupama inviting her to Bombay for doing job.

After Shamanna's transfer, the family of Anupama shifts to another village where she meets Savantri, the school ayah. She suggests Anupama that she should worship the village goddess who is very powerful and does not reject the prayers of sincere devotee. Anupama informs Savantri that she has visited many religious places but of no use.

Anupama's disease is increasing. She finds a small white patch on her arm. There is no sign of cure. On the contrary, it is spreading more on her body. She comes to know that the patches will spread rapidly over her body and the doors of her in-laws will be closed for ever because her mother-in-law has told her to come back only if she is cured from the disease. Anupama decides to pray the goddess of the village as Savantri has suggested. But after seeing one more patch on her arm she thinks that visiting goddess is useless. But at least she can cry outside the home freely. While going to the temple she overhears two women Indira and Sharda who are also visiting the goddess. They are talking about Anand's family. From them Anupama comes to know that Girija is married to a person who is on a very high position in his office. Anupama is shocked by what these women talk. They are of the opinion that Anand and his family members are deceived by Anupama. Indira informs Sharda that Radhakka is searching for a new bride for Anand. Till this moment Anupama was sure that she was still loved by Anand but now she comes to know reasons for not writing to her. She remembers his sentence *'till death do us apart.'*

Anupama has played many roles on the stage—Samyukta, Vasavadutta, Noorjahan and countless others. But in the real life though Anand has not taken part in any play, he has surpassed Anupama in acting. But the writer has raised certain questions in the mind of readers.

> What would he have done if his mother and sister had fallen pray to the affliction? Would he have deserted them as he had her? He would probably have sympathized with them and taken care of them, but when it was his own wife, the woman he claimed to love, he had abandoned her. (p. 75)

Anupama knows that Anand came to India for the marriage cremony of Girija and without meeting her he has left for England. Anupama sometimes reaches at the top of the hill thinking suicide. But some unseen power holds her back. She compares herself to Girija and thinks that she is superior to Girija in every sense. Just a small white patch is pushing her to death. She realizes that it is not her fault that she has white patches. She thinks why she should die for a husband who doesn't even care about her. Anupama is practical enough to change her decision. She calms herself and decides to return home.

> She looked down at the valley again, and saw it in a different light. The sun had risen higher; there were numerous wild flowers getting ready to blossom; birds were flying out from their nests in search of food. Life had begun to have new meaning for her. (p. 79)

Anupama prays to the goddess, "Give me the courage to live, no matter what happens." Anupama has made the decision to go to Bombay and with the help of Sumitra find a job.

Anupama stays with Sumitra and her husband Hari Prasad when she comes to Bombay. Anupama and Sumitra visit Elephanta caves, Victoria Terminus, Borivali Park and so on. Anupama is always conscious that she is guest in their house. She feels that it will be best if she moves out as soon as possible. In the office of Gopal Athrey, a friend of Hari Prasad, Anupama gets the job of a clerk. Anupama after receiving her first salary sends some money to her father as she thinks that it is her duty. She even offers Sumitra money to cover her expenses but it is Hari who stops her by saying he cannot take money from her as she is just like a sister to him. The financial independence makes Anupama confident. In the office there are many other girls who have come from various regions of the country. They have become friends of Anupama now. Dolly and Anupama become good friends. Anupama constantly feels that she is in need of accommodation. She is afraid of closeliness to Sumitra and Hari because it may end in unhappiness. When Anupama gets Deepavali bonus she buys a silk sari for Sumitra and silver bowl for Hari.

Dolly, a new friend of Anupama is supposed to go to Australia after her marriage but she meets with an accident. When admitted in the hospital, Dolly is in need of blood. Anupama donates her blood for Dolly as the doctor tells her that leukoderma cannot pass on through blood transfusions.

After attending a colleague's marriage, Anupama goes straight home instead of going to office. But to her surprise she finds Hari at home. He has come to collect his baggage as he is going on tour. Anupama goes into bedroom and shuts the door behind her but does not lock it. She starts to change out of her sari, when suddenly she feels a pair of hands grasping her from behind. It is Hari. Hari's intentions are clear. He wants sexual pleasure from Anupama. She gathers her courage and slaps his face hard. The accidental arrival of sales-woman and her knocking on the door give a chance for Anupama to rescue herself from the clutches of Hari Prasad.

Anupama has decided that she will change the accommodation before coming back of Hari from his tour. She requests her friend Dolly to find an accommodation for her. Dolly is ready to give a spare room outside small colonial style bunglow with a fairly large garden. Anupama has started getting bored at office. Her job as a clerk does not nurture her talent and creativity and it is not challenging enough for her.

Anupama gets new job of lecturer in Sanskrit in one of the colleges in Vile Parle. At the time of interview, she has been given the responsibility of directing a Sanskrit play staged by the college in inter-collegiate events. Anupama is overjoyed with the responsibility as she is craving for this sort of job.

Dolly, after her marriage, leaves for Melbourne with her husband. Dolly's mother goes to Goa. Dolly has given Anupama the total charge of the Bunglow. She has told Anupama that she can stay there without paying any rent.

Anupama meets with an accident and she is admitted to the hospital where Dr. Vasant and Dr. Satya work. When Anupama is admitted in the hospital she is unconscious and when her purse is opened Dr. Vasant finds a collection of Sanskrit plays *Bhasa Natak Chakra* translated in Kannada. Dr. Vasant takes the book to his room for reading. He finds that in margin Anupama has written her notes. And those indicate that Anupama has depth of knowledge and has a different sort of vision for Sanskrit plays.

Vasant finds that Anupama has a rare collection of books. There is a good link between Vasant and Anupama. Both are Kannada speakers and both are interested in Sanskrit literature.

Dr. Satya is interested in Dr. Vidya who is his junior. But as it is his bad luck, Dr. Vidya is marrying another doctor who is settled in the U.S.A. As Vidya is more calculating instead of marrying Satya who is not that much rich, she chooses a doctor whose parents are also doctors and are rich. Satya hardly eats anything for few more daysand later suffers from jaundice. He is in need of good food, care and rest. Satya does not want to go to Mysore, to his native place. When Dr. Vasant asks Anupama to help the situation Anupama suggests that Satya should come and stay with her at her home in the outside room. She treats Satya and takes his care as a child because Anupama is of the opinion that a patient is like a child.

Anupama suggests Satya to forget the past. Satya says that she doesn't know what is it to fall in love and then lose the person you love. Anupama has not told anything about her past to Vasant and Satya. Now she tells Satya that she is married and her husband has abandoned her for another woman due to her white patches. When Satya comes to know about the past of Anupama, he is shocked. Anupama tells Satya,

> Who says life is fair? It is better to understand the vicissitudes of life and solve our own problems in the manner we find appropriate. (p. 116)

When Satya asks Anupama if she considers herself unfortunate, Anupama's answer is philosophical. She says,

> No Satya, of the thousands of flowers that blossom on a tree only a few will bear fruits. But of those few fruits, insects and squirrels will eat some. The tree doesn't keep anything for itself. Does that mean the life of that tree is wasted? I have great friends and good students, and I am economically independent. I neither worry about the past nor brood over the future. I accept life as it comes and I don't have any regrets. (p. 117)

In the last chapter of the novel we are told about the reaction of Dr. Anand to Anupama's disease. In England when he sees the Parijat tree his mind recollects Anupama. He receives letter from his mother informing him about the white patches of Anupama. In the letter it is mentioned that Anupama had white patches before the marriage and she was taking the treatment secretly. Anand knows full well that there were no patches on the body of Anupama even after the marriage. But he doesn't dare to tell his mother that Anupama is innocent and she is suffering from the disease recently. He dares not to respond to Anupama also. Anand thinks of his unborn children. Though it has not proved that the disease is hereditary, he does not want to take risk. He comes to India for Girija's marriage but without meeting Anupama he goes back to England. Radhakka wants that Anand should remarry. Without giving firm answer to his mother Anand returns. But Radhakka assumes it positively and started searching for the bride for Anand.

After completing his degree Anand continues to practice

in England. One day he sees a couple. The wife is using crutches and husband helping her. There is also a baby in his arm. The husband tells Anand that as he is a God fearing person and as he has taken a vow, he has to help her until death. The incident opens the eyes of Anand. He thinks of Anupama. He knows that he has done injustice to Anupama.

Some months later Anand comes back to India. He starts practice at his home. One day he comes across the love letter written by the boyfriend of Girija. The letter clearly indicates that there were sexual relations in between Girija and her boy-friend. Radhakka was also aware of the affair. Now Anand starts comparing Girija with Anupama. Girija after having sexual relations with her boy-friend is living with her husband happily and Anupama having no fault of her own is suffering loneliness. Anand decides to visit her.

Anupama receives a telegram from the village. It is about the death of her father Shamanna. The last link with her past has been severed. Later on she gets a letter from Sabakka asking for her forgiveness and sending the money continuously. Anupama is disgusted with the situation. The people have treated her as bad omen are now demanding help from her.

Once Anuapama asks Vasant, "How do you define beauty?" He answers,

> One's beauty is seen in one's nature. A good human being who is compassionate to others, who tries to understand the other person's difficulties and reach out to them in their hour of need has real beauty. (p. 132)

Anand goes to place of his father-in-laws. From there he goes to Hunase village where Shamanna was transferred but his search for Anupama is futile.

The relationship between Anupama and Vasant proceeds further. Vasant proposes Anupama.

> Now I want to go back to my village and serve the people there. That is my dream. Will you be part of

> my life and complete my dream? Will you share my happiness and sorrows in future? (p. 138)

Anupama does not give any response to Vasant.

Anand is in Bombay to attend the International medical conference. He meets his friend Dr. Prakash Apte. Prakash makes Anand to attend a Sanskrit play at Tata Theatre. Unwillingly Anand goes for the play. But to his great surprise the play is directed by the Anupama. The play which is staged is Bhasa's *Swapna-Vasavadutta.* The play is about the prince Udayana who is deeply in love with Vasavadatta. Anand comes to know that probably he never loved her as Udayana loved Vasavadatta though she had all the qualities of Vasavadatta.

Next day, after collecting her address from the office of Tata Theatre, he goes to meet her. He remembers Anupama's words in her introduction to the play. *In any community, land or race, a woman always wants her husband to love only her:* When Anand walks in, Anupama is speechless. She smiles sadly. There were so many things that she had once wanted to tell Anand. She has devoted her mind, soul and body to him but in return she has got wounds only. Anand feels uncomfortable as Anupama is silent. Though white patches have covered her body, in her eyes there is confidence. Anupama asks certain questions which are not answered by Anand.

> . . . Did you speak when you first got to know about my condition? Was it my fault that I got this white patch? It is my fault that I am a poor man's daughter? (p. 146)

> Had I known your attitude towards life, I would have told you to marry somebody else. Suppose you had got leukoderma, do you think I would have left you for some other man? (p. 147)

Anand wants to begin a new life with Anupama, but Anupama rejects the proposal. She says, *"How can you possibly expect a burnt seed to grow into a tree?"* She asks Anand to leave her alone. She is economically independent now. And the economical support has given her enormous strength.

Vasant is also eager to know Anupama's decision. Anupama requests Vasant to forget his idea because she does not want to be entangled in the circle of husband and family. She wants to follow a different path. She also promises Vasant that she will not forget his friendship. She tells Vasant,

> You should marry someone like you, with a simple and compassionate heart, preferably a doctor, who can also help you in your work. Please remember that whenever you come to Bombay, this Mahashweta will always welcome you as a friend and her house will be open to you. We have become good friends. Let us remain so, and not complicate our relationship by getting married. (p. 150)

Anupama gives Vasant a pleasant present of a sweater which she has knitted for him and requests him to wear it during cold weather.

Mahashweta has become successful in presenting the real life of people suffering with leukoderma. But real success of the novel lies in the post-script of the novel. Sudha Murty has narrated an incident of marriage in the post-script. She was invited for a marriage ceremony. The bride after engagement caught leukoderma. The would-be-husband hesitated to get married with the girl having this disease. But in the mean time bridegroom read the novel of Sudha Murty, the novel *Mahashweta* and decided that he should not behave like the hero of the novel. So he decided to marry the engaged girl and for this marriage Sudha Murty was invited. Certainly, slowly but steadily the change is at hand.

Works Cited

Murty, Sudha (2007), *Mahashweta,* New Delhi: Penguin Books India.

14

Anita Desai's *Fasting, Feasting*: A Tale of Entrapment

Suchi Agrawal

Anita Desai's *Fasting, Feasting* (1999) tells the story of two middle-class families and the allegorical struggles of the individual members to find individual identity and happiness. This meticulously constructed prose gravitates towards the position of women in the family and explores socially ordered gender imbalance in domestic life. Featuring a traditional Indian family in a provincial town of India and a typical American family in suburban Massachusetts, Desai utilizes comparison and contrast as an effective writing mechanism. Unique in her approach and successful in execution, Desai's illustration of dichotomies within the two families range as obviously as the novel's title and as subtly as a meal choice.

Fasting, Feasting certainly is a dichotomous novel – in style and substance. The first half of the book recounts the experiences of Uma, the oldest daughter of a middle-class family that inhabits "a small provincial town" far removed from the bustle of Bombay. The second half takes place in western Massachusetts, where Uma's brother, Arun, is attending college and boarding at the suburban home of the Pattons, also decidedly middle class. Inevitably, readers will draw comparisons between the two families, one living with the legacy of colonialism, the other enjoying the largesse of a new imperial power.

Uma, a plain girl with a mystical bent, suffocates in a patriarchal system of arranged marriages. She has neither the looks, intelligence nor self-confidence to attempt a career, an option her mother and father have vetoed in any case.

Arun, a dutiful but sullen child, must cope with the pressure of being the favoured son. Forced to study day and night to qualify for a superior university, he feels trapped by the very education meant to liberate him – even if he is privileged to pursue that education in a country devoted to self-actualization.

It is no surprise that this novel should create conflict. *Fasting, Feasting* takes as its subject some of society's most uncomfortable and pathological aspects, and it refuses to redeem them with aesthetic flourish. It is stern, unflinching and tragic.

The novel, as the title suggests, is about practices of the body. It enters households from their refrigerators, dining tables and kitchens, and it recounts human relationships in the language–not only of fasting and feasting – but also of greed, craving, taboo, disgust and every other kind of relation to food. With its two linked novellas, one set in India and the other in the United States, the novel gives an excruciating account of how society can seize control of individuals – especially women – through such practices as eating, and remove them from everything they intended to be.

The problem with writing about things that are so everyday is thaf it is difficult to find characters who are alert enough to them to see their drama. Anita Desai solves this problem by introducing a naïve observer into both halves of the book: Uma in the first, who is slow and captive and, in the second, her brother Arun, who leaves India for the first time to study in the United States, and finds himself assaulted by the strangeness of the mundane.

Fasting, Feasting is a novel, ultimately, about the operations of the family, and it is savage in its critique. For Desai, the nuclear family is a mad and petty realm, whose power is maintained only by the exclusion of nearly everything that is alive and interesting. Her Indian and American fathers share an equal paranoia about the intrusion of alien elements into the home, which becomes, therefore, a bleached-out zone. The women who dwell in its small circle suffer from claustrophobic tics, and they sustain themselves with impossible fantasies of transcendence: conviviality, travel and death. It could not be more bleak.

The novel as it is implied in the title itself, presents a contrast between the two cultures, the one, Indian, known for its pious and longstanding customs representing 'fasting,' and the other, American, a country of opulence and sumptuousness epitomising 'feasting.' The plot unveils through the perceptions of Uma, in India, and of Arun, in America. Both of them are entrapped, irrespective of the culture and enveloping milieu, by oppressive bonds exercised by their own parents, Mama Papa. They are just MamaPapa or PapaMama but remain nameless throughout the novel. Yet, this namelessness does not indicate their anonymity but signifies their universality. They are the prototypical parents found everywhere in the middle-class families of India, who discuss, plan, plot, control, govern the activities of their children, be it marriage or going abroad for studies. And in their over-domineering concern, they tend to ignore the inadvertent possibility of entrapping their own offspring.

Thus, they do not give contingency to the fact that perhaps their children too can have a life to call their own. May be even their own preoccupations, their own priorities, maybe an agenda for themselves that goes beyond what they actually want for their children. The novel begins with a snapshot of MamaPapa in a contemplative mood:

> "The parents sit, rhythmically swinging, back and forth. They could be asleep, dozing—their eyes are hooded—but sometimes they speak."

That is when a sudden deluge of ideas hit them and they order their eldest daughter, Uma, to carry them out without delay. Uma is asked first to inform the cook to prepare sweets for her father, with neglectful impatience that she has been already asked to pack a parcel to be sent to her brother Arun in America. While she comes literally running on her toes, she is entrusted with an additional job of writing a letter to their son. Somewhere in the middle of the novel, the reader understands that it is the usual scene that goes on in the household of MamaPapa.

> "All morning MamaPapa have found things for Uma to do. It is as if Papa's retirement is to be spent in this manner—sitting on the red swing in the veranda with Mama, rocking and finding ways to keep Uma occupied. As long as they can do that, they themselves feel busy and occupied".(133)

In this manner, living under the demanding rule of MamaPapa, Uma is repressed, suppressed and is imprisoned at home. The first part of the novel tells us in a flashback as how she became a reluctant victim of entrapment at home. The second part of the novel shows how her brother Arun, who leaves his home for higher studies, feels trapped by the very education that is meant to liberate him.

Usually, at home, it would be an oppressive atmosphere even if one of the parents is overpowering. With regard to Uma, both of her parents appear to have merged into a single identity MamaPapa/PapaMama, as if they have a "Siamese twin existence"(6). Hence, whenever MamaPapa say something, and whoever says it, it comes with double the intensity and power that it cannot be defied at all. "Having fused into one, they had gained so much in substance, in stature, in authority, that they loomed large enough as it was; they did not need separate histories and backgrounds to make them even more immense"(6). Despite a slight variation in the roles they have chosen to play, Papa's of "scowling" and "Mama's scolding"(10), in terms of opinion, they never differed from each other. Therefore, if one refused there would not be any "point in appealing to the other parent for a different verdict: none was expected, or given"(14).

Further more, the women are not allowed for outings usually, but when Papa feels that the women laze around the house too much, then they would be taken to the park for a walk. On one such occasion, Uma gets easily distracted and fails to keep pace with her Papa. Though Papa is far away, and she is left in the company of Mama, she would not dare attempt to buy some eatables on her wish though it is highly tempting: "Uma finds saliva gathering at the corners of her mouth at the smell of the spiced, roasted gram but decides to say nothing"(12-13). In the end, Uma is blamed for being "slow" when all the while Uma could not reconcile herself as why they are hurrying just to go back home.

Likewise, the children are not allowed to have any sense of privacy even when they have grownup. They are not allowed to shut any doors in the household. For this meant secrets, especially nasty secrets, which are impermissible: "It meant authority would come stalking in and make a search to seize upon the nastiness, the unclean blot"(15).

MamaPapa also decide which of their children should have education and how much of it. As far as Uma is concerned, a pleasant escape from her claustrophobic conditions at home is her school-going. The convent school for her is "streaked with golden promise"(20). Hence, she always goes early to the school and later finds some excuse to linger there for longer time. Conversely, she feels deprived during dull weekends when she is left at home: "There were the wretched weekends when she was plucked back into the trivialities of her home, which seemed *a denial, a negation of life* as it ought to be, somber and splendid, and then the endless summer vacation when the heat reduced even that pointless existence to further *vacuity*."(21)

Regardless of Uma's verve for convent education, she is forced to stop going to school when Mama gives birth to the third baby, Arun. Even as Uma shows disagreement, she is coaxed, cajoled and finally threatened to accept her Mama's decision:

> But ayah can do this—ayah can do that—' Uma tried to protest when the orders began to come thick and fast. This made Mama look stern again. 'You know we can't leave the baby to the servant,' she said severely. 'He needs proper attention.' When Uma pointed out that ayah had looked after her and Aruna as babies, Mama's expression made it clear it was quite a different matter now, and she repeated threateningly: 'Proper attention' (31).

Later, Uma looks forward towards her marriage to give her the much-needed relief, yet, unfortunately, she returns home frustrated after a deceitful marriage and subsequent divorce. Back at home, she gets a rare job offer through Dr. Dutt, but MamaPapa refuse to send her. When Dr. Dutt persists on taking Uma for the job, Mama lies of an illness for which she needs Uma to nurse her. In like manner, when Uma receives an invitation for a coffee party from Mrs. O'Henry, MamaPapa refuse to send her to the party because of the apprehension that Mrs. O'Henry might ensnare her and convert her into a Christian nun.

Reduced thus to a baby-sitter at her earlier days and an unpaid servant for her self-centred parents for the rest of her life, Uma finds no escape from her entrapment. Uma experiences, however, a brief repose of happiness and freedom once when she is allowed to accompany her ailing aunt, Mira-Masi, on her pilgrimage. During her stay at night in an ashram, Uma finds a strange link of her life with the barks and howls of the dogs:

> At night she lay quietly on her mat, listening to the ashram dog bark. Then other dogs in distant villages, out along the river bed and over in the pampas grass, or in wayside shacks and hovels by the highway—barked back. They howled long messages to each other. Their messages traveled back and forth through the night darkness which was total, absolute. Gradually the barks sank into it and drowned. Then it was silent. That was what Uma felt her own life

> to have been—full of barks, howls, messages, and now—silence (61).

At this juncture, one is reminded of Anita Desai's characteristic way of making her internally turbulent protagonists find expression through association with external surroundings. Thus, for instance, in *Cry, the Peacock,* Maya's feelings of isolation and longings are coupled with those of the crying of the peacocks. Still, one locates a kind of sublimity in the agonised inner cry of Maya when it is likened with peacocks. When Uma's pain is related to the barks and howls of dogs, the poetry of Maya's anguish is to be seen in sharp contrast to that of the excruciating poverty of Uma's entrapment.

Catering to the whims and fancies of MamaPapa, but keeping her remorse selfcontained, at one point of the novel, Uma feels utterly friendless and alone, even when she is at home and surrounded by her MamaPapa. In desperation, she thinks of writing a letter to a friend to share her grief but it only ends up with the realisation that she has none to confide with: She could write a letter to a friend—a private message of despair, dissatisfaction, yearning; she has a packet of notepaper, pale violet with a pink rose embossed in the corner—but who is the friend? Mrs. Joshi? But since she lives next door, she would be surprised. Aruna? But Aruna would pay no attention, she is too busy. Cousin Ramu? Where *was* he? Had his farm swallowed him up? And Anamika—had marriage *devoured* her? (134).

However, it would be wrong to presuppose that Anita Desai shows Uma's unattractiveness, clumsiness and dullness of mind as causes for her entrapment. Uma's polar opposite, her graceful, beautiful and brilliant cousin, Anamika's confinement is more poignant. While Uma's failure in her school exams pressurises her to stay at home, Anamika does so excellently in her final school exams, that she wins a scholarship to Oxford. Yet, Anamika lives in a patriarchal society that considers higher education to be the prerogative of males, and marriage as the major preoccupation of females.

The scholarship obtained is used only as a means to win her a husband who is considered an equal to the family's prestige. Anamica's parents are unperturbed by the fact that he is so much older than her, so grim-faced and conscious of his own superiority, and is "totally impervious to Anamika's beauty and grace and distinction" (70). But it is Anamica, who starts another life of entrapment the moment she enters her in-laws' house. Anamica's husband is a typical 'Mama's boy' to the extent he could be a silent witness to his mother's beating of his wife regularly. Anamica, who won scholarship to Oxford, spends her entire time in the kitchen cooking for a very large family that eats in shifts—"first the men, then the children, finally the women"(70). After a miscarriage, which followed a brutal beating, and the belief that she could not bear more children, finally, the family ties her up in a nylon saree, pours the kerosene over her, and burns her to death.

Here again Desai is not implying that the un-burnt brides and the well-settled ones may live a content life. In this regard, she portrays the story of Aruna, Uma's smart and pretty younger sister who makes a discreet choice and marries "the wisest, ... the handsomest, the richest, the most exciting of the suitors who presented themselves"(101). Aruna's marriage to Arvind who has a job in Bombay and a flat in a housing block in Juhu, facing the beach is just like a dream-come-true. Yet to live that dream-life fully she transforms herself and desperately seeks to introduce change in the lives of others. She cuts her hair, takes her make-up kit wherever she goes, and calls her sister and mother as 'villagers' once they refuse to accept her sophisticated and flashy style of life. For that reason, she avoids visiting her parents' home and the rare occasions of her short visits are spent in blaming the untidiness of the surrounding and the inhabitants. Even she goes to the extent of scolding her husband when he splits tea in his saucer, or wears a shirt, which does not match, with his trousers.

In this way, Aruna's entrapment is different from the rest. She has liberated herself from the customs and dominating home rules that bind the rest of the characters like Uma and Anamica. Yet, in negating those codes, she ensnares herself in her mad pursuit towards a vision of perfection. And in order to reach that perfection she needs to constantly uncover and rectify the flaws of her own family as well as of Arvind's. When none other than Uma sees through the entrapment of Aruna, she feels pity for her:

> Seeing Aruna vexed to the point of tears because the cook's pudding had sunk and spread instead of remaining upright and solid, or because Arvind had come to dinner in his bedroom slippers, or Papa was wearing a t-shirt with a hole under one arm, Uma felt pity for her: was this the realm of ease and comfort for which Aruna had always pined and that some might say she had attained? Certainly it brought her no pleasure: there was always a crease of discontent between her eyebrows and an agitation that made her eyelids flutter, disturbing Uma who noticed it (109).

While Uma, Anamica, Aruna present the female versions of entrapment in *Fasting, Feasting,* Arun pictures the male version of it. Unlike his sisters, right from his birth, Arun desists eating the food of his family which is symbolic of its values. Much to the dismay of his father, he shows his preference for vegetarian food. Simply because it revolutionised the life-style of his father, Arun can not be forced to eat non-vegetarian food. This, of course, is a cause of disappointment for Papa.

Nonetheless, Arun cannot fully come out of the clutches of Papa, especially, in terms of his education. And ironic enough, it is education, which instead of offering the desired autonomy, paves way for Arun's entrapment.

Papa, in order to give "the best, the most, the highest" (119) education to his son, takes charge of Arun's life from his childhood. Although Arun's school examinations are over, Papa cannot allow him to go to his sister's house in Bombay during holidays, since he has planned that time for taking up entrance examinations and preparation for sending applications to go abroad for 'higher studies'. However, in the eyes of Aruna, her father's manic determination to get a foreign scholarship for Arun, is actually on account of his unfulfilled dreams, which he tries to impose on his son. That is why, when the letter of acceptance from Massachusetts finally arrives, it stirs no emotions in Arun.

Anita Desai, in portraying the stories of entrapment in *Fasting, Feasting,* presents one version after another; each contributing together to a master version, and each simultaneously subverting the other towards an open and contingent version. Accordingly, in the story of Uma, we find her unattractiveness leading to her eventual entrapment. Yet, if we pass a final verdict on this account, we would be proved erroneous since Desai presents the versions of Aruna and Anamica, Uma's appealing sister and charming cousin, respectively. Beauty cannot offer them escape from entrapments; in truth, it is rather their good looks that victimise them. Further, if we think again that it is Uma's lack of education that has led to her entrapped situation, Desai presents us the subversion of Anamica, where foreign scholarship fetches her an equal match but fails to provide her the required escape, it suffocates and kills her literally. In like manner, if as Uma thinks, "A CAREER. Leaving home. Living alone" (130) would bring in the necessary freedom from entrapment, Desai presents us the story of Arun, who leaves home, lives alone for a career but feels the pangs of entrapment despite it.

Also in providing a male version through the story of Arun's entrapment, Desai negates any feministic verdict based on the other female versions of entrapment that is likely to put the blame on the patriarchal, male-centred society. Thus, Anita Desai, often described as one of the finest writers of this country, has moved from her earlier, typical way of sympathising with her characters, females especially, to a different level of sensibility now. Where it would be easy to presuppose her overt feministic concerns in a novel like *Cry, the Peacock,* it would be unwise to approach her *Fasting,*

Feasting with any such preconceived notions. Desai herself speaks out in a recent interview that she has been deliberately shifting her focus from female characters to male characters. She rather feels she needs to address and voice out themes which concern males too. She says:

> "Specially in my earlier work I found myself addressing the same things over and over again: very much about the life of women, specially those women who are confined to home and family, also the solitude from which a person can suffer even if living within a big family or surrounded by crowds. But after several years and several books I began to feel suffocated myself by the confinement of these subjects. I felt I was limiting the territory to such an extent that it created a kind of suffocation even for me. So I deliberately opened the doors, to widen the canvas, and started writing more about male characters and their lives, because I felt they had a wider experience of the world, and I could address a greater variety of experiences."

Works Cited

Costa, Magda. "Interview with Anita Desai, *Lateral* (March 2001).

Desai, Anita. *Fasting, Feasting* (London: Vintage, 1999)

15

Indian Ideology in Vikram Seth's Novels

Prerana Sinha

To Vikram Seth, the noted Indo-Anglian writer of late twentieth century, recognition in the literary field came globally through *The Golden Gate,* published in 1986. It was seen as a brilliant example of a Verse Novel based on Californian life imbued in lust and materialism. In 1993, Seth got instant fame and publicity for the celebrated novel, *A Suitable Boy.* By this time the Indo-Anglian authors were being seen as serious writers of merit, and Seth was ensconced, perhaps, as the most popular Indo-Anglian writer whose novels are still in demand. Six years later, Seth's another novel *An Equal Music* was launched amidst much fanfare and hype, more so because Salm an Rushdie's *The Ground Beneath Her Feet* too was launched simultaneously and both these novels were assumed vying for the international award, Booker's prize.

Vikram Seth won awards and fame for all the three novels. This fact definitely makes one curious as to what thought and philosophy goes into churning such prodigious works; there must be some uniform ideology that he must have followed in one novel after another. What is most intriguing is that Seth adheres to his ideology in novels which are so dissimilar in the treatment of subject and sensibility; while the first one was based on American society, the second was conceived on Indian subcontinent and the recent one, *An Equal Music* deals with the life of European musicians, Seth's works in fact reveals that whatever sensibility he might be using, he still retains his Indianness.

According to my findings, Seth re-establishes the Indian belief in constancy, stability, fidelity in relationships and makes a sound family system as the foundation in the novels. It is a marvel that while other Indo-Anglian novelists have mostly viewed passion and lust as an important thread in their novels; Seth has not only rejected it, but has also shown the repercussions of such indulgences. All this he does brilliantly by being sometimes omniscient, sometimes semi-omniscient narrator by splitting, varying and incarnating in his characters. He appears to be guided by Jonathan Swift, the Augustan satirist's saying, 'Man is rationis-capax' ie. man is capable of rationality. Like the authors, namely Fielding in the eighteenth century and Jane Austen in the nineteenth, Seth too makes his characters pay for their errors until they realize their follies. Regarding sex passion he seems to emphasise what D.H. Lawrence underlined in his letter to friend, Frieda: "I think when one loves, one's very sex passion that nearly drives one mad, is far away from real love" (Moore, p. 244). In *The Golden Gate,* Liz., the central character while discussing her love relation with John confides in Phil saying,

> . . . Well, love's fun
> At first . . . but living with someone
> You love, can be less than appealing
> If everything's just great in bed
> Yet nothing's shared inside your head.
>
> (Seth: *The Golden Gate,* p. 240)

She even adds:

Passion's a prelude to disaster" (Sonnet 11: 20, p. 244)

The foundation of Liz's relationship with John has only been sexual passion. She realizes that for a permanent relationship it is important that the woman and man share intellectual proximity as well or else the marriage becomes a complete disaster. Liz realizes another important factor that true love should also give a sense of freedom to both; it should not prove itself a 'tightening tether/A habit-forming drug, a crutch', (Sonnet, 11:13 p. 240).

Liz has experienced the passionate love of John who is so possessive about her that he fails to see her true identity, her intellectual wants. Phil on the other hand recognizes it and encourages her in meeting her goal. John is unable to see the truth because he is himself full of complexes. In fact, the lack of parental love has made him weak; he is unable to see the reason. Above all, he lacks sensitivity to understand the reason behind the homo-sexual relationship between Phil and Liz's brother, Ed which according to Seth is a serious flaw. Seth exhibits a very tolerant outlook towards this taboo subject. If John lacks tolerance, Seth cannot forgive him until he willfully admits his mistake.

It appears quite ironical that Seth is ready to forgive the two men indulging in such a relationship but not John whose sin is not of that magnitude. The reason is simple: man only commits mistake and it is therefore expected that he must atone for his mistakes; a moral seer will never tolerate its non-acceptance. The two men, Ed and Phil, realizing the sin that they were commiting, soon discontinue as Ed's sense of religion has made him realize.

> The point is that my body is
> Not mine alone—I don't disdain it
> But it's God's Instument . . . (Sonnet 4:52, p. 98)

To the author what matters most is relinquishing whatever is wrong, for sooner or later, the erring person will be forgiven. Moreover, to err is human so we have no right to socially or morally ostracize or castigate anyone; no matter how serious his crime is.

While Liz and Phil get married, it is John who is left forlorn and unhappy. He pays heavily for his flaw and only towards the end, he realizes that he is a failure who could not get his soulmate; in the end he is a saner person.

Seth's next novel was out and out an Indian novel, titled *A Suitable Boy.* In essence, the novel is search for suitable boys. Mrs. Rupa Mehra is the widow in search of suitable boys for her daughters. The novel begins with the solemnization of the marriage of her elder daughter, Savita while she is equally anxious about the marriage of her second daughter, Lata which she has presumed to be fraught with greater problems as Lata is intelligent who would not accept any boy suggested by her mother and is not beautiful like Savita. Lata, therefore, has to assess the problems confronted by her mother due to her widowhood, a social stigma in Indian society that forces her to stoop low in arranging marriages, the consideration of dowry and consequent dependence on her son, Arun and his impudent wife. Lata has also to judge people, relationship of husband and wife as she examines the wedded life of her sister who remains completely devoted to her asthmatic husband, to her in-laws, and later to her child, who is born not just to her and her husband but to the entire clan. Regarding true love she realizes that Savita and her husband shared a compatible relationship because first they had come to love each other and secondly their yearnings did not stretch beyond their limits. This relationship she perceives in contrast with the married life of her brother, Arun Mehra who had married Meenakshi Chatterjee as he had got attracted to her vivaciousness, her external beauty. She feels they are not successful life partners as Meenakshi is neither faithful to her husband as she has an illicit relation with an Englishman nor is she careful about running her household within the limited salary of Arun Mehra. Moreover, she does not take care of her daughter and worst of all she is impudent and callous with her mother-in-law. On the other hand, Lata can clearly see how religiously her mother was carrying out the duties which she had to manage on her own. In spite of the problems and hurdles, her mother retains her bravery, steadfastness and resolution; occasionally, she would remember her husband who was spiritually and morally a great sustaining force in her otherwise difficult life. Lata too matures and understands the reason behind the restlessness and anxiety of her mother for all the family members. She analyses the role of the wife, the mother in the Indian society as underlined by the author. As per the Indian tradition, Mrs Mehra is every inch a typical mother. Regarding the role of the Indian mother, Sudhir Kakar emphasizes:

> The mother functions as the external ego of the child for a much longer period than is customary in the West and many of the ego functions concerned with reality are later transferred from mother to the family and other social institutions. . . . Every detail of behaviour is regulated. Relationships are codified. (Kakar, p. 59)

Lata's choice of prospective husband has to be according to her perception of the individual in totality in relation to the society she belongs to. She knows she too like her mother and her mother's mother should exercise self-control and a marital order by being receptive to the likes and desires of family.

Lata comes across three suitors and she has to make a sagacious and an unbiased judgment of her life partner. Lata falls in love with a muslim boy, Kabir. But the courtship stops sooner than it begins because the mother hailing from a middle-class Hindu family would not accept it. Moreover, he is still studying. Lata understanding the encumberances and visualizing the impossibility of their relationship going any further makes things clear to Kabir. Moreover, Seth too does not seem to approve of Kabir as a suitable boy as he is not decisive. Instead of taking the problem as a challenge, he simply quits.

Another suitor that Lata comes across is Amit Chatterjee, her sister-in-law's brother. He makes advances towards her. Once again her mother stops its possibility mid-way. According to her, the boy has two disqualifications: firstly, he is a Bengali and more importantly, "Poet, wastrel! Who has never earned an honest rupee in his life . . . ." (Seth: *A Suitable Boy,* p. 486) Her obvious choice is a decent, Khatri, industrious boy, Haresh Khanna. In contrast with the ultra-modern, elite Amit Khanna, she prefers Haresh who is simple, down to earth who would not demand dowry. However, Lata too is not so dumb that she would blindly agree to her mother's choice. She is intelligent and prudent enough to judge things. She is nevertheless, carried away by Kabir's good looks and later by Amit's romantic advances. But being a product of Industrial World she cannot remain impervious of the realities of material life. Amit does not fit into her image of a husband for her he is non-serious, a flippant youth who would not be able to shoulder the responsibility of a marriage.

As regards Kabir, her experiences and feelings are distraught with pain. She feels hurt and jealous when she is told that Kabir has been seeing someone. She realizes, its passion, a negative feeling that is the harbinger of suffering and confusion which might wreak destruction and despair. Lata would rather opt for self-control, rational calm and social order through chastity and strict monogamy. Considering divorce rates, extra-marital relations, casual promiscuities and the frequency of crimes of and for passion, especially in the West, Lata's commitment to self-control and a planned marital life is undoubtedly an Indian concept.

Seth like the older writers wants to emphasise that true happiness and fulfilment of a couple lies in tolerant participation in the family matters and renunciation of sexual domination. Emotions, desires, romance are necessary in life but these things should not override man's duties in actual life. Seth belongs to that Indian culture where saints and people like Mahatma Gandhi were born, where this icon had sought for freedom of India through self-control, termed *ahimsa* and *satyagraha,* it was again for the same reason that he had later embraced celibacy.

Seth glorifies the social order that is so central to the family system that in itself has been the greatest armour and strength for Indians which is unfortunately dying in the West and hence he makes it as the core, the root of a stable, secure life. Moreover, Lata finds Haresh an adaptable man who is self-made, anti-snobbish and who cares for her mother's sentiments and above all; he has also agreed for a teaching career for Lata. There are chances that the two would make a mature, compatible couple.

Seth's third novel *An Equal Music* was on a very different theme: Seth's predilection for music that is brilliantly brought through the lives of String quartet players living in Europe. The author has portrayed the complex lives of these artists. He has successfully built a corollary with the self-enclosed, obsessive love of Michael, one of the players and Julia, his beloved whom he had not met for the last seven years, where both have to strike a balance between familial responsibility and professional life. For, Julia is already married and has a son also but Michael wants to revive their love. Julia too, much as she may wish to return to her love, will not be able to do so, as she is now somebody's wife, and more importantly she is a mother or Madonna. It is commendable that even though the story percolates around the life of English people, Seth retains the Indian ideology of preference for family life, subjugation of lust and passion and a complete adherence to a chaste social order. Both indulge in lust and passion but it only leaves them guilty and unhappy.

It is significant to note Michael's utter desolation and disillusionment who tries to probe the meaning of their relationship through religion. He says to himself, "Adultery and sin: ludicrously, there are no gentler words. But Julia cannot accept this brimstone" (Seth: *An Equal Music,* p. 169).

Seth has appropriately used stream of consciousness technique to envisage Michael's trepidations and conflicting thoughts in the novel. By the interior monologue device, Seth is successful at mirroring Michael's guilt, his consciousness about his position as an intruder who is trying to disrupt the tranquillity of Julia and her family.

He ruminates over the conjugal relation of Julia and her husband in the last seven year: "Let us measure it in stacks of photographs, in school fees, in shared meals, in the mellow, delights of the connubial beds, in hard times shared" (Ibid, p. 212).

Michael's discomfiture is wonderfully conveyed. He cannot ignore the reality, the fact that Julia's existence cannot be treated in isolation, she has to be conceived in totality: a woman who has seen different times in her life; good and bad. He realizes that marriage is much beyond a sensual relation; it is a commitment of inter-personal trust, faith, concern and love. Michael feels it would be criminal to disengage Julia from the security and warmth that she is getting in her married life.

It is pertinent to underscore Julia's troubled expressions about the moments she and Michael shared with each other. She writes to Michael:

> I have to learn peace again, for my own sake and for Luke, and for James, who looks lost and tired. I have become restless with you and uncertain, and afraid, and guilty, and unsustainability, stupidity, full of joy and pain . . . (Ibid, p. 324)

Julia feels she has lost her peace of mind; she has become restless, perhaps afraid that her married life might get wrecked. The solution to their wretchedness according to the author is music; what Shakespeare had observed: 'If music be the food of love play on. Give me excess of it, that surfeiting . . .' (Shakespeare, p. 1).

Truly, music can become the soul of one's life, it can sustain a person amidst his turbulences and despair. Michael has to find a way to make Julia's life worthwhile as in an illness she has become deaf. Michael realizes that he has to unselfishly think of giving her a purpose for living. He encourages Julia to play despite her deafness. Michael achieves an uncanny sense of satisfaction and fulfilment as he sees Julia involved in it; his triumph is he has managed to yield to another musician's craving for music.

Michael ultimately ends up as a rich character despite having indulged in adultery as he has succeeded in giving an equal music to Julia by enabling her to breathe life into her handicap and in return she is able to give life to art and art-lovers. After seeing Julia perform at the solo recital Michael achieves great satisfaction and his feelings are exquisitely expressed in these evocative words of Seth:

> Music, such music is a sufficient gift, why ask for happiness, why not hope to grieve? It is enough, it is to be blessed enough to live from day to day and to hear such music. (Seth: *An Equal Music,* p. 381)

Michael is happy even in his unhappiness and solitude. He would lead his entire life, with no qualms. Indeed, music can be as redeeming and become an expression of sublime beauty and divinity in the hands of artists and Seth has accomplished it. He is able to understand the value of music because of his training in Indian Classical Music. Moreover, being born in the country of *'Music samrats'* like Tansen and Bhimsen, it is not surprising that Seth is able to feel its pervading effect so well.

The primary aim of literature is to mirror life fully and the onus of generating good literature lies in the hands of writers who can educate and sustain the readers. Such writings become pertinent and imperative in today's fluid world, where values of life are fast annihilating. By making the negation of passion in all forms and affirmation of a simple and chaste life, the underlying theme of all his novels, essentially an Indian ideology, Seth's contribution will always be cherished and remembered.

Works Cited

Kakar, Sudhi, *Hinduism: A Fettering Faith: Political Consciousness in*

Indian English Writing, ed. M.K. Bhatnagar, Bahri Publication, 1991.

Moore, Harry T. (ed.) *The Life and Works of D.H. Lawrence,* Harry T. Moore, Great Britain: Unwin Books, 1951.

Seth Vikram, *A Suitable Boy,* Viking Penguin India, 1993.

——, *An Equal Music,* Viking Penguin India, 1999 p. 169.

Shakespeare, William, *The Twelfth Night or What You Will,* Act 1, scene 1, ed. Stanley Wood, George Gill & Sons Ltd., 1966.

16

Shahshi Deshpande's Best Articulation of her Vision: *The Dark Holds No Terrors*

C.P. Sharma

The Dark Holds No Terrors is Shashi Deshpande's most favourite narrative till today because it embodies her vision most artistically and effectively. In the foreword to the Penguin edition of the novel, she admits it in clear terms.

> All authors, like most parents have their favourite children; but unlike parents, authors can, without any compunction declare their partiality *The Dark Holds No Terrors* is of all my novels the one dearest to me. Perhaps this is because it is one which came closest to the vision I had of it when I conceived it. Perhaps it is because it was this book which gave me the never-to-be experienced-again happiness of a first acceptance. (p. 6)

No doubt she does not specify or spell out what her vision is, a close reading of the novel explicitly demonstrates that it is a feminist vision, which calls out for a space and a voice for every voiceless, silent and silenced woman. Her novels probe into the territory of the interior lives of the middle-class women who are engaged in an unending battle against the age-old discrimination of patriarchy and the daily nameless humiliation, of day-to-day existence. Her texts provide a detailed account of the gender injustice in the contemporary India. Her female protagonists, who are exceptionally sensitive and independent, reach out to the outside world in an attempt to find answers for the ontological questions which keep gnawing at their heart.

Like the other female protagonists of Shashi Deshpande, Sarita, the central figure of *The Dark Holds No Terrors* hails from the urban middle-class society of contemporary India. Through her heart-rending tale of injustice, violence, guilt and terror the novelist tries to portray all those bewildered and tortured women who in spite of being intelligent, independent, sensitive and attractive are condemned to lead a miserable life of an unhappy marriage. One of the pioneering feminist discourses, the novel daringly foregrounds sexual violence within the framework of the marriage which is legally and socially sanctioned. The author deliberately uses the word 'rape' to delineate the male aggression or 'invasion' of the female body even in the case of a lawfully wedded couple. The nightly onslaught on the wife's body against her will is a beastly act of violence, which reduces the woman to an abject, disgraceful non-entity. In the prologue to the novel which is marked out in italics, the novelist vividly paints Saru's nightmarish ordeal thus:

> All first it was a nightmare of hands. Questing hands that left a trail of pain . . . . And the nightmare was compounded of lips and teeth as well? Hands and teeth? No, hammers and pincers. I could taste blood on my lips.... Now there was no waking. The dream, the nightmare, whatever it was, continued. Changing now, like some protean monster, into the horror of rape . . . it was a monstrous invasion of my body. I tried to move, twisting my body, wriggling under the weight that pinned it down. It was impossible. I was pinioned to a position of an abject surrender

> of my self. I began, in sheer helplessness, to make small whimpering sounds, piteous cries. The small pains merged all at once into one large one. And still the body above mine, hard and tense, went on with its rhythmic movements. The hands continued their quest for new areas of pain. Now the horror of what was happening to me was lost in a fierce desire to end it. I could not, would not bear it. I began to fight back, hopelessly, savagely. (pp. 11-12)

The misery and ignominy of Sarita becomes doubly oppressive and relevant as we learn that the rapist is none other than her husband. The words and images are carefully chosen and skilfully crafted into the fabric of the narrative. The hands, lips and teeth all become viciously alive, and like monsters they maul and bruise the passive, helpless female form. The brutal sexual act is described with an honesty which is almost shocking. The horrendous scene inevitably jolts us to an awareness that in the hegemonic order of patriarchy: the male is always a master and the female a slave.

Sarita is neither illiterate nor an economically helpless female dependent on her husband. She is no Savitri of R.K. Narayan's *The Dark Room* weeping and whining but unable to leave the house. On the contrary, Saru, being highly educated, has a profession of her own. She is a successful and prosperous lady doctor. But her husband Manu, whom she has married for love defying her mother, is only a low-paid teacher in a third-rate college. A typical egoistic male, a product of patriarchy, he soon starts resenting the superior status of his wife. When they go out together, there are nods, smiles and respect, but these are for her, and not for him. She describes the situation thus:

> And so the esteem with which I was surrounded made me inches taller. But the same thing which made me inches taller made him inches shorter. He had been the young man and I his bride. Now I was the lady doctor and he my husband.

> a+b they told us in mathematics is equal to b+a. But here a+b was not, definitely not equal to b+a. It became a monstrously unbalanced equation, lopsided, unequal, impossible . . . . (p. 42)

With rare subtlety Shashi Deshpande strikes at the root of the unequal relationship between man and woman; the woman must follow the shadow of man, but no man will like to live in the shadow of a woman. This reversal of the conventional social order, this unbearable anomaly in the patriarchal hierarchy rudely affects the marital life of Saru and her husband. While he keeps up a normal relationship with his wife during the day in the darkness of the night in the bedroom he becomes a beast and tries to show his superiority and manliness by raping her ruthlessly. Apparently, this drives her to exasperation, and despair to a total disintegration of her self. She calls herself a 'two in one' person: a public self which goes round in a white starched apron healing the sick and a private self which like a trapped and bruised animal, whimpers and cries out against the terrors looming in the darkness of the night.

When Saru comes to know that her mother has passed away after a prolonged suffering from cancer, she decides to go home to her father. Though she tells her husband and children that she wants to be with her father at this hour of grief, she knows in the heart of her heart that it is nothing but a desperate attempt on her part to get away from the fearful and tortuous experiences of the night:

> To get away from this house, this paradise of matching curtains and handloom bedspreads. This hell of savagery and submission. But what if I carry my own hell within me? Then there is no hope for me at all. But that too I have to know. And therefore I am going home to my father. (p. 28)

After an absence of fifteen years when she reaches her parents' home, the most haunting figures are her mother and her brother who are no longer alive. Her mother dominating and discriminating her against her brother Dhruva, had accused her when she was only a child that she was responsible for the death of her brother. She realises that the terrors of the dark from which she was fleeing are related not only to her sadist husband, but also to the burden of guilt, which she has been carrying within her for being responsible for the accident in which her younger brother died.

The section which deals with Saru's unhappy childhood is a feminist attack on gender discrimination, which unfortunately forms an integral part of the socialisation of a girl child in the male-dominated society of India. Her mother consciously and systematically persecutes her because she is a girl and she has different sets of rules to follow. Dhruva is different because he is a boy. He is more important because as a son he will carry the family line forward and he alone will light the pyre of his parents. As for a daughter, she is only a temporary inmate of her parental home. She has to be given away in marriage to another family with a dowry. Therefore, she is always a liability and a burden. Saru remembers at the depth of her heart that while Dhruva's birthdays were celebrated with worship, on her birthday there was only a festive lunch. After his death her birthdays were passed over in silence. Her mother represented those 'patriarchal matriarchs' who would internalise the social mores, customs and conventions so completely and unquestioningly into herself that she would feel that perpetuating them through her daughter was the natural and inevitable duty of a mother. The following bits of dialogue between the mother and the daughter lay bare the truth:

> Don't go out in the sun. You will-get even darker.
> Who cares?
> We have to care even if you don't. We, have to get you married.
> I don't want to get married.
> Will you live with us all you life?
> Why not?

You can't.
And Dhruva?
He is different. (p. 45)

The difference in the upbringing of a boy and a girl is brought out very clearly here. Marriage and man should be her natural and necessary destinations. She is groomed to fill the social role prescribed for her by patriarchy. Woman exists only in relation to man, and she has to conform to this.

True, as a child Saru was deeply hurt by her mother's obvious preference of her brother. Back home now as an educated discerning adult, she sees herself as the victim of gender discrimination and the hegemonic values of a male-dominated society. "One is not born, but rather becomes, a woman," Simon de Beauvoir correctly affirms. Tracing the root of female oppression in such prescriptive social mores, Shashi Deshpande interrogates the established social norms according to which the female mind is conditioned to accept submission and silence as a natural process.

In almost all her novels the author repeatedly refers to another social custom prevalent in Brahmanical society, and that is the confinement in which women are kept during menstruation. She is the first Indian writer to refer to the female body and a woman's private experiences like menstruation and childbirth in the most uninhibited manner. Saru describes her initiation into womanhood as a humiliating experience in the following words:

> It was a torture. Not just the three days when I couldn't enter the kitchen or the *puja* room. Not just the sleeping on the straw mat covered with a thin sheet. Not just the feeling of being a pariah, with my special cup and a plate by my side in which I was served from a distance, for my touch was, it seemed, a pollution. No it was something quite different, much worse. A kind of shame that engulfed me . . . (p. 62)

A polluted and polluting being, a woman must consider

her body as a matter of shame. Inevitably, Saru refers to her own self shamefully as "a dark, damp, smelly hole". Her mother grimly reminds her that she is now grown up, and so she should be hidden in the folds of her clothes and must take care that her body's not exposed to male gaze, not even to her father: "You should be careful now about how you behave. Don't come out in your petticoat like that. Not even if it is your father who's around." (p. 62) The mother on behalf of the phallocentric society makes sure that control, concealment, confinement, passivity and self-effasiveness should become a way of life with the daughter. Thus, subordination and a sense of shame are ingrained into the mindset of the girl child. Consequently, Saru grows up to be afraid of and ashamed of her sexuality, and even as a married woman she, in spite of having enjoyed sex, always feels in her subconscious mind a deep-rooted fear of, and repulsion to this instinct.

As the narrative moves backward and forward, filtering through the flux of the consciousness of its female protagonist, there are many a reference to the socially constructed image of the woman as an ideal wife and as an ideal mother. When Saru enters her father's home after many years, the first thing she notices is the absence of *tulasi*. *Tulasi* worship is one of the rituals which every pious wife as *pativrata* must observe in order to ensure that she dies a *sumangali* before her husband's death. Saru wryly comments that her mother's wish was, however, granted. Looking at her photo hanging on the wall once again Saru says sardonically that the huge *kumkum* mark (a mark of her haloed married status) on her forehead blots out everything else, suggesting thereby the obsession of the Indian woman with the image of herself as a blessed wife. Without a man she is a cipher. Therefore, there is rejection and disgrace for a woman being a widow. The ominous presence of a widow on any auspicious occasion is banned. Sudhir's mother whom Saru meets once again on her return home is one such lesser, inferior being. She envies Saru's mother who was fortunate in her death, no matter she had died a miserable death.

Another condemnable ritual still practised in the Brahmin families of Karnataka and Maharashtra is the naming ceremony of the bride. Her maiden name chosen by her parents is discarded and the husband's family gives her a new name. This ceremony is symbolic of the death of the wife's former self and a rebirth to suit and conform to the rules and values of the new home. Most women proudly accept this demeaning custom as a routine matter. But Saru is appalled at the injustice meted out to women by such ceremonies. She vehemently criticises the passive acceptance of such cruel practices in the name of tradition and religion. She tells Smita, her classmate, that she would never call her by her new name, Geetanjali. While Smita is complacent and proud that her husband has fondly chosen the name for her because he was reading Tagore at the time of their marriage, Saru and her feminist friend Nalu go all out to condemn it. Saru asks: "This drastic change of identity, changing both the names that identified you for so many years . . . How then do you know yourself, and who you are?" (p. 118)

Likewise, Saru, with all her feminist zeal, refuses to accept the stereotypical images of womanhood—woman as an angel in the house virtuous and self-abnegating to be valourized. Saru is intelligent, attractive, sensitive and strong, but at the same time she is rebellious, rude and demanding. She does not mind using her professor to rise in her profession. Not only Boozy's influence but also his money is welcome to her if it can help her to set up her practice. She toys with the idea of having an affair with him in order to spite her impotent husband. But she drops him when she comes to know that he is a homosexual. Earlier in the book she dismisses the sacrificing ideal of womanhood in a contemptuous manner:

> Stupid, silly martyrs, she thought; idiotic heroines. Going on with their tasks, and destroying themselves in the bargain, for nothing but a meaningless modesty. Their unconscious, unmeaning heroism, born out of the myth of self-sacrificing martyred women, did not arouse either her pity or her admiration. It made her angry . . . (p. 107)

Thus, Saru deconstructs and subverts the stereotypical image of a wife as virtuous and enduring as a *pativrata.*

Saru demolishes another mythical image of an Indian woman, viz., that of a mother. Like Deshpande's other protagonists, she rejects the sacrosanct status given to motherhood. The ambivalence in the mother-daughter relationship with its bitter-sweet nature is central in *The Dark Holds No Terrors.* Saru never sees her mother as a role model. Perhaps it is her mother's strict adherence to tradition and her total submission to the male hegemony, which drives her away from her mother. With shocking resentment, she tells her:

> If you are a woman, I don't want to be one, I thought resentfully, watching her body. The cleft which ran down her back, a deep furrow, dividing her body sharply in two. The two buttocks sharply outlined by the kind of sari she wore, tucked in between her legs. The way her hips moved as she walked. I can remember walking as stiffly as possible, holding my pelvis rigid willing it not to move, so that I would be as unlike her as possible. (p. 62-63)

This is certainly an unusual reaction for a daughter and a very unusual image of a mother. However, towards the end of the novel, Saru feels guilty of having deserted her mother and of not having tried to cross the bridge, which had kept them apart. She herself has never felt the contentment or fulfilment of a mother. Not that she has no love for her children. She describes her mixed feelings at her first delivery thus:

> Sometimes she wondered at herself. Was she an unnatural, unloving mother? She had sworn that she would never fail her children in love and understanding as her own mother had done. That she would be to her children all that her mother had not been to her. But the children had started off a disappointment. She had been buoyed up through all the months of pregnancy by the thought of a miracle

> awaiting her. The miracle of motherhood. But when, after a day-long struggle, she had felt, through a haze of pain and shock, Renu's head forcing itself out, she had been outraged at the indignity of it. Her posture, her grunts, her cries, the pain which made an animal out of her . . . Was this the prelude to motherhood? (p. 161-62)

The birth of Saru's first child is vividly described by Deshpande without any inhibition or social taboo, not as a gratifying experience of sacred motherhood but as an undignified animal experience. Thus, the writer deconstructs the 'miracle of motherhood'.

Saru condemns the stereotypical representation of woman, marriage, man and wife in strong terms in her speech made at Nalu's school on the topic, 'Women and Profession'. While she delivers the speech on the expected lines, in an aside she says that she should have told them the following:

> But if you want to be happily married, there is one thing you have to remember. Have you seen old-fashioned couple walking together? Have you noticed that the wife always walks a few steps behind her husband? That is important, very important, because it is symbolic of the truth. A wife must always be a few feet behind her husband, If he is an MA, you should be a BA. If he's 5'4" tall you shouldn't be more than 5'3" tall. If he is earning 500 rupees, you should never earn more than four hundred and ninety nine rupees . . . . Don't ever try to reverse the doctor-nurse, executive-secretary, and principal-teacher role. . . . Women's magazines will tell you that marriage should be an equal relationship. That is nonsense. Rubbish. No partnership can ever be equal. It will always be unequal, but take care that it's unequal in favour of your husband. If the scales tilt in your favour, god help you, both of you. (p. 137)

Saru's ironic words, wrenched out of her own wretched experiences, conjure up an absurdly comic-tragic picture of the conventional image of a happy marriage. With characteristic feminist rage Shashi Deshpande, through her protagonist, strikes at the unequal power structures of patriarchy. Axing at the root cause for feminine oppression, Saru relentlessly goes on to say:

> They will tell you about economic independence and an independent identity. Forget the words. If Draupadi had been economically independent. If Sita had been an independent identity, you think their stories would have been different? No, these are things that have been voluntarily surrendered, consciously abandoned, because that is the only way to survive. And what, in the long run matters more than survival? (pp. 137-38)

Besides these internalised feminist concepts that we find mirrored in the character of Saru, there are also direct references to feminism and feminist agenda. Saru refers to Vidya, a friend of Manu, whom she had met in the early years of her marriage. She wryly describes those intellectual parties where Vidya, a 'women's libber' (those days feminism was not a commonly used word), accused Shakespeare for his limited vision:

> Now, now, let me explain. What I'm saying is that his is a typical man's view of life—the man at the centre, the woman always on the periphery . . . look at the way he made the women always subordinate to the men . . . Look at Hamlet, Lear, Othello. And look at Ophelia, Cordelia, and Desdemona. Poor, feeble shadows. And when you come to a conflict or a climax, the woman recedes into the background. Just look at the way he disposed of Lady Macbeth. And how splendidly she starts off, really! (pp. 155-56)

Saru sardonically states that when she met her years later married and mothered:

> She had, she told me, given up acting because Ashwin

> doesn't like the idea of my going on the stage. His family disapproves too. They don't mind my associating with the theatre occasionally, but no acting, directing or anything like that.
>
> And the family, I found out later had made a fortune out of producing hooks, buttons or something like that. (p. 156)

Saru's classmate Nalu, whom she meets when she returns home, has also become a feminist, but of a different kind. She is a spinster who spends her time. and energy on her young students. It's through her that Saru first learns about 'a room of one's own' and an introduction to Virginia Woolf. However, she feels that Nalu is only a theoretical and theorising person. She analyses every situation with a clinical, professional approach, which lacks human touch. Saru has toyed with the idea of confessing to her about the crisis in her life. But she knows that Nalu would never be able to look at the situation in its proper context:

> I could talk to Nalu about myself and my problem and may be she would understand better than most people would. But to her I would be a woman, my problems a part of women's problems. But this is mine, Saru's, and has as much to do with what I am, apart from my being a woman. It's only I, it's Manu and I, and how we react against each ather. (p. 121)

Saru does not want that her story should be taken as a woman's story. She feels that her tragedy lies not in the fact that she is a woman, but in the fact that she is Saru. The root cause of their suffering lies in the sad truth that both Saru and Manu have a different mind set, temperament and, above all, a complex character fraught with contradictions. Perhaps the key to Shashi Deshpande's vision of feminism lies here; generalising and trying to weigh every man-woman relationship on the scales of feminist strictures or an ideology is not her forte.

Saru's journey to her parental home can also be seen as

a feminist journey in search of identity, self-hood and individuation. She had, as an adolescent, fought a feminist battle against her mother to break free. She remembers that in that battle her father had stood by her. After getting a first division in her intermediate, she had made up her mind to join the medical college. But she knew that her mother would never agree with her. She said that they could not afford to waste so much money on her because they had to get her married also. Between marriage and education she chose the latter. Her first victory against her mother takes her further away from the matriarch. When she falls in love with Manohar, a flamboyant literature student, she takes it as an opportunity to prove herself against her mother. She enjoys shocking her orthodox mother by choosing to marry a man from a lower caste. When she settles with Manu and starts her medical practice, she thinks that she is a liberated woman. She has rejected her mother's notions of marriage as the destination and destiny of a woman. She has proved her independence. Later when she sets up her own practice and becomes rich and famous as a lady doctor, she should have been at peace with herself. But it is not to be. When her loving husband turns a monster in the night because he is unable to accept her success, she realises the vulnerability of being a woman. Though she is emancipated, she is still not really free or liberated. She had thought that she would find her identity away from the confines of home. But now lost in the quagmire of surrender, submission and savagery, she sees her own feminine self-fragmented and splintered around her. Once sitting in her consulting room, she cuts a piece of paper into bits to the horror of the nurse, and says to herself that they are the bits of her mind falling on the ground. The hollowness of her existence or non-existence makes her almost crazy. Apparently, despite being emancipated, when locked in an unequal relationship with a man, the female passivity, vulnerability and the legacy of patriarchy continue to dog a woman. Breaking free from these shackles needs immense courage, resilience and willingness for a brutal self-criticism. When Saru arrives at her father's home, she is in this second final stage of her feminist struggle for freedom and individuation. Sitting quietly, she goes through the entire gamut of her tumultuous experiences spanning the different stages of her life from early childhood, adolescence and youth to maturity. She thinks of herself as a guilty sister, an undutiful daughter and unloving wife, and she accepts "these selves to become whole again". All this leads her to grasp the reality of her situation which is beautifully put by the novelist as follows:

> My life is my own . . . Somehow she felt as if she had found it now, the connecting link. It means you are not a strutting, grimacing puppet, standing futility on the stage for a brief while between areas of darkness. If I have been a puppet it is because I made myself one. I have been clinging to the tenuous shadow of a marriage whose substance has long since disintegrated . . . (p. 220)

So at last to retrieve her own splintered self, Saru turns to the darkness within herself. She must exorcise the monsters and terrors lurking in the dark. At the end of the novel when she rushes out to attend to one of her patients, she has come out of a cathartic experience — she has forgiven her mother, her father and her brother. The very fact that she agrees to meet Manu shows that she is no longer afraid of him. And —more importantly she is able to turn to her professon, in her own interest, not to prove herself successful and rich but to realize her true and uninhibited free self. After agonizing trials of errors through 'progression and regression' she moves to self-discovery and strength. Look at the ripeness and maturity reached through her feminist self-exploration:

> All right, so I'm alone. But so's everyone else. Human beings . . . They're going to fail you. But because there's just us, because there's no one else, we have to go on trying. If we can't believe in ourselves, we're sunk. (p. 220)

No doubt life is a continuous process marked by change

and renewal. Indeed, the novel ends, as all modern feminist texts do, without a closure; like Henry James's great novel, *The Portrait of* a *Lady,* it is an open-ended narrative. The feminist journey to selfhood and individuation is a process which is ongoing.

Works Cited

Deshpande, Shashi. "Note from the Author", *The Dark Holds No Terrors,* New Delhi: Penguin Books, 1990.

(All subsequent references to this novel are trom this edition and have been absorbed in the text by giving page references in parentheses.)

Beauvoir, Simon de. *The Second Sex in the Norton Anthology: Theory Criticism,* ed. Vincent B.Leitch, New York: Norton & Company, 2001.

17

Nayantara Sahgal's Retrieval to Past: A Persuit of New Dimensions

Sandhya Saxena

Nayantara Sahgal's odyssey as an eminent exponent of political novel remains unhindered, despite odds and obstacles. Commencing her carrier with *A Time to be Happy,* published in 1957, Nayantara continues to explore new horizons even in the 21st century which has witnessed the publication of her latest novel *Lesser Breeds* in the year 2003. She clearly exhibits the deterioration in values in almost all the important spheres of post-Independence Indian milieu against the backdrop of pre-Independence India, and successfully evolves a wayout of the impasse to stem the rot. Nayantara's political analysis extends extensively from the days of immediate pre- and post-independence era to the days of Emergency in 1975 and even beyond that. However, in her last three novels she recedes into the past because "from there on" she has "no further to go"(Sahgal, pp. 16). She declares, "It was like barking against the wall so I branched off into the forties and now back to the twenties" (Ibid.). A crusader for values, Mrs. Sahgal wrote fiction with a purpose. Hence, the anticipatory nature of her fiction remains unquestioned. The visionary in the novelist is shocked to see the endemic apathy towards values and democratic ideals and wakes up to novel dimensions in the later novels.

The fictional world of Mrs. Sahgal presents almost a chronological account of the decay and degeneration of values in Indian politics of pre- and post-Independence era.

A Time to be Happy (1957) is set in the immediate pre- and post-Independence period when there are hardly any glimpses of those fissures which later set in. In those early days politics had not assumed its devilish face and people were still trying to recover from a slumberous state. *This Time of Morning* (1965) provides a clear picture of the post-Independence scenario indicating not only a passage of time from midnight to morning but also a passage of idealism which is candidly visible in the daylight. The novel reinforces a murky note struck in the previous novel regarding the post-independence era as one finds all canons of decency and decorum overthrown in unscrupulous hunt for power. In *Storm in Chandigarh* (1969) the novelist portrays how the regional feelings are exploited to blot the totality of progress in a democratic set up. The linguistic bifurcation of the Punjab into Haryana and the Punjab about twenty years after the Partition of India in 1947 sets forth the situation here. The mounting tension and conflict between the newly-carved states bring on sufficient causes of anxiety for those who strove earnestly for the emergence of India as an independent nation. Further retreat from Gandhism is brought undisguisedly in *The Day in Shadow* (1971). The novel depicts the post-Nehru era when Delhi had become a place of feverish activity and Gandhism had been perverted to wield political power and influence over the masses. Healthy political values and democratic conventions were awfully threatened in the post-Independence era. *A Situation in New Delhi* (1977), ostensibly set in the 1960s, records the gloomy atmosphere consequent to the void created by the death of Pt. Nehru. The inefficiency of the politicians and the decline of values in political arena were responsible for the distrust and distress of young men like Rishad who, for the betterment of the country, involved themselves in violent action, following the doctrines of the Naxalite Movement. *Rich Like Us* (1985) focuses on the anguish of an intellectual artist at the disintegration of values that led to the declaration of Emergency in India. At this juncture Nayantara discerns, "with *Rich Like Us,* I have reached the end of the road. It exorcised that whole shame making national experience [i.e., the Emergency] from my system" (Chaddah, *The Sunday Tribune,* 4 June 1987).

In her earlier novels Nayantara continues to move into the labyrinths of colonial experience as well as colonial hangover in order to bring out competent ex-colonial leaders. In *This Time of Morning* "Kailas Vrind and Kalyan Sinha both have similar goals but different ways of setting about the task. Who amongst them, is the better excolonial?" (Jain, p. 99) Through her criticism for the political forces she comments upon the lack of commitment and dedication among most of the bureaucrats and leaders of the post-Independence era. The discussion on the *Bhagavad-Gita* between Dubey and Trivedi in *Storm in Chandigarh* is a noticeable endeavour to project the difference between the past and the present. Men of Trivedi's generation had worked for the 'other' though most of Dubey's contemporaries worked for 'self. "They were a different breed – insensitive, power hungry and status conscious" (Sahgal: FSF, p. 74). The post-Independence era with its characteristic state of doubt, confusion and uncertainty stands in sharp contrast to the pre-independence epoch which is an emblem of commitment, dedication, ideals and values. The excruciating experience of most of Nayantara's protagonists reveals that it is virtually impossible for them to survive in a totally different world. Simrit's story in *The Day in Shadow* is apparently the story of India on various levels.

> "Like Simrit, India is bewildered by the economic laws and needs and tries to relate to her numerous children at levels of communication which do not materialize. The question which is raised over and over again is what have we inherited and -how we set about making the best of it" (Jain, p. 102)

Nayantara's novels signify how the humanistic principles and moral integrity have lost their way into the mazes of political rivalry and selfish bureaucracy. In her two successive novels – *A Situati n in New Delhi* and *Rich Like Us* – Nayantara objectively evaluates the situation. Devi's dilemma after Shivraj's death, in *A Situation in New Delhi,* is symptomatic of India's own perplexity. Even in sixties, it is still a colonial India yearning and striving to survive after its break with the idealism of the past. *Rich Like Us* demonstrates a total collapse of democratic ideals and human values.

After this terrific experience Nayantara changes the course of her political journey and goes back to the golden aura of pre-Independence India when Indian leadership, though enslaved, ardently aspired for values and ideals. The indication to her journey back into the glory of the past can already be noted in her novel *Rich Like* US'. Sonali's resignation from her government job and her decision to join Mr. Brain's project about the study of mid-seventeenth to the mid-eighteenth-century Indian history suggests that there is hope only in the study of the past of the nation, and there is a necessity of reviving the moral values of the bygone days. Hence, Nayantara goes back to the 1920s in her next novel *Plans for Departure* (1986) which is both a love story and a mystery set in a continent poised for revolution and a world on the edge of World War I. *Mistaken Identity* (1988) is a story of love and obsession that brilliantly sums up the turmoil in the twilight years of Empire. *Lesser Breeds* (2003) studies the significance and relevance of non-violence in a violent unequal world. Beginning with 1932, the novel ends in 1968 when disarmament still remains a distant dream.

Nayantara's later novels stand widely apart from the earlier ones both in thematic minutiae as well as in narrative devices. In *Plans for Departure* and *Mistaken Identity* Nayantara warns her fellow citizens of the disastrous consequences of caste discrimination and communal disharmony in a secular republic. India, to Mrs. Sahgal, has been "a unique proposition based on the most civilized human instincts – a sort of meeting place of the human race, where the search for identity has worked itself out, by and large, peacefully and creatively, through different traditions of music and dance, arts and crafts, food, speech, poetry, dress and manners, in fact all that goes into distinguishing one lifestyle from another." (Sahgal "India's Identity . . ." p. 48). The harmonious blend of diverse cultures quite different from one another, gives the notion of "collective selfhood" to India. In her above mentioned novels, particularly in *Mistaken Identity,* Nayantara presents a vision of a world that "has not been broken up into fragments by narrow domestic walls". (Tagore: *Gitanjali*).

In her previous novels (upto *Rich Like Us)* Nayantara had been assiduous in concentrating on the concurrent problems only. But in the later novels she outstandingly emerges as a visionary writer.

In *Plans for Departure,* the novelist presumes how class conflict and caste discrimination harbour horrible consequences. In the novel, she presents the problem of untouchability through the eyes of a British missionary Marlowe Croft whose preoccupation with the establishment of a church in the remote hill station called Himpur verges on cynicism. Moreover, he is more concerned with the construction of a church and Christianizing the natives than with the solution of the problem. He refers to the crusade of Mahatma Gandhi in South Africa to emphasize his own view that India won't be able to attain freedom "until untouchability is rooted out." (Sahgal: *Plans for Departure,* p. 40) His efforts to motivate the sweeper boy for attaining human dignity are really appreciable. However, a deeper probe into his character reveals that his is a narrow approach of a missionary rather than that of a reformer like Gandhiji. In order to uproot the social stigma like untouchability Mahatma Gandhi stressed the need of self-purification instead of conversion to other religions.

Marlowe Croft and Henry Brewster, in the novel, appear to be two sides of the foreign ruler. Social problems attract Marlowe because "Christian propaganda was his job" (Ibid., p. 49). Henry also comments, "The Church was one more expression of white solidarity" (Ibid., p. 49). Henry's disapproval of Marlowe's plans of interference with the religious belief and custom of the natives is possibly because it may cause an insurrection and he is there to "keep peace and to collect revenue" (Ibid., p. 100). Neither Marlowe's consideration for untouchables nor Henry's rejection of the Christian propaganda can be interpreted as crusades for the betterment of the natives. Nayantara's implication, here, is that foreigners will take privilege if we fail to solve our prevailing problems, overthrowing our narrow precincts. She receeds into the 1920s and draws an appropriate atmosphere to caution her countrymen against the menace called casteism. It is a threat to democracy and may prove to be fatal to the freedom of the country. The politicians misuse it, today, for political benefits as missionaries took its privilege for propagating Christianity in the East.

Mistaken Identity which initially appears to be the story of a royal princeling Bhushan Singh, his mistaken identity and his several love affairs, ultimately assume a very profound meaning. It begins with the tales of the youthful love of a feudal lord for a Muslim girl, Razia to whom he is not united into marriage because of the protest of society. Despite failure, his vision of communal harmony and human unity is not distorted and, finally, he gets married to another Muslim girl. For Mrs. Sahgal, Bhushan is the true heir to the legend of Kabir whose corpse changed into flowers when his Hindu and Muslim followers quarrelled over the way of the dissolution of his corpse, "The legend lives on in Bhushan Singh for whom there are not merely these two communities that we as Indians partake of, but that we are indeed each other, joined from the gut, and that this, in essence, is full blooded meaning of India. (Sahgal: "India's Identity...", p. 52) The novel concludes with a union between people of different religions, social backgrounds and political beliefs. In the end, Bhushan's mother, the 'ranee' of a decadent Maharaja steps out of her palatial prison house to be united to her Muslim lover, comrade Yusuf and her son marries the comrade's daughter. The ending symbolizes a political as well as a social revolution. The final union implies that "the solution to India's problems is this marriage of opposites, of contraries, not merely the upholding of truth in the singular" (Jain, p. 105). With this king of prophetic ending Nayantara thinks of this novel "as a hymn to racial impurity and in praise of the mixtures that have combined to produce the modem Indian, in this case with the interlocking of two traditions, Hindu and Muslim, within an individual life". (Sahgal: "India's Identity . . .", p. 51).

Lesser Breeds marks the beginning of Nayantara's journey outside the political framework within India alone. She no more bothers about the political upheavals, decline of values, horse trading and other synchronous issues in Indian politics. In her latest novel the novelist propounds a new equation; India's quest for identity in the coexistent world is projected against the hectic activity of the past. The novelist focuses on the struggle of a nascent democratic country to survive amidst the waves of oil crisis, trade wind and disarmament proposal. The novel probes into the national history of 1930s through Nurullah, an English teacher who arrives at Akbarabad and encounters a non-violent resistance movement against British rule. For about a decade he lives with a family of great eminence, profoundly dedicated to non-violence. Contrarily, Nurullah finds himself stubbornly resistant to the same creed when he departs. While Nurullah doubts the efficacy of non-violence, Pete Ryder, a European researcher regrets the violent uprising in 1942. He has firm faith in the theory of non-violence. He feels that the non-violent movement of 1942 would have been more effective had there been no violent uprising: "May be they concealed their gravity and extent of the non-violent rebellion, too, for reasons of security.... Why would they make a 'dangerous new weapon' public knowledge" (Sehgal: *Lesser Breeds,* p. 216). The novel also depicts how the British rulers imposed their decisions on India even after Assembly Election. They thrust India into Europe's war (the Second World War) without the consent of her elected legislators. Indians were not given the right to self-governance. "An Indian Military Academy was not set up till 1934, and when the Viceroy's war broke out in 1939, of the thousand majors in the Indian army, only eight were Indians.' (Ibid., p. 153) Previously non-violent movement had already shaken the foundations of British Empire and the occupier had not yet recovered from the terror of Indians Mutiny of 1857. In such circumstances "an armed Indian was a fear somerisk" in the "kind of world it was, made up of Europe and the lesser breeds whom Europe had a right to rule. Armed or unarmed revolt made no difference to that right". (Ibid)

The first part of the novel entitled 'Company Bagh' is provided as a backdrop to the second segment 'An Island called America'. The experiences of Nurullah and also those of Shan, in their own dependent country are contrasted with their fabulous feelings in a free country, America. The amiability and humanity of Edgar and Leda Knox to Shan and Nurullah serves as an antithesis to American Government's indifference towards India. The novel also hints at how India's hopes with America were badly shattered. The novel examplifies what Nayantara writes elsewhere; "Roosevelt had been a champion of India's struggle for freedom. He had sent emissaries to the leaders of the national movement and interceded with Churchill for a speedy transfer of power, but the war ended, Roosevelt died, and no one of his vision or calibre took his place." (Sahgal: *Point of View*, p. 178) adds," To be considered America's friend one had to enter its pacts, join its military line up. 'you are either for us or against us' was the refrain that symbolized the nightmarish Dullesian delusion on which American policy in Asia was based . . ." (Ibid.). For the countries with recently attained freedom, it was practically impossible to be partial to any of the Powers, or else, their freedom would have been endangered. Eknath, in *Lesser Breeds* also feels the same, "When I opted for Foreign Services after Independence, little did I know I'd be answering the same questions for the rest of my career. 'Why haven't you joined our military pacts against Communism?' 'Because we don't want cold war, hot war, holy or unholy war'...'Why haven't you thrown open your markets to our manufactures?" (Sahgal: *Lesser Breeds*, p. 362).

He feels like having a 'bellyache' as a representative of India.

Eknath finds himself vulnerable at the failure of disarmament proposal "for a comprehensive test ban, a freeze on missile materials, a ban on the use of nuclear weapons and a steady reduction of weapon stocks" (Ibid, p. 361). He realizes, "The West is still The World, makes the rules, calls the shots . . . It's 1966 but nothing's changed" (Ibid, p. 361).

The denouement of the novel marks the disillusionment of the narrator himself. He was once committed to non-violence, convinced that "it was the path all people would have to take of battle, fatigue and exhaustion, if not wisdom." (Ibid., p. 369). However in the concurrent global contingencies it is discarded as mere fantasy. Finally, the novelist envisages another crisis that may threaten the international relationship in future; "The roughest chapter of trade is about to begin. Oil and allied treasure will exact a more terrifying price than pepper, gold and nutmeg, or teak and diamond ever did. Asia, and who knows, Africa, will be the battlefields of war immemorial." (Ibid., p. 369)

Nayantara's last three novels (among those published so far) display a total shift from the earlier ones. The narrative, in these novels, moves from present to past and vice versa to emphasize how the remnants of the past may have vital significance in the present and future as well. New dimensions are introduced in narrative techniques also. In *Plans for Departures* the colonial experience is turned inside out. It brings to light another form of post-colonial consciousness. Instead of identification with Gandhian India, there is an undisguised criticism of religious barriers and outworn attitudes, of bureaucratic insensitivity and political manoeuvrings through the central narrative consciousness of Anna Hanesn, a Danish woman bred in a democratic set up. Anna is at a distance from both British imperialism and Indian experience. Here, Mrs. Sahgal detaches herself from India and analyses her from outside. Thus she changes her position within her fictional world.

In the two successive novels Nayantara makes another experiment — that is, shifting from women-centred to male-centred narrative. Bhushan, in *Mistaken Identity,* is a loafer, a man with a lover's instinct. His passion for love is the leitmotiv of his life. The novel presents the fantastic event of the elopement of Bhushan's old mother perhaps because, fantasy is required to strengthen reality. Tossing between fantasy and reality the novel strikes the need of self-discovery. There are many like Bhushan and his old mother waiting to be liberated from their mistaken identities in order to identify themselves with their true selves.

In *Lesser Breeds* the central narrative consciousness is that of Nurullah whose quest for self-discovery makes him learn what he owes to the city of Akbarabad. He has an exclusive role as a narrator. He thinks of himself as "a bystander merely Nurullah, a newcomer to flowers, caught in twist and traps of history, I (he) had no hand in Shaping." (Ibid., p. 114) However, his reflections as well as discourses with Pete Ryder in the midst of proceeding narrative and his intimacy with the pivot family in the novel make him an integral part of the story. His status is that of an onlooker who, voluntarily or involuntarily, happens to be indispensable to the mainstream of the novel.

A distinct demarcation is apparent between Nayantara's previous and later novels so far as themes and technical devices are concerned. To broaden the fences of her fictional world, she shifts from Indian female narrators to Anna Hansen in *Plans for Departure,* and finally, to male-centred narrative in her latest novels. Her retrieval to past spells out her disillusionment with the co-existent world and expands her fictional frontiers. As a sensitive artist Nayantara Sahgal is anguished to notice a retreat from values in both political as well as personal life. In one of her responses to life, literature and politics she asserts; "My fiction was about a demythologized India whose people were much the same as virtuous or as rascally, as anyone else. They had wanted to be free, and once free they wanted to run their own lives. In the course of doing so the golden landscape of freedom decayed, power corrupted and idealism became a ghost but one that still haunted the house. (Sahgal: *The Journal of Commonwealth* Lit. vol. 30 Nos.) Mrs. Sahgal wrote with the purpose of resurrecting the 'ghost of idealism' and reinvigorating it with fresh vigour and vitality in each successive novel.

Works Cited

Jain, Jasbir, *Problems of Post-colonial Literature and other Essays,* Jaipur, Printwell, 1991.

Quoted in R.P. Chaddah, "A Rich Reward", *The Sunday Tribune,* Jan. 4 , 1987.

Sahgal, Nayantara, "I Find It Very Hard Not To Write", An Interview with Talveen Singh, *Debonair* (July, 1988).

——, *From Fear Set Free,* New Delhi: Orient Paperbacks, 1962.

——, "India's Identity in Mistaken Identity", *'Point of View' A Personal Response to Life, Literature and Politics,* New Delhi: Prestige Books, 1997.

——, *Plans for Departure,* London: Penguin Books, 1987, p. 140.

——, *Lesser Breeds,* Harper Collins Publisher, India, 2003.

——, "The Myth Reincarnated", Address at the conference on "New Cartographies: Commonwealth and Post Colonial Literature", St. John's College Oxford, 6 April 1995, Pub. in *The Journal of Commonwealth Literature,* vol. XXX no. 1, 1995.

Tagore, Rabindranath, *Gitanjali,* New Delhi: UBSPD, 2004.

18

Kamala Markandaya's Women Through Male Narration

Sudhir K. Arora

Narration is an art which is not easy to acquire. Kamala Markandaya is gifted with the art of narration. She has attempted all the narrative paradigms successfully. To explore the technical aspects is itself a technique that requires the plurality of approaches. One vision will be partial. To look through one vision may be right from one point of view. But none can shut his eyes from other approaches which may be equally valid for exposition and exploration. One may be right from one's own angle but the others' angle cannot be ignored. It is a fashion to search out the image of woman in the novels of a novelist particularly when the novelist is a woman. To study woman from woman's angle is common. To study female characters from male narration is a new approach and is equally valid. If male narrations are taken into consideration, they may also be helpful in throwing light on the female characters. If male narrations are properly deconstructed, they will themselves reveal what they think of women. In this paper, I have attempted to deconstruct some male narrations from Kamala Markandaya's novels in order to trace out the forms of image of women.

Let me start with Kamala Markandaya's popular novel *Nectar in a Sieve* which is a story of Rukmani's struggle against the odds of life. "It is a thing that might happen to anybody." he said, "Do not fret. Come, dry your eyes and sit up here beside me" (*Nectar in a Sieve,* p. 9). This statement of Nathan shows his innate goodness and his cooperative attitude towards his wife Rukmani. He consoles her that every girl has to leave her house. He asks her not to worry and soothes her inviting her to sit beside him. The narration shows that Nathan has a kind of respect for woman and is mentally prepared to treat his wife as a companion. When Nathan is in joyful mood, he takes Rukmani in his arms and raises her up. He shows her love before the onlookers and his happiness can be seen in his statement which also reveals the importance of Rukmani in his life. "I am happy because life is good and the children are good, and you are the best of all" *(Nectar in a Sieve,* p. 61). Life seems to be good because of his wife and children. He calls her the best of all. He states that it is due to Rukmani that life has become good.

When Rukmani tells Nathan about the young men who are eyeing Ira, Nathan becomes angry and says: "My daughter is no wanton . . . Not only men but women look at her, for she is beautiful" *(Nectar in a Sieve,* p. 34). He is proud of his daughter who is beautiful but when he sees the same daughter parading at night, he asks her not to go. Ira replies that she will not let anyone die from hunger and for this she will parade. At this he loses his control and calls her "A common strumpet" *(Nectar in a Sieve,* p. 103). Actually in society one who sells her body for any cause is treated to be a strumpet. When he calls her so, he wishes to show the mirror of the society where such woman is not respected.

Now let me quote four narrations to point out what a man thinks of a barren woman:

> "Mother-in-law," he said, "I intend no discourtesy, but this is no ordinary visit. You gave me your daughter in marriage. I have brought her back to you. She is a barren woman." *(Nectar in a Sieve,* p. 54)

> "I have waited five years," he replied. "She has not borne in her first blooming, who can say she will conceive later? I need sons." *(Nectar in a Sieve,* p. 54)

> "I do not blame him," Nathan said. "He is justified for a man needs children. He has been patient." *(Nectar in a Sieve,* p. 54).

> "I would," he replied, with a hint of sorrow in his eyes, "for she was a good wife to me, and a comely one, but I have waited long and now I have taken another woman" *(Nectar in a Sieve* 65).

These four narrations clearly indicate one thing that only a fertile woman has a status while a barren one is treated like a barren land. Ira's husband comes to return Ira because she is a barren woman. He frankly tells Rukmani that he has waited for five years and cannot wait now. There is no guarantee that she may conceive. He needs sons. His statement "I need sons" shows his concerned for growing his tree of his family and only son can continue it. He does not say "I need daughters". That shows the patriarchal nature of the society where a son is preferred to daughter. Nathan also considers his case right and does not blame him. His statement "He is justified for a man needs children. He has been patient" seals the way of the patriarchal society which allows a man to re-marry for producing sons. Ira's husband does not wait for long and takes another woman. A barren woman, however, may be good wife and comely one, is neglected and returned to the family.

Some Inner Fury is mainly a narration of the love story of Mira and Richard but along with it, other plots are inserted. On the one hand there is love of Mira and Richard while on the other hand there is a pair of Kit and Premela whose chemistry does not tally. Mira and Richard while loving respect each other's identities. There is no possession in their case but in the case of Kit and Premela there is more of possession than of person. Mark the narration for a wide gap that he has made because of his incommunicativeness:

> Kit was equally incommunicative: there is a tradition, perhaps not only in India, that the best way to ensure this is to keep them as far as possible in ignorance and so now Kit insisted, blandly, that there was nothing to tell." *(Some Inner Fury,* p. 117)

The above narration takes the reader into the male viewpoint that it is better not to share with the women. Kit follows it and does not let anything know to Premela. He follows this tradition which does not allow even sharing with the wife. He believes that there are certain domains in which women should not interfere or encroach. He tells his wife nothing as he does not wish any encroachment on her part. In a very dominating tone, the following narration seals her points of view:

> Certain domains belong to men alone, and Indian women learn early not to encroach. Kit knew he would not have to remind Premela a second time. *(Some Inner Fury,* p. 117)

It is Govind, the freedom fighter who puts a mirror before Kit in order to show his true image. He blames him for the death of Premela. Premela loved her husband Kit who never loved her. It is Kit who does not know the meaning of love. Mark Govind's narration that presents the insensitivity of Kit towards his wife Premela:

> "She loved you," he said, "You never loved her—you do not even know the meaning of love. You gave nothing-not even a home. You drove her to the village—you drove her to her death." *(Some Inner Fury,* p. 240)

Kit is dominating and over-possessive to the point that he never offers his wife what she deserves. His narrations depict his notion of considering women inferior to men.

A Silence of Desire is the story of Dandekar and Sarojini who desire to silence their queries but are themselves silenced because of misunderstanding which is responsible for digging a trench in their relation. When the silence becomes communicative, misunderstanding is removed and harmony is restored in their relations. In the beginning, Dandekar is satisfied with his domestic life as his wife provides him all the essential things that are expected by him. Though he poses to be modern, he is traditional regarding the image of Indian woman. He differentiates between Indian women and Western women when he says: "Our women are not like that. They do not flaunt themselves in front of men either before marriage or after. They are brought up differently" (*A Silence of Desire,* p. 24).

Seeing a photograph, Dandekar becomes suspicious of Sarojini. He imagines: "A married woman did not have men friends who were not known to the husband, the family one of the girl's idols perhaps a teacher, a film actor?" (*A Silence of Desire,* p. 34) He goes to the office and is much disturbed to hear the remark of Joseph that "Women are sly cats, you never know what they're going to be up to next" (*A Silence of Desire,* p. 37). When he comes to know that Sarojini did not visit Rajam, he becomes more suspicious. The remark of Joseph about women tortures his mind and inwardly he experiences a kind of depression that makes him feel "dispirited, vulnerable, and somewhere around the perimeter of his mind, seeking entry, snuffled the thought: all women are the same" (*A Silence of Desire,* p. 37). Under such impression, he calls her wife "a soiled woman" and spies on her. He expresses his anger before her: "Yes. And if I had watched you sooner, it would have been better for us, all of us, because a soiled woman is no good to anyone, not even to her children, do you understand that (*A Silence of Desire,* p. 71). Such narration is nothing except his depression which he feels out of insecurity because of his wife. Mark the Dandekar's narration for his attempt to show his male supremacy:

> What were you doing? You say you, a married woman, were with this man in his house but you do not say why or what for. Am I not your husband, entitled to know? Or am I some kind of hireling

> gigolo to be told only as much as is good for him? *(A Silence of Desire,* p. 85)

Dandekar who is suspicious of Sarojini's behaviour interrogates her. He makes her realize that she is a married woman and is not expected with any other man except her husband. He asks her what she was doing with the man. He makes her remember that he is her husband and being a husband he is entitled to know about her whereabouts. If she does not let him know, what is he to her? Is he only a hireling gigolo or libertine? The excerpt clearly reflects the dominating nature of Dandekar who while living in male dominated society talks only of rights over woman. His jealousy is quite clear here as he cannot tolerate his wife with any man. It also reflects that Sarojini has not shared the secret with her husband. If she had shared, it would have been better.

When the same Dandekar comes to know the truth about the growth in his wife's womb, he feels stunned and wishes: "If only you had told me . . . why could you not tell me?" *(A Silence of Desire,* p. 87) He persuades her to get it operated but Sarojini has faith in the healing touch of the Swamy. He shares with Chari and tells him about his incompleteness without her. He asks her to relieve his wife from the talon of the Swamy. Mark the narration for his love for Sarojini: "My wife is part of me now—I did not realize it in all the years it has been happening, but I know now that without her I'm not whole" *(A Silence of Desire,* p. 140). This narration shows that he loves her and without her he is incomplete.

Dandekar sees the world with the specks that he wears. He never tries to see his wife with her specks. If he had seen her through her specks, he would have not found her a soiled woman. The narration mode is better in this novel as it takes the reader into the mind of Dandekar. With Dandekar, he goes through the same experiences. The image that Dandekar offers about woman is partially true as he never sees the things from Sarojini's points of view.

Possession is the possession not only of talent of a young boy Val but also of his body over which Caroline claims and exploits it for her physical satisfaction. Mark the narration for exploitative nature of Caroline:

> He said, bitterly, speaking in Tamil so that the rush of thought should not be dammed by dearth of words: "She does not care for me. She cares only for what I can do, and if I do it well it is like one more diamond she can put on the necklace round her throat for her friends to admire: but when I do nothing I am nothing to her, no more than a small insect in a small crack in the ground. It was not a slip of the tongue, a manner of speaking: it is what she thinks of me when I am as I am now. *(Possession,* p. 55)

The above narration traces out some hidden factors of the hypocrite nature of Caroline who presents her as the well-wisher and guardian of Val's talent but in reality she is not so. She does not care for him. What she cares, is his art that she exploits for her personal gain. It is pity that he is no more than a small insect in a small crack for her if he does not produce anything unique. His use of words like 'insect', 'crack' and 'ground' clearly reveal his pain over his exploitation. Through the narration of Val, Caroline seems to be possessive and hypocrite.

But the same Val is obliged toEllie as she is his inspiration for his art. He takes her to the triumphal tours as he considers her right to go with him because she has been his model. His success is her success. Sample the narration for the honour he gives to Ellie:

> "Between conscience and care, Valmiki made Ellie accompany him on his triumphal tours. He insisted that she should. It was her right, she had been his inspiration, his model, his success was at least partly hers" *(Possession,* p. 123).

A Handful of Rice is a story of the vagabond Ravi who is transformed into a householder on account of the love of Nalini. When he sees Nalini, he utters: "What a girl like that, and half a man's troubles would be over" *(A Handful of Rice,* p. 25). He imagines that his troubles will automatically come to an end if he gets such a girl for his wife. While eating, he dreams of a family and a house for him and his wife. Mark the narration for his dream of a wife and a house for her: "If I had a wife, he thought as he ate, she would cook for me, it would like this everyday—but what had he to offer to get himself a wife?—I'll buy her a little house, small but nice" *(A Hanaful of Rice,* p. 11). This is the image of a girl that he thinks about. He wishes to give him for someone and that someone will be his wife. For her, he dreams of buying a small but nice house. He thinks of a traditional image of woman who will cook for him and create an atmosphere of love that will release him from troubles.

Now take one more Ravi's narration to point out image of women:

> Ravi had sisters and so he knew the strict watch that was kept on young unmarried girls in their community, in all communities except shameless ones like the Europeans *(A Handful of Rice* p. 40).

This narration exhibits clearly that strict watch is kept over the girls in Indian society which is male oriented in nature. It also offers a difference between the European women and Indian women. The European women are said to be shameless on account of their shamelessness. Ravi has the first hand expenence because of his sisters who are kept under strict watch. The narration offers a traditional image of Indian young unmarried girls who are strictly watched lest they should go astray.

The Coffer Dams is the story of the builder Clinton who has a passion for "His work. The Dam" *(The Coffer Dams,* p. 26) and neglects his wife "Unpredictable Helen" *(The Coffer Dams,* p. 25). As a builder he succeeds but as a husband, he fails. He is jealous and possessive by nature. He is jealous of Bashiam because Helen goes to meet him in order to have the first hand knowledge of the native people. Note the narration for his over-possessive nature:

> "She is mine, he said, stubbornly; why should I let her go? What I have I hold. But knew this to be an illusion, having touched the emptiness where she had fled him, so that the bolsters began to sag under the weight of knowledge." *(The Coffer Dams,* p. 126)

The narration shows his mastering nature. He thinks that his wife is his wife and he has the right over her body and soul. Notwithstanding educated, he does not consider her a person. He succeeds in making the dams but fails to make the building of relations. Being husband, he does not take her into confidence and in his drunken state, rapes her.

On the other hand, there is Bashiam who is cooperative and feels the pulse of Helen. Mark the narration for his affection that he feels for Helen when she is shivering with cold:

> They rose. She was shivering. Bashiam said, 'Are you cold?' and without waiting for an answer put a shawl around her, draping it over her head and shoulders. *(The Coffer Dams,* p. 83).

Seeing Helen shivering with cold, Bashiam puts a shawl around her. Offering the shawl is not important. What is important is his feeling for Helen. This mutual feeling is missing in Helen-Clinton relation. If there had been Clinton in place of Bashiam, he would have not noticed Helen. For Bashiam, Helen is a person—living person who has her identity.

The Nowhere Man is Srinivas who loves his wife Vasantha so much that in his later years he misses her and the gap is not filled even by the presence of Mrs. Pickering. Even in her company he feels spiritually isolated. When Srinivas throws her ashes into the river, he recalls the memorable moments that he passed with her. To him, she was a thoroughly Indian as is clear from the narration:

> . . . he could hot help feeling with Vasantha, who in her breath and bones had remained wholly Indian. She would have liked her remains committed to the

> currents of an Indian river, though she had scrupulously refrained from such onerous impositions; and now, watching her ashes drift away downstream. *(The Nowhere Man,* p. 40).

The policeman tells Srinivas that the river is not meant for throwing the rubbish. Srinivas reacts to the statement of the policeman and very emotionally replies: "It was not rubbish," said Srinivas, and found to his dismay that his throat was working painfully. "It was my wife" *(The Nowhere Man* 41).The last sentence "It was my wife" shows his love for his wife. The death of Vasantha leaves a gap that becomes wider in spite of the company of Mrs. Pickering. In the end, he feels that he is a nowhere man looking for a nowhere city. He praises Mrs. Pickering who shares with him. For him, she is a friend who shares his house and keeps it well. Laxman asks him about her identity. Srinivas introduces her thus: "A friend", replied Srinivas "She shares the house with me. Have you not noticed how well kept it is? A pigsty" he said slyly, "no more" *(The Nowhere Man,* p. 64).

The scenery of *Two Virgins* reveals lesbianism, sex, dance, abortion and amorous glances, etc. Women dominate this novel as the title clearly reveals that it is the story of two virgins. However, male characters like Appa, Devraj, Mr. Gupta, Chingleput, Manikkam, etc., have registered their presence but mostly they are introduced through the consciousness of the sisters. Mr. Gupta is the film director who comes to the village for a documentary film. Lalitha acts and impresses Mr. Gupta who invites her to the city for being actress. She reaches the city where she is exploited sexually by Mr. Gupta. Mark the narration for his taking an advantage of innocent girl:

> Lalitha is a woman with the natural desires of a woman, he said. His voice was very hoarse.
>
> Of which you took advantage, Appa accused.
>
> I am not made of stone, said Mr. Gupta, huskily. *(Two Virgins,* p. 220).

This narration throws light on his nature of exploiting the girls. He calls Lalitha a woman with the natural desires of a woman. It may be true that Lalitha comes to the front to press the sex-button and Mr. Gupta takes an advantage of Lalitha's innocence. When Appa charges him with the exploitation of his daughter, he very frankly tells him that he is not made of stone. Hence, Mr. Gupta treats girls only as a possession or a means for entertainment. He is greedy for sex and does not feel any scruple for exploiting the girls for sex on the name of roles in the film. Today, in the society there are thousands of Mr. Guptas who make many Lalithas victim of their lust tempting them with the roles in the films.

The devil always appears in pleasing shape. This is true in case of Chingleput who is the well-wisher of Saroja. Appa calls him "a shrewd man" *(Two Virgins,* p. 103) but Saroja sees in him a companion with whom she shares her troubles and takes guidance from him. But the same man shows his real motives when he clasps her. Mark the words that he utters before Saroja:

> Your whole life is in front of you. He clasped her. His organ was hard, was nuzzling her body. Don't be afraid, I'm a man, I can't help it, said Chingleput. *(Two Virgins,* p. 250)

This narration reflects the inner working of his mind that somewhere there is a hidden pattern that jumps through his organ against her body while clasping. If he had been her real well-wisher, the feeling of lust would have never come out. Why does he tempt her saying that the whole life is before her. Mr. Gupta took the advantage of Lalitha who could not gather herself and drowned in the river of his temptations. But Saroja is not a girl to be tempted easily because of Lalitha's case. She understands Chingleput's real motives when she feels her organ nuzzling her body. He shows that he is a man and asks her not to be afraid. But Saroja becomes fearless and is not trapped. The narration peeps into the mind of Chingleput who shows that he is Saroja's adviser and friend while he is a man waiting for an opportunity to exploit her sexually.

The Golden Honeycomb has the three main inspiring (female) native bees—Manjula, Mohini and Usha who provide honey of Indian culture to Rabi who motivates other bees—the masses for a revolution against the foreign bees who were stealing the Indian golden honey to take it to their soil. Mark the narration for embracing the native (female) bee Usha in place of the foreign one-Sophie:

> A woman of a pared and lucid grace with whom he could talk, or be still, who could move him, and move with them, effortlessly picking up where he left off their common strand. A woman who was at one with him, their lives interlocking at more than one level, with whom it pleased him to feel, he could wait, or not, to come together. In their own country, in their own time. *(The Golden Honeycomb,* p. 455)

The above narration reveals that Rabi feels good in the company of Usha who makes him relaxed by providing an outlet for his viewpoints. He moves with her and discusses with her. He plans for future with her. She is a woman who will prove not only to be a good wife for him but also a companion with whom he can share his feelings. This narration shows that a woman is a companion for man sharing with him in joys and sorrows.

The Dewan shows his broadmindedness in allowing Usha to talk and move with Rabi. When Vatsala informs him about the relationship of Usha with Rabi, he says: "It's natural . . . . Their attitudes are not dissimilar. It's bound to bring them together" *(The Golden Honeycomb,* p. 385). When two persons of similar attitude meet, none can stop them to meet them. Hence, he thinks that there is no harm in meeting Usha with Rabi.

Pleasure City is mainly a story of the friendship of Tully and Rikki in changed atmosphere. Rikki is much influenced by the female characters and also influences them in their own way. Let me begin with Mrs. Bridie who influences Rikki. Rikki portrays Mrs. Bridie thus:

> . . . tall, bony woman with her yellowing skin and

> her tired eyes, who looked so different from everyone around. . . . He thought about her bosom. So flat, he could feel through the stuff of her dress, not at all like the full globes of his mother. He thought it must be so from never having brimmed with milk for children. *(Pleasure City,* p. 6)

From this narration, the image of Mrs. Bridie's physical features comes before the readers. Mrs. Bridie is different from other women because of her physique which is of tall stature. She is bony with yellowing skin and tired eyes. Her tired eyes indicate that she feels a kind of isolation in life. She has not the freshness in her personality partly from her physical frame and partly from her discontented life. Rikki observes her bosom which is flat and not like his mother. He surmises that her breasts are not global because of being childless, they were never brimmed with milk. She is the woman who is responsible in shaping his personality. She is the woman who has the potential for moulding the character. It is she who possesses "the key to locked, mysterious boxes that he barely knew existed except for the barest outlines that were showing up hazily in the distance" *(Pleasure City,* p. 6).

Note the narration for the image of Mrs. Pearl:

> Grey curls with blue lights in them, a dumpy figure not improved by the flowered costume — a glance and he had placed her firmly in the brigade of aged and authoritative ladies that overflowed the camp" *(Pleasure City,* p. 137).

This narration is from Rikki about Mrs. Pearl who is a new arrival at Shalimar. From this narration, she appears to be not only short and plump but also aged and authoritative lady. She is wearing the flowered costume but it does not make her impressive.

Corinna, the wife of Tully comes to Shalimar to meet her husband. To Rikki, she seems to be a horseman. He presents her as a horseman with a woman's long flowing hair. The outfits—the turban, the shirt and the trousers—she was wearing gave the impression of a horseman. "It was long and silky, a woman's flowing hair; the turban, and the shirt and trousers she was wearing, had led him to suppose a horseman" *(Pleasure City,* p. 106). Tully appreciates her for her confidence and balance. Her riding is worth seeing as she keeps balance. For Tully, she has:

> poise, confidence, command, comes up superbly from initial crouch to upright and hold the position. Balancing finely, she rides the skimming plank with her body, guides it in subtle diagonals, her first work is dazzling. *(Pleasure City,* pp. 131-132)

After analyzing male narrations about women, I can surely say that somewhere in their mind in spite of asserting their favour for women, is the seed of male dominance and they wish to grow it as far as possible. But when they counteract women, they have to retreat and finally make an adjustment with them. Nathan in *Nectar in a Sieve* has illicit relations with Kunthi even after marriage and does not feel guilty. Rukmani who has not the physical relations with Kenny has a kind of fear in her mind and does not let her husband know of it though this platonic kind of relation is outcome of his treatment. Nathan favours Ira's husband when he comes to return his daughter as she is barren. Somewhere they have developed the feeling that they are men. Yet, Nathan loves his wife, praises her for her skill in running the family and recognizes her importance in family. He respects woman in Rukmani and that is the reason why Rukmani lives with him happily facing all the odds in life. Kitsmay in *Some Inner Fury* is possessive by nature while Richard is cooperative. Kitsmay does not love Premela and expects from her to be modern. He does not allow her to interfere in his matter and asks her to be busy with her own affairs. It is Richard who loves Mira and treats her in a friendly way even after her leaving him for the sake of the countrymen. Dandekar in *A Silence of Desire* expects Sarojini to be submissive. In the beginning she is modest and submissive in nature. He is jealous by nature and does not wish to be disturbed in his daily routine. He fails to fathom Sarojini's faith and fidelity and doubts her for having relation with the Swamy. But when he comes to know, he shows his care for his wife and asks her to go to hospital for cure. He works on doubts and does not listen to what his heart says. Sarojini makes him realize that she is still faithful to the family. He has to accept her significance in the family and without her, he thinks that home is not home. In *Possession,* Val is a Tamil Brahmin boy who does not exploit but is exploited by Caroline physically and mentally. He is shown with the three women—Caroline, Ellie and Annabel. He makes physical relations with all these three women though Caroline forces him to be in such relation. He respects Ellie as he feels that she is bleeding inside and has many things in her nature that are similar to him. Where is his code of conduct when he makes relations with other than Caroline? No doubt, Caroline forced him to be indulged in illicit relation but what's about his relations with Ellie and Annabel? Ravi in *A Handful of Rice* falls in love with Nalini at first sight and wishes to make her his wife. He feels that it is she who can change his life and will make an end of his trouble. No doubt, she changes his life and proves to be a sheet anchor for him. He rapes his mother-in-law in his drunken state though he feels sorry after it. In his frustrated condition, he beats his wife but is ashamed of his behaviour. In *Coffer Dams,* Clinton is thoroughly possessive and greedy for sex and work. He wants to have dominance over Helen but she makes him disillusion and goes to Bashiam for exploring her space. Mr. Srinivas in *The Nowhere Man* is indeed a cool and calculative man who loves his wife for her devotion and friendly nature. In *Two Virgins,* Mr. Gupta, Devraj and Chingleput belong to the world where men have hunger for sex. They think women only as commodities and will not miss any opportunity to exploit whenever they find it favourable. Rabi in *The Golden Honeycomb* is a young man who respects woman in his mother and woman in his beloved Usha. When he has sex-encounter with Jaya, he regrets. In *Pleasure City,* Rikki again respects woman in Mrs. Bridie and is helpful to every woman who comes in his contact. Male narration displays many designs of the image of women. To men like Nathan, Richard, Ravi, Srinivas and Rabi, women are 'Persons' who have the potential to run the family and support men whenever the situation demands while there is the other category of men like Dandekar, Clinton and Mr. Gupta who think of woman as 'Possession'.

The discussion clearly exhibits the image of women through male narration which is an innovative technique that Markandaya has used. She makes her male characters speak so that their comments may reveal the facts which they have in their mind concerning women. No doubt, her male characters show their dominance over women but her women characters pierce the needle into balloon of their ego and air comes out. Her male characters realize their incapability in running home smoothly. First they are proud but later on they become meek and submissive to the women who make them understand that they are not commodities that can be purchased, used and thrown.

Works Cited

Markandaya Kamala .....*Nectar in a Sieve,* New York: Signet Books, 1954.

—— *Some Inner Fury,* London: Putnam & Co., 1955.

—— A *Silence of Desire,* London: Putnam & Co., 1960.

—— *Possession,* London: Putnam & Co., 1963.

—— *A Handful of Rice,* New Delhi: Orient Paperbacks, 1966.

—— *The Coffer Dams,* Delhi: Hind Pocket Books, 1969.

—— *The Nowhere Man* (Originally published in 1972), Bombay: Orient Longman (Sangam Books), 1975.

—— *Two Virgins* (Originally published in 1973), rpt., Vikas Publishing House, 1975.

—— *The Golden Honeycomb,* New Delhi: B.I. Publication, 1977.

—— *Pleasure City,* London: Chatto & Windus, 1982.

19

Repression, Eruption, Edification of Sita in Anita Desai's *Where Shall We Go This Summer?*

V. Sunitha

"During the formative period the mind lends itself to easy modelling" says Swami Chidbavandha (p. 6) in his book *The Student*. This statement underlines the susceptibility of the formative days. The enlightenment and illumination of parents in the form of proper nurturing and guidance shows the child the way to reach the destination though inundated by commotion. It's like the tender buds that blossom and spread fragrance after receiving sunlight. Antagonistic to this, the permeated and perpetual darkness makes the bud droop and wither away. This is applicable in the life of the central character of the novel, Sita. The dark shade that has enclosed her during her salad days leads her to the dark. Rejection, repudiation, emotional fracas and the consequent repressed feelings of infancy disintegrate and dismantle Sita's stance as a housewife and mother. Her father's deportment and her mother's run off exasperate and leave a deep scar on her psyche.

Sita's parents play a derisive role in bringing her up and hence their influences handicap her from being an ideal parent and justify her position as a mother. Her abraded psyche culminates in whimsical decisions. One can speak volumes on the emotional tantrums that gobble away her sanity. Prolonged repression at the ignorant age erupts and explodes when it finds likelihood. Dearth of emotional outlet appends her woes. The water stored in dams is deployed for harvesting but Sita's pent-up agony denies her affability with others. The novelist finally ties her to a string called acceptance and pulls her back from the abyss that she fantasized to dwell in. Perhaps the novelist is very cautious in projecting Sita, where she does not want her to sway to the nihilistic dominion that conquered Maya's psyche in Desai's *Cry, the Peacock* and Dimple's in Bharati Mukherjee's *Wife*. The novel backs up many incidents that are a glass case of Sita's inner fracas and turbulence. Her whimsical whim to conserve her child in the womb receives more attention in the novel. The *raison d'être* is the muddled world that is unfit for her child's survival. Of course a mother is certainly possessive and defensive of her child but Sita's notion of containing the child in the womb suggests her queerness.

Both maternal and paternal blood ties are indispensable entanglement for an individual's ideal growth. But Sita is stripped off from the love of both the parents. If her father's laxness has some part in ruining her psyche her mother's abscond forms the other part. Sita, in her girlhood is tossed into the ocean of predicaments by stripping off affiliation, acceptance, sense of belonging and attachment. "She belonged if to anyone . . . to this whole society. . .and saw no reason why she should belong to one family alone?"(p. 77) Commenting on her nomadic life and belabouring on sense of belonging Anant says, "Belongingness in a family gives one the feeling of personal involvement to the extent that one feels himself to be an integral and indispensable part of the system" (p. 63-72). As nemesis would have it poor Sita's juvenile days are rendered null and void in terms of kinship. She internally yearns for the proximity and closeness of her father, brother and sister in vain.

The word mother is annexed with connotations,

'protective', 'devoting', 'caring' etc. Kakar too joins in extending support to the point that highlights the significance of mother, "Indian child experiences his mother as a good mother and her presence as nurturing and fear spelling."(p. 83) But abscond mother of Sita owns the credit of appending her with rudeness, arrogance, recalcitrance, excruciating heart ache, agony, trepidation etc. This fact too should be considered for her perverted demeanour. Sita is presumptuous in extending a stalwart support to her act of running away to the island by endorsing her mother's retreat. Her words to her spouse Raman, spotlights her background of disintegrated family. "I think that is the urge my mother felt when she ran away to Benares I had to run away too to the island"(p. 135). The defeatist instincts within her robs her from the guts to face the reality because, "a mother dead and lost is far more easy to accept than a callous deserted mother" observes Bande Usha (p. 117) in her "Psychological interpretation of childhood in Anita Desai's novels". It is the lack of maternal and paternal nurture, love and care that robs of Sita from reciprocating it to her children. Her incapability and sadistic impulse regulates her psyche. The unattained love of her childhood leaves it unattainable even to her children.

For the half part of the novel Sita's father deserves special attention, because it is he who has poured life into but failed to nurture his daughter by providing congenial environs to his daughter. Dissimilar to this, we see, Maya's father in Desai's *Cry, the Peacock* overprotects his daughter and hampers her adjustment in her marital life. Sita's father makes the tender bud Sita to droop and go flaccid by nullifying reinforcement and back up to her. He is the superannuated hero of the novel. His reverence in the island merits him with titles such as 'God', 'Gandhian', 'saint', 'charlatan' etc. His attainments and achievements are manifold. His triumph in obtaining an elevated place in the hearts of the villagers through his magic deeds, on the other side, highlights his utter failure in tending his son and daughter. Portrayed and celebrated as a man of accomplishment by the village folk, has accomplished only in exacerbating the ordeal of his daughter by hurling her as a discarded object. His demeanour towards his daughter has stamped her prospects. Ignorant Sita, as a slender girl is repressed and cannot voice out and verbalize her profound longing for care and concern. Her emotional hunger is not satiated by her heroic father. His chameleon existence is an unresolved enigma to his descendant. But she is fascinated by his enthralling powers and this is what, which has dragged her to the island after a lapse of twenty years.

Another input the novel discloses is Sita's sensitivity to the fact that Rekha is her step sister and her father's whole attention is exclusively for Rekha. Sita is an, "unworthy offspring of the illustrious and well remembered father"(p. 25). His subservient notion on her, negligence and bias has left deep imprints on her psyche. Consequently, her adolescence is marred; her otherwise sane mind becomes crippled, berated, launching her in the province of berserk. Her inferiority complex inundates her in the ocean of catastrophe and mishaps. Densely packed and congested feelings of childhood unwrap, explode and blaze in all possible ways during her adolescence. Raman, adds fuel to the fire and helps for its combustion by placing twigs called cold attitude, immune temperament, lack of intimacy, failure to picture the inner cravings of wife, etc. Sita throws her into drastic actions because her psychological, ethical and sentimental issues are at loggerheads.

A probe into Sita's conjugal affinity brings into exterior myriad evidences that bear testimony to her wedlock where love has vanished into oblivion. Sita is carried only by doldrums and depression and not by love after her life with Raman. Raman has succeeded in business, has the ability to bear his backache but has failed to probe into the inner recesses of his wife. He fortifies his notion on his wife as maniac rather than analysing her idiosyncratic temperament that dictates her, to impede the child. Barely physical intimacy with negation of emotional attachment has ruled out Sita from unassailable feelings. Hence she says to her child, "I shall keep you safe, we shall go nowhere"(p. 117). This substantiates her unguarded state.

A close study of Sita's psyche unfolds her bottled up feelings where all her wants and pining for a congenial household, affinity with her father and sister are retorted by the overwhelming detachment. Her marriage did not guarantee love and protection. This shatters her personality, unties the link between thought, emotion and behaviour. Schizophrenic Sita retreats from reality and personal relationships due to the intolerable vagaries of childhood. Denial of love throughout her life thwarts and exasperates her. Absence of emotional vent of her oppressions shape her as a square peg in a round hole, she breaks into violent eruption of emotion, uses terse words and appears to be rigid. The cause for Sita's freakishness is nothing but her claim for the injustice meted out to her. It is a protest on the prejudice dispensed on her. The feelings of retribution and avengement that reside in her vents into wrath and she reviles, denigrates and traduces everything around her. Her retract from the normal state of affairs reaches the limits of preposterousness and unlikelihood.

Sita's life is deleted of the subtle aspects which eventually burden her psyche with obstinate and adamant demeanour that cannot be divested unless others adhere to her whims and fancies. Predominantly, she satiates her inner urge by snapping the ties with her in-laws and directs Raman to own a separate house for them. This makes transparent of Sita's demeanour that repudiates human afflictions. Even Raman's friends are obnoxious and displeasing to her as she averts their encroachments and loathes their intrusion. Her craving for seclusion ventures to distance human contact. Fine qualities like patience, forbearance and endurance are absconding in Sita as she is swamped and overwhelmed by exasperation.

Sita's eccentric demeanour and her abhorrence to everything in her vicinity accounts for her dementia. Already weighed down by four children and heavily pregnant with the fifth child in the womb her dejection and disheartenment is interminable. Monotonous household, repressed psyche, angst and agitation, oversensitivity and volatile nature cannot surpass her grief and mental torment. The brutality and turbulence that she witnesses in the chaotic world diverts her from normal life. Habitual and simple things are amplified as vigorous images gaining access to the world of berserk. Its magnified replica blurs her vision betraying her as a perturbed individual. Her psyche is infected with the petty things that magnify as violence and horror according to her vulnerable mind. The affluent life in the Bombay apartment is only a showpiece that did not embellish her inner 'self' that is wrecked in the pandemonium of ordeals. Financial constraints did not hit her but it did not assuage her inner tumult. Her typicality is brought forth by dictates over her children and getting appalled and nauseated by the insignificant happenings around her.

Deluged by the widespread apprehensions of brutality, Sita cannot come to terms with even trivial happenings around her. The events that can be easily shrugged off and discarded march to the extent of leaving a deep scar on her psyche. Servant's wrangle, her son's assembling and obliterating of blocks, her daughter's crumbing of a new sheet of buds, children enacting the scenes from movies, etc., reverberate ferocity and trigger her wrath. The feelings of collapse are liquefied in her blood and veins where it is unfeasible to redeem her from its tyranny. That's why she perceives her daughter is insensitive while she crushes the buds and her son is terrible when he destroys the blocks. She feels that, "the creative impulse had no chance against the overpowering desire to destroy" (p. 41). It insinuates the hostility and antagonism of the younger generation where she is assured of the destructive forces that will gulp down the creativity, construction and innovation.

Sita wants everyone to be attuned to her thoughts and ideas where any disorder to her whims and fancies may cause havoc in her. She insists her daughter to join in art class by negating her ambition to join in a medical college. Just like the Indo-Pakistan war boosts patriotism in Adit of Desai's *Bye Bye Blackbird* and thereby he resolves to shift his ambience, the novelist authenticates Sita's fight and unguarded feelings in this novel by disclosing the scenes of Vietnam war in the newspaper, to which she is shackled and let down with the notion, "survival seemed hopeless. How civilizations survive? How could the child? How could she hold them whole and pure and impeached in the midst of this bloodshed?"(p. 50). She is of strong conviction that turbulence and cruelty would overpower her and lead her to an unbearable wreckage, that would divest the life of her as well as her offspring. "She finds herself unbearable in her distress, the drama of her distress"(p. 32) because "it's all like living in the wilds, the black cloud of melodrama"(p. 39) for her. Horror and terror are the hallmarks of her everyday life. This is comprehended when she says to Raman, "one may be attacked, one's children may be attacked"(pp. 43-44). To grapple with reality one needs to be even-minded and stubborn in withstanding the odds and trials that goes with it, but pathetically the cynosure of this novel is at loggerheads with her family or human affinity. This does ventilate her eccentricity and idiosyncratic nature.

Sita's word, thought and deed may be dear to her, but the same thrusted upon others cause melee. Anyone unwilling to submit to Sita's dictates becomes the ground for her quarrelsome and argumentative demeanour. Her ill-temper, annoyance, irritation and uncontrolled behaviour make her children poor victims where they have to be hushed up when she hurls slippers, etc., on them. Perhaps it is her repressed childhood and her inability to restrain her overflowing unconscious, establishes despotism over her family members. The treacheries and betrayals of childhood deep by affect her psychologically. Her outbursts for trivial things is comprehended through Moses' words, "angry because it rained, angry because there was no food-always angry mad people are like that"(p. 143). Perhaps Moses designation 'berserk' endorses her recalcitrant demeanour that is the upshot of repression in salad days.

Sarah, in Desai's *Bye Bye Blackbird* smokes; it is habitual to the women of alien soil. But in *Where Shall We Go This*

Summer the novelist calls reader's attention to Sita's inner trepidation by bringing into reader's focus her smoking habit, "a thing that had never been done by any woman in their household and even by man only in secrets"(p. 44). It is nothing but an outlet of the suppressed and seething violence concealed inside her. The smoking appears as a port in her storm of difficulties, through this she seems to reveal her blow for blow, her avengement, revenge and slap at the callous immunity of her husband. Perhaps she relishes in the sadistic pleasure that is derived from visualizing Raman's torment. It is paradoxical and incongruous to note that the novelist has named her 'Sita' after the model of docile and submissive Sita in classical literature who fhas to undergo fire ordeal to prove her fidelity. Rao substantiates this view, "Sita, especially has left the tradition of her namesake far behind and has taken to smoking and neurotic outbursts as a result of this growing incompatibility"(p. 47).

The frown and the disgust in her countenance mirrors her inner mind that is worn and tattered completely depriving her to fit into the roles of wife or mother. She is ill-equipped mentally and physically to cope with the pregnancy because, "control was an accomplishment that has slipped out of her hold"(p. 29), which makes her succumb to terrible predicaments and explode to Raman, "It's not easier, it's harder, harder, it's unbearable"(p. 29). Desai hollows out the inner fissure of Sita through her deeds where she, "continues to huddle, twists her fingers, smokes bitterly through the nights and displays her agony"(p. 29-30).

The arrival of Rama in the epic the *Ramayana* is to redeem his wife Sita from the atrocity of Ravana. In this novel the arrival of Raman to Manori island rescues Sita from the clutches that haunt and diminish her mental faculty. The parsimonious and niggardly island did not confer the alms of miracle which she pleaded to attain but it can be certainly extolled for re-routing her back to the mainland from the detracted path that she was ambling with muddle. Amid the deception the island leads her to know the other side of her undeveloped 'self'. Her father fixation gets falsified. The enchanting magic of the island vanishes by opening the curtain which pictures the actuality of his father. In short, an uneducated woman studies her psyche in the island.

The Serpent and the Rope is a semi-autobiographical story of Raja Rao that can be drawn parallel with the present novel. The serpent in the title refers to illusion and the rope to reality. But in *Where Shall We Go This Summer?* the island is projected as the image of both illusion and reality. The growth towards self knowledge is the theme of both the novels. In *Where Shall We Go This Summer?* it is Sita who attains growth towards the self and in *The Serpent and the Rope* it is concerned with the Brahmin Ramaswamy.

Thus the doors of reality unbolt and entitle her journey to the island as 'self discovery'. From the domain of the unreal world Sita crosses the threshold and seeks entry into it. A red carpet welcome is rolled out to her by 'realization'. There is certainly a magic existing in the island, if not Sita wouldn't have become sane at the end of the novel. The novelist reconciles Sita's wrangle and unbalanced position by tethering her to a string called acceptance. This is symbolically represented when she rummages about her husband's footprints in order to place her own on it which is a sign of her submission. She irons out the culmination of harsh realities by reconstructing herself and taking a diversion from illusion and thus proceeds to capitalize on reality.

Marget Atwood's *Surfacing* and Desai's *Where Shall We Go This Summer?* both expose the interior journey of their chief protagonists. They try to rediscover themselves by journeying back to the past. This reverse journey transfers them into new human beings. In *Surfacing* the nameless narrator journeys back to the island where her father lived. Her trip tc the isolated island explores her inner 'self. She "surfaces to rediscover her lost innocence with a new acceptance of herself and her spiritual powers in the natural world"(p. 120) asserts Urs Vikram Raj. It is nature that educates them with reality of life by elucidating their self-created problems.

Shakespeare's play, *As You Like It* conceptualizes human life in a significant way. Human beings seek entry into the stage of life to enact the drama of life, by their birth and exit by their death. Similarly Sita seeks entry into the island, into the stink of the island air her ignorance evaporates, her passion as an actor no longer resides, steering clear the way to the main land. She finds the means of fulfilment in her relationship to the world.

Despite expecting the world to tune to her rhythm, Sita transforms to the tunes of reality. This welcome change is after manifold turmoils, obsession that has evolved into positive note by stuffing shrewdness, forethought and prudence into Sita's psyche. Her apprehensions are tamed and acclimatized. Her anxiety is temporal and terrestrial. The island experience lays road to Damascus. It lets her to the realization of the futile pursuit of holding back the birth.

In an interview with Atma Ram Desai makes it clear that, "suicide would have been too melodramatic an alternative for the middle aged woman"(p. 27) that's why she makes her protagonist of *Where Shall We Go This Summer?* to visualize a new horizon amidst the sea of disarray, rather than drown and die in it. The concept of Art of Living becomes apparent to her. Docile Sita becomes obstreperous only to metamorphose into an amenable woman and "harmonize the opposites of life"(p. 116) utters Naiker. After her reincarnation melodrama of insanity blurs and she becomes edified to cope with the real world. Perhaps this is the message the novelist seems to riposte for the current mayhems.

Works Cited

Anant. S.S., "Conflict Resolution Through Belongingness" Manas, 26, Nos. 1-2, 1979.

Bande, Usha, "Childhood in Anita Desai's Novels: A Psychological Interpretation *Indian Women Novelist,* set I Vol. II, Ed. R.K. Dhawan, New Delhi: Prestige Books, 1991.

Desai, Anita. *Where Shall We Go This Summer?* New Delhi: Orient Paperbacks, 2006, (Subsequent page number citations appear in parenthesis in the text.)

Kakar, Sudhir. *The Inner World* New Delhi: Oxford University Press, 1978.

Naiker, Basava Raj, "Marital Disharmony in Anita Desai's Novels" *Indian English Literature* Vol. I New Delhi: Atlantic Publishers, 2002.

Rao, Vimala. "Anita Desai's Where Shall We Go This Summer? : An Analysis", *Commonwealth Ouarterly* 3: 9, 1978.

Ram, Atma. "An Interview with Desai", *World Literature Written in English,* XVI: I (April 1977).

Swami Chidbhavanandha. *The Student* Tiruparaithurai: Sri Ramakrishna Tapovanam, 1998.

Urs, Vikram Raj, S. N., "Discovery of the Self: An Interior Journey in Margret Atwood's Surfacing and Anita Desai's Where Shall We Go This Summer?", *Indian English Literature,* Vol. I ed. Basava Raj Naiker, New Delhi: Atlantic Publishers, 2002.

20

The Psychic Trauma in Anita Desai's *Cry, The Peacock*

V. Sunitha

Anita Desai's first novel *Cry, the Peacock* is a psychological novel that narrates the story of estranged and detached couple Maya and Gautama, who live in their own worlds. Their attitudes, outlooks and perspectives to life are diametrically opposed. Their dispositions are incompatible. Maya is over-emotional and highly-strung while Gautama is calm, placid and phlegmatic. His practical outlook to life is beyond Maya's self-love and imaginary world. He is a diligent and industrious lawyer who is more dedicated to his profession than probing into the fanciful world of his wife.

The novel *Cry, the Peacock* opens with the death of Maya's pet dog Toto. The readers are introduced to Maya's deranged state of mind when she reacts to the death of her pet. She is 'overwrought' and uncontrolled by looking at the staring still eyes of her dead dog. Toto's death fuels conjectures and speculations on theological, spiritual and existential questions causing an emotional void in her psyche. The death of the pet hardly brings any change in Gautama. He accepts it with positiveness and conviction.

Maya stands for 'Maya', an unreal world and Gautama stands for real and actual world. If Maya is a Hedonist and epicurean, Gautama is a Puritan. She embellishes and adorns the glory and beauty of the sensuous world with great diligence. Her excessive love for life with all its pleasure and rapture makes her delightful and fine. Her aesthetic appeal and ornamental tendency is inhospitable and unwelcoming to an empirical and feasible man like Gautama. He is a well-reasoned, sound and intelligent man with a rational outlook to life. His legal profession also attributes to his well-proportioned nature. His philosophical and theoretical perspective is antithetical to Maya's temperamental and passionate nature. She obtains inexorable gratification if she is entangled in the love of her husband. Her world is confined and restricted from external realities.

Maya, rich in sensuous and voluptuous thoughts of love is stripped of her wishes and desires, as Gautama is cold and unattractive. He is repulsive to the seductive temptress Maya. He is least enchanted to be lost in the world of physical beauty and warmth of flesh. Young wife Maya is left adrift and unfastened by Gautama. Their tastes, approaches, attitudes, behaviours are in conflict. The gulf between the couple has grown wide because of the discrepancy in age. Maya finds herself in hell, as she has failed to accustom with Gautama and accepted him as he is, due to her immaturity. It is a clash between illusion and worldly knowledge. Gautama is impassive and never cares to attend the needs of his wife but Maya is overflowing with her abundant thoughts of love and passion, which have thrown her into the pit depriving her of worldly knowledge. Her fabricated world, which is impregnated with bliss and ravishment, is bereft of aloofness and neutrality of Gautama. It is beyond the bounds of her possibility to fit into the pattern of Gautama's framework of life. The misunderstanding between the couple grows constantly with no hopes for its subsidence. Neither of them attempts to understand and alleviate the enlarging polarity between them. Amorous and lustful Maya is uncared for and unwanted by the ascetic and austere Gautama. Being caught in the clutches of mental disorder, she exterminates Gautama and herself at the end.

Sensual pleasures are of no value to Gautama, who on account of his strict adherence to profession leaves no room for Maya's fulfillment of emotional urges. He is much absorbed in attending his clients and money making rather than to probe into the demented psyche of his wife. His files and papers increase his revenue. He proves to be a hard workingman striving to establish well in his profession but fails to be a good husband as he does not spare his valuable time for the petty things of the household. He is concerned with his own business while Maya yearns for his presence and craves for his love. His wish for material pursuits is so extensive that Maya and the marital pleasures concerned with her are completely nullified. He proceeds according to his thoughts and plans. He is a balanced man uninhibited or unrepressed by feelings or sensations. His self-discipline and firmness in the attitude and approach has sharpened him into a *yogi,* who is unappreciative and unresponsive to worldly pleasures.

Aloofness and dispassion are what Gautama practices and enjoys in imposing them to his passionate wife. He teaches her that attachment breeds problems and pain to humanity and advocates her to remain detached. Her need for him is banned and restricted by his pontification from 'the Gita'. Perversely, Maya longs for pleasure and thrives in sense objects. Sensual attachment is her ruling passion. It is beyond her knowledge to distinguish pleasure and pain and remain indistinguishable to good and evil. "Maya lacks intellect and reason as much as Gautama lacks emotion and sensuousness and therefore they cannot come close to each other by transcending their limited visions of life. Given this, the catastrophe is the logical outcome of their temperamental disparity" (Panigrahi and Viney, p. 74). This incongruous couple entangled in the knot of marriage is destined to mutilate beyond recovery.

Gautama's age and his attitude to sex remains an intractable difficulty to her. Her seductive behaviour has no power to hold him in her trap of love. Gautama blows out Maya's burning urge for sex. She wishes for her femininity to be subjected under his masculinity. The gratification of her feminine instincts is possible by Gautama's masculine traits. She extends welcome to play upon her soft, delicate flesh. To be confined under his virile powers is what she aspires for. Her virginal and chaste beauty would flourish after Gautama's physical touch. She is of strong conviction that her feminine elegance and grace would get blossomed and illuminated by her mate. Each and every moment of his company is valuable and precious for her. She can resist and battle against any odds provided Gautama accompanies her all the time. Her overpowering love for Gautama makes her to admit to him, "when you are away from me I want you, because I insist on being with you, being allowed to touch you" (Desai, p. 97).

Maya disrobes and uncovers herself to beguile Gautama and coaxes him to play the game of love. She surmises that her undressing would certainly cajole Gautama's sexual urge. Flooded with the carnal desires she wants to win Gautama's eulogy to her lustrous beauty but in vain. She hopes that her charm and luster of youth would captivate and pull him for sexual act, which would abate her blazing sexual desire. Gautama's drowsiness and insensitive sleep is the rejoinder for her preparation. She becomes sad and helplessly thinks of her weakness for him. As her attempts to excite and conjure him fails, she dislikes and detests her own state. She becomes conscious of his uncompromising nature. She devalues herself and feels frivolous and worthless.

In her early childhood Maya visits an albino astrologer. His prediction of death to either of the couple in the fourth year of their married life forms a strong base in the subconscious mind of Maya. Right from the beginning of the novel, the readers notice Maya's preoccupation with the prophecy. Though the disastrous thoughts of the death are suppressed in the initial stages of her married life during the fourth year, it occupies a predominant place in her psyche, leading her to tread on the paths of disaster and ruin. The prophecy that can be easily neglected and ignored with an unorthodox outlook shrouds and envelops Maya by curbing her sanity and augmenting her mental illness. Eventually, it ends as obsessional neurosis.

Maya yearns for a life of sensations. "She experiences the world through the senses while Gautama looks at it through reason and commonsense" (Jain, p. 28). Gautama's overwhelming odour of, "smoked cigars, of whisky, of manhood" (p. 14) are exceedingly tempting to Maya. Her inexpressible attraction to his debauched state accentuates the extent of love that she bears for him. In fact, she is lured by his intoxication and hankers to remain in a trance like state under his male domain. Gautama's physical touch with conversation is what she observes as love of husband. She is immature to realize anything other than her conception of love. His tender touch of her hair and her cheeks to lessen her worries on Toto's death, in spite of being a momentary feel, is strong enough to open the vistas of happiness to her. She forgets all his indifference towards him. Her internal as well as external pressure subsides and she confesses, "I was flooded with tenderness and gratitude, I thought of him as my guardian, my protector, the one who has seen to the burial of my pet and come to wipe the strands of hair out of my wet eyes and speak to me softly" (p. 15). It is purely an emotional love. It is this dichotomy between the profane and divine love that further widens the chasm between them. Rajeshwar observes: "Maya cherishing her attachment to sense objects and Gautama religiously professing non-attachment and in the process both unconsciously contributing to the ever widening chasm of misunderstanding between them". (Rajeshwar, p. 16)

Gautama couldn't recognize Maya's passion, emotions, lust, etc. It's only an elderly man's relationship with a child. He fails to see the woman in her. Her flesh remains famished and unfed. Her biological needs are unavailing and abortive. And it is the suppressed vengeance that bursts forth at the end. It is Gautama's detachment that brings him the despondency of death. Though Gautama is a balanced man he is unaware of his wife's sentiments and changing moods. His absence of aesthetic sense is not in harmony with the decorative and elegant thought of Maya. She assures that her husband is not a companion to her in real sense because hardly is he, aware of anything that concerns her and so Maya is bereft of satisfaction in life. Maya's excessive longing for love and Gautama's immoderate aversion and detachment exhibits the exact picture of their matrimonial bond.

One might misinterpret Maya's love and libido for Gautama. It is not only the act of sex and the inflow of his male organ that may convince her. His embrace and emotional attachment would lift her to paradise. In her sleep with him, she fancies to brush her hand with his hand, twine his hair with hers. She cries out for a romance that "goes deeper than flesh and thought" (p. 90) which would inebriate and intoxicate her psyche. The night time agonies are inexplicable to her. It is unfathomable to anyone who did not experience it. The rejection and pejoratives of Gautama are strong enough to turn cool nights into hot summers. It is an excruciating pain in her heart. External pain or wound can be get rid of by consuming proper medication but the question: "What is the remedy for the internal angst of Maya?" remains unanswered.

It is sarcastic to note the conjugal bond of this mismatched couple. One is imploring for love and other retreating from it. Miserly and niggardly Gautama cannot offer love alms to his wife who is beseeching for the same. In spite of this utter loveless state, their married state extends for four long years. It is a wretched, forsaken life devoid of communication and rapport. As Maya is untouched by Gautama's doctrine so is Gautama unruffled by Maya's tantrums. She asks him, "Is there nothing in you that would be touched ever so slightly if I told you I live my life for you" (p. 97). "Maya's creative search for love and harmony and wholeness is genuine and desirable though not completely possible" (Sarup, pp. 15-16). She is forced to conclude that Gautama is 'an inhuman dry stick' (p. 96) untouched by any and not have 'the faintest knowledge of me' (p. 97) due to his hostile retort. Their life is woebegone due to their myopic sight that hampers the mutual respect and understanding between each other. Both of them hold responsibility for their despicable nuptial knot.

Gautama's senility may not be the sole stumbling block hampering his way to attain the sacred love of the conjugal bond. It is not even an approved fact that decrepitude debilitates sexual urges. He is neither sexually aroused nor alive to the world but enjoys with his cronies. It is idiosyncratic and eccentric to note Gautama's etiquette. The novel doesn't articulate Gautama's abhorrence or hatred for Maya. It only pronounces his distaste and lack of sexual appetite. Is it the disparaged virility or the rational thinking the impetus for his allayed libido? So, it is not only Maya but Gautama too stands in need of psychic therapy.

It is unreasonable of Maya, a connoisseur of all things in life, to anticipate an industrious and tireless man to count the stars in the sky. It is absurd to have such a fatuous supposition. A man who is not able to notice the odour of limes, not able to hear the singing voice, doesn't have the aesthetic sense to discern and realize the beauty of lawn, who never burdens himself with Toto's death, one who entails himself completely in his vocation, is fit enough to be damned to death according to her. This is the dictate of her tarnished psyche and she follows it resulting in killing him. The episode of Gautama has come to a halt. She can gaze at the world with a refreshed hope. She can put an end to all her cravings and the consequent frustration. "*Cry, the Peacock,* is the story of a hypersensitive young woman Maya, pitted against a taciturn husband. She lives a life of acute sensitivity and dies in her quest to find fuller of life" (Bande, p. 14). But, Maya cannot pursue her life according to her anticipation after Gautama's death. Her psychosis handicaps her brain and hampers her survival. Overpowered by the self-destructive forces, she commits suicide.

The novel dotes on the doleful existence of unloved, uncared and mismatched couple. Maya is unheard of an ideal pair. She is strange and exotic to archetypal love. Neither she is told of an absolute or consummate husband nor wife as her father has fed her only by the fictitious fairy tales. Maya's friend Leela who has fallen in the pitfall of love with a tuberculosis patient has to sustain all his juvenile behaviour in the name of marriage. Her guise of love is to extricate herself from the society that cruelly darts at the destitute. She undergoes the pangs of the wedlock. Sikh's wife exhibits her mismatched marital bond by openly condemning her husband in the party. Nila, Maya's sister-in-law is a divorcee due to her maladjusted married life. Porn, one of Maya's friends wishes to snap her husband from her in-laws. As she fails in persuading him she complains against him. Mr. Sapru also joins in the list of discontented marriage. The incompatible couples that Maya comes across in and around her becomes the source of her distress.

Marriages are made in heaven is an old saying. Its new version is, 'Marriages are made in heaven but are suffered on the earth'. It is debatable whether the present-day marriages are confined to this dictum. It is doleful to dot the scrupulousness of today's modern couples and their unbalanced life that breaks-up in dissolution. The personality rupture is mushrooming day by day. A sound life cannot be lead unless the couples adhere to the concept of mutual understanding. "Metaphorically, the novel calls for reconciliation and balance, communication and understanding between spouses. Since marriage implies a space of sharing and mutual risk, both the partners have the responsibility to flow towards and into each other, so that they can avert tragedy. If this is not possible they should part without violence, without killing each other" (Kher, p. 23).

Works Cited

Bande, Usha, "Introduction", *The Novels of Anita Desai: A Study in her Character and Conflict* New Delhi: Prestige Books, 1998.

Desai, Anita, *Cry, The Peacock,* (New Delhi: Orient Paperbacks, 2005, (Subsequent page number citations appear in parenthesis in the text.)

Jain, Jasbir, "Anita Desai", *Indian English Novelists,* (Ed.) Prasad Madhusudhan, New Delhi: Sterling 1982.

Kher, Indernath. "Madness as Discourse in Anita Desai's *Cry, The Peacock*". *Commonwealth Novel in English* Vol. 5. No. 2, 1992.

Panigrihi, Bipin B., and Viney Kirpal, "The Individual and the Search for Self-identity in *Cry, The Peacock*", *Indian Women Novelists* set I Vol. III ed. R.K. Dhawan, New Delhi: Prestige Books, 1991.

Rajeshwar, M., "The Dynamics of Attachment and Non-Attachment: Maya and Karma Yoga as Aspects of Technique in Anita Desai's Cry, The Peacock" .*The Journal of Indian Writing in English* Vol. 24, No. 2, July 1996.

Sarup, Madan, "An Introductory Guide to Post Structuralism and Post Modernism", Athens: The University of Georgian press, 1989.

21

Chemmeen: An Ethnic Novel of Kerala

Basavaraj Naikar

Thakazhi Sivasankara Pillai (1914–) happens to be one of the internationally known Malayalam writers. He was born in a village, Thakazhi, ten miles south of Alleppey in Kerala, the land of coconuts. Sivasankara Pillai hailed from an agrarian family. His father was a farmer by profession, gentleman, scholar and connoisseur of Kathakali, the great Dance Drama of Kerala. His brother Kunju Kurup was one of the great Kathakali dancers of his times. His home provided a rich background of Sanskrit culture and the indigenous arts of Kerala. As a boy Sivasankara Pillai absorbed these valuable influences unconsciously.

He was educated in the primary school at Thakazhi, the Middle School at Ambalapuzha, Kuruvilla High School near Haripad, the Law College at Trivendrum. Sivasankara Pillai came in contact with the lives of fishermen and fisherwomen. Later on when he returned to the same village as a young lawyer, he had many fishermen as his clients. When he was in High School, he came under the influence of Kainikkara Kumara Pillai, scholar, critic and dramatist. Sivasankara Pillai had started writing poetry in his formative period, but Kumara

Pillai turned him from poetry to prose. When he was studying at the Law College at Trivendrum, he was influenced by the National Movement, which was in full swing. At the same time he became a member of a small intellectual group, which met regularly at the residence of A. Balakrishna Pillai, editor of *Kesari,* an exclusive literary journal. During this period Sivasankara Pillai extended the frontiers of his knowledge by his wide reading in English and European literature and other areas. He was deeply influenced by Freudian and Marxian thought.

He began his creative writing career as a short story writer. His first volume *Puthumalar* (*New Blossoms,* 1934), a collection of short stories was a sensational success. It was soon followed by his first novel, *Yegalinle Pratiphalam* (*Reward,* 1934), which was sold out within a few weeks of its publication. His other important novels are *Patitapankajam* (Fallen *Lotus,* 1945), *Tottiyude Makan* (*The Scavenger's Son,* 1971) *Rantitangazhi* (*Two Measures, 1948*), and *Kayar* (*Coir,* 1988).

Sivasankara Pillai entered the Malayalam literary scene in the 1930s shocking the refined sensibility of the elite class. Apart from being influenced by Freudian and Marxian thought, he was also involved in the progressive writers movement, which insisted on the depiction of the downtrodden and their protest. As he grew older and more mature, he was disillusioned with the literature of propaganda and political ideology and developed his own deep and comprehensive humanist vision of life based on the authority of his authentic experience without any external colouring of doctrine or ideology. He became the champion of the common man and inaugurated an era of social realism in Malayalam literature and reached the height of transcendental realism. When his novels were translated into English and other European languages, he had earned international recognition for Malayalam language also. As R.E.Asher says, "It makes us feel that Malayalam Novel can be proud of having a novelist like Thakazhi and that the language will be noted at international level as the language in which Thakazhi wrote."[1]

Sujit Mukherjee has a very insightful observation about Sivasankara Pillai's novels. According to him the English translations of Pillai's novels by different translators are not equal in their performance. Hence the original qualitative hierarchy of his Malayalam novels is upset in their English translations. "The less but perhaps not undemonstrable explanation lies in the varying levels of success in translation -very high in V.K.Narayana Menon's rendering in *Chemmeen*, very low in M.A.Shakoor's work in *Two Measures of Rice* or the anonymous hand in *The Iron Rod*, a mediocre achievement in R.A. Asher's version of *The Scavenger's Son*. Never again has Thakazhi impressed in English translation so much as he did in *Chemmeen*, and the blame for not being able to retain his early following has probably to be attributed to his translators."[2] Though *Chemmeen* enjoys the highest position among Pillai's novels on account of the excellence of translation, yet it has certain gaps in it. Sujit Mukherjee draws our attention to this factor: "It is now known that Narayana Menon not only translated *Chemmeen*, but also abridged the original and carried out editorial revisions, with the full permission of the author with whom he was in regular consultation while the work was in progress."[3] In Goethe's opinion, one of the tests of the greatness of a work of art are its translatability. A translated work is generally compared to a queen, whose beauty shines through in spite of the rags she might be wearing. In spite of the translator's abridgement and editorial revisions, *Chemmeen* succeeds in revealing its beauty of vision and capturing the attention of the international reader.

Chemmeen may be described as an ethnic and provincial novel about the fishermen community of coastal Kerala as it deals with the different aspects of fishermen's lives in a very realistic manner and creates a vivid local colour of the region. The fishermen's continuous struggle with the sea for survival, their crushing poverty, the values and ideals of the community and their violation and the resultant tragedy, etc., have been captured by Sivasankara Pillai in a very authentic and convincing manner. The novel, obviously, testifies to Pillai's keen observation of the fishermen's community, deep understanding of human nature and the artistic ability to articulate his vision of life.

The novel begins suddenly with a dramatic scene, where Karuthamma, the protagonist, is chatting with her childhood boyfriend Kochumuthalali. The dire poverty of the fishermen is problematized very clearly by the novelist. Karuthamma, a girl of about sixteen years, who is quite innocent, tells her boyfriend, "You know my father is going to buy a fishing boat and a net, which will then be our own" (p. 3), and asks him to lend some money to her father to fulfil his ambition of owning a boat and a net. Pareekutti pleads his inability to lend the money. Since both the boy and girl are on the verge of adolescence, they discover the awakening of amorous feelings in them through mutual gazing and talking. When Karuthamma notices that Pareekutti's eyes are riveted on her bare breasts, she becomes conscious of her sexual identity and feels shy about it. She tells him, "Don't look at me like that" (p. 4). "She shrank from him, crossed her hands in front of her bare breasts and turned around. She realized she had only a single piece of loincloth covering her" (p. 5). Both the boy and the girl discover their sexual selves and become shy like Adam and Eve in *Paradise Lost*. "Her breasts were a symbol of the exuberance of youth, throbbing with life. When he looked at her and fixed his eyes on her breasts, Pareekutti had felt as if his nerves were on end and shivering. Was that why the laughter ended? Karuthamma had only a single piece of cloth worn round her waist. She had nothing underneath. And the single piece was a thin one" (p. 5). The childhood friendship between Karuthamma and Pareekutti has slowly matured into friendship and juvenile love.

The whole action in this ethnic novel takes place against the backdrop of the fishermen community of Kerala, which has its own frame of values, ideals and norms to be strictly followed by the members of the community. The love that has been burgeoning between Karuthamma and Pareekutti is something that is forbidden by the norms of the fishermen's community. When Panchami, the younger sister of

Karuthamma and Pareekutti observes the private conversation of Karuthamma and Pareekutti, she carries tale to her mother, "Mummy, Karuthamma was standing behind the boat on the seashore laughing away with our Kochumuthalali . . . You should have heard them laugh, Mummy" (P.6). Karuthamma's innocent meeting and talking with Pareekutti is not approved by her mother, as such behaviour runs counter to the norms of their community. When Chakki asks Karuthamma, "Do you understand what you are doing?" Karuthamma rationalizes her action by saying, "I asked him for the money that we still need for the boat and the net" (p. 7). The mother rightly snubs her by telling her that it is none of her business to ask for money from the boy. As Karuthamma is still very young, innocent and ignorant, she does not know the code of behaviour enjoined by the community on its members. It is, therefore, the duty of the mother to alert and enlighten her daughter about it. ". . . Chakki was a fisherwoman brought up in the tradition of that seafront. She was the inheritor of some old truths and of a way of life" (p. 7). According to the fishermen's community, chastity is the highest ideal to be followed by the women of the community. Chakki believes in the philosophy of the community, which is expressed through a folk-myth, "When the first fisherman fought with the waves and currents of the sea single-handed on a piece of wood on the other side of the horizon, his wife sat looking westward to the sea and played with all her soul for his safety. The waves rose high on the sea. The whales approached him with their mouths gaping. The sharks charged the boat with their tails. The current dragged the boat into a terrible whirlpool. But he escaped from everything miraculously. Not only that. He came ashore with a very big fish. How was he saved from that storm? Why didn't the whale swallow him? How did the boat survive the attack of shark? How did the boat sail out of the whirlpool? How did all these things come to pass? Because, on the shore a chaste and pure woman was praying steadfastly for the safety of her husband at sea" (p. 8) Chakki, who believes in this philosophy, reminds Karuthamma, "You are not a little girl any more. You are a fisherwoman now" (p. 8). She inculcates the philosophy of the community in her daughter's mind, "This wide-open sea contains everything my child. Everything. Why do you think all the men who go out there come back safely? It is because of the women at home who live clean lives. Otherwise the currents in the sea will swallow them up. The lives of the men at sea are in the hands of the women on shore" (p. 8). She explains the myth further; "Do you know why the sea goes dark sometimes? That is when the anger of the goddess of the sea is roused. Then she would destroy everything. At other times she would give her children everything. There is gold in the sea, child, gold" (p. 8). Chakki highlights the value of sexual purity for women in the fishermen's community. "Purity is the great thing, child. Purity. The strength and the wealth of the fishermen lie in the purity of his wife... My child, you must not be the cause of the ruin of the seafront" (p. 9). Chakki wants to forestall the possible danger to the fishermen's community by the juvenile fallibility of Karuthamma.

After being slowly indoctrinated with the philosophy of the community by her mother, Karuthamma begins to think about Pareekutti's identity and learns by herself that Pareekutti does not belong to the fishermen's community and that he is a Muslim. In the patriarchal community of the fishermen, the so-called love, especially inter-caste love is not sanctioned at all. It is only the arranged marriage, which is socially approved. But in the novel love as well as caste is problematized by the novelist. Though precautioned by her mother, Karuthamma is not in a position to take any firm decision about Pareekutti, as she happens to be mentally immature. The amorous feeling that is stirred in her heart has been growing more and more powerful as days go by. Her emotion overrides her thought. That is the reason why she yields to her instinct and follows Pareekutti stealthily at the opportune times. One night she happens to hear Pareekutti's singing at night and feels an irresistible urge to go out of her hut and meet him. Initially she tries to control herself by plugging her ears with her fingers, but the song cannot be shut out. While she is undergoing the inner dilemma, she overhears theP. conversation of her parents, especially her mother's premonition about her, "Some Moslem boy will get your daughter into trouble. That's what is going to happen" (p. 11). The parents think loudly of selecting a suitable groom for her and arrange her marriage at the earliest. Karuthamma knows that the Muslim boy has already got her into trouble.

Next morning Karuthamma's father gently reminds her of her mother's warning and asks her, "My child, be on your guard" (p. 14). Being advised and alerted by her parents, Karuthamma decides to tell Pareekutti that "He must not stare at her breasts the way he did. And one more thing. He must not sing in her vicinity" (p. 14). Next time when Pareekutti comes to her hut, Karuthamma puzzles him by asking him if he is a Muslim. When he asks her if she cares for him, she replies that "I shall care for you - always" (p. 18). Thus the love affair between Karuthamma and Pareekutti continues in spite of all kinds of hindrances.

Ironically enough, the emotional life is intertwined with economic life in the novel. Pareekutti, for example, has gifted a big quantity of dry fish to Chemban Kunju. Obviously Pareekutti has an ulterior motive behind this act. As he is secretly in love with Karuthamma, he wants to earn the sympathy of Karuthamma's parents. Chemban Kunju, because of his poverty and struggle for survival cannot understand the sexual significance of the gift. Since Pareekutti is in a position to lend some money to people, Chemban Kunju thinks of borrowing some money from him so that he may be able to buy a boat and a net of his own. But Karuthamma does not take her father for borrowing the money from Pareekutti as she thinks that he may cheat the poor boy by not repaying it at all. When she articulates her doubt, her mother scolds her for considering her father to be a 'thief'. She asks Karuthamma, "What is that Moslem boy to you? Why does all this hurt you so much?" (p. 20) As a woman Chakki can understand the secret feelings of her daughter and expresses her premonition, "It seems as if you are going to ruin the seafront" (20). Like any responsible mother, Chakki wants to prevent the possible emotional entanglement between her daughter and the Moslem boy. But Karuthamma does not like her secret lover to be cheated by her parents. Compelled by the economic necessity, Chemban Kunju borrows some money from Pareekutti and begins to search for a boat and a net.

When the neighbours and companions of Chemban Kunju come to know about his plan to buy a boat and a net, they begin to guess as to how he might have earned so much money. Some of them begin to build myths about him, "Some said that he had got bars of gold from the depths of the sea; that one day he found a piece of black rock, which had been washed into the seashore and it turned out to be a bar of gold. Others said that his good fortune was due to his foresight. But that was hard to believe. Every one of them worked as hard as he did, and they made no more than enough to live. How could he have saved so much?" (p. 24) The fishermen's initial puzzlement gives way to jealousy. Because of jealousy, the fishermen revoke the norms of the community according to which there are four castes of fishermen —Arayan, Valakkaran, Mukkuvan and Marakkan. They know that among these four castes, only a Valakkaram is to be permitted by the Headman to buy a boat and a net. They feel that since Chemban Kunju belongs to the Mukkuvan caste, he has no right to buy a boat and a net. The ethnic community of the fishermen of Kerala, like the larger Hindu society, is divided into castes, which are based upon professional specialization and indirectly contributing to the complementarity of division of labour. The other fishermen meet the headman of the community and bring to his notice Chemban Kunju's wrong prioritization in buying a boat and a net without his permission and not arranging the marriage of a nubile daughter. "Ramanmuppan and Ayyakunju, the two elders of the seafront and two others, as the representatives of the community, went to see the headman. They took with them the usual tributes. They wanted to place before him a matter that was affecting the whole seafront.

Chemban Kunju has a grown-up daughter. He has not given her away in marriage. She is a grown girl gadding about the seafront. That was the main complaint" (p. 33). Ayyankunju draws the Headman's attention to Chemban Kunju's violation of the norms of the community and anachronous action, "While that girl is wandering about single on the seafront, Chemban Kunju has gone away looking for a boat and a net for himself" (p. 33). The wants to assert his authority in spite of the changing time.

Chemban Kunju buys the boat from the celebrated Vaalakkaran Kandakoran of Pallikunnath. It was a famous boat in its time; Kandakoran has sold it to Chemban Kunju as he has fallen on bad days due to his extravagance. Achakunju opines that "The glory of Pallikunnath has come to Chemban Kunju along with this boat" (p. 38). But when Chemban Kunju returns home happily after buying the boat, he is depressed to hear the gossip of the fishermen about his negligence of his daughter's marriage. Chemban Kunju attributes all this gossip and slander to envy. Once again he borrows some thirty rupees from Pareekutti to meet the expenses.

In order to silence the gossip mill of the seafront, Chemban Kunju wants to fulfil the formality of seeking the headman's permission to buy a boat and a net. "Next morning Chemban Kunju went to see the Headman of the seafront. The headman was very angry at first, but he soon cooled down. He got Chemban Kunju to agree that his daughter would be given away in marriage as early as possible. Chemban Kunju would also take to the headman a share of the day's catch. Chemban Kunju complained of the jealousy of the fishermen of the village. The Headman assured him that he would see to it" (p. 41).

After seeking the permission of the headman, Chemban Kunju feels the financial pinch again. He requires another five hundred rupees to buy the accessories and launch the boat. Again he sends his wife to borrow the money from Pareekutti. Luckily Pareekutti has some money with him as he has sold some dry fish the previous night. He, therefore, lends the money to Chakki, as he knows their predicament.

While the economic problem of Chemban Kunju is solved for the time being, the love between Karuthamma and Pareekutti has been growing stronger. When Pareekutti happens to meet Karuthamma, she experiences thrill, shyness and nervousness simultaneously. By now she has been able to understand that she loves him, but yet cannot articulate it. "She wanted, in fact, to tell him so much, to ask so many questions. She even wanted to ask him if she could be converted to his religion. She stood there in the shadow of the boat on the seashore. He could not take his eyes off her heaving breasts. And she did not ask him not to stare at her" (p. 43). Karuthamma feels a new sensation of love for him, but cannot express it voluntarily. It is only when Pareekutti asks her, "Karuthamma, do you love me?" she answers "Yes". When he asks her further, "And you love only me?" she answers, "Yes, only you" (p. 44). Karuthamma feels shocked by her recognition of her inner feelings. "Her own voice shook her like the sound of thunder as she regained her consciousness and realized the full force of what she had said. She looked Pareekutti in the face. Their eyes met. They had said everything that had to be said. They had opened their hearts to each other" (p. 44).

Chemban Kunju is very happy to launch his new boat and seems to enjoy the grace of the sea-goddess. Both husband and wife feel that their economic problem is solved forever. Chakki expresses her sense of gratitude to Pareekutti when she happens to meet him, "It was because of you that the boat was launched today. But for you, it couldn't have happened" (p. 48). She promises to repay his loan after the *chakara* season is over. Pareekutti innocently replies that he does not want the money back as he has given it to them on Karuthamma's request. Chakki feels angry at this suggestion by Pareekutti and wants to return his money compulsorily. She does not want to be obligated to him and use her daughter as bait. She understands the sensitiveness of the issue, as she knows the philosophy of her community too well. "Chakki asked a little angrily, 'Why should you give money to Karuthamma? What is she to you?' She continued, her voice growing louder, 'No, that won't do. We don't want anything like that. You must take back the money.' Pareekutti realized that Chakki was serious. He said nothing. Chakki said, like a mother giving him good advice, 'My son, we are of the fisherman's caste. You don't belong to our community. You and Karuthamma played together as children on our seashore. That was long ago. We shall give her in marriage to a good fisherman. And you should marry a good girl of your own community" (p. 49).

The new boat has brought good luck to Chemban Kunju. On the first day itself Chemban Kunju is able to collect a big quantity of sardines. The good luck and success has already changed Chemban Kunju's behaviour without his knowing it. When he returns to the shore many traders and children have already gathered there. "Chemban Kunju looked as if he knew none of them" (p. 53). When Pareekutti asks Chemban Kunju, "Will you trade the fish with me?" Chemban Kunju asks him callously, "Have you the money? I must have cash down" (p. 54). Far from showing any sense of gratitude towards Pareekutti, Chemban Kunju sells the fish to another trader, Khadar Muthalali. Pareekutti swallows the insult and keeps quiet helplessly. Chakki "had seen the transformation that had come over Chemban Kunju" (p. 54). Chakki says, "When he saw the fish, he was transformed into the devil himself" (p. 54). The success in Chemban Kunju's life has given him a new strength and confidence. He has become arrogant without knowing it. In his arrogance he even pushes his own youngest daughter Panchami, who goes near the boat to gather some *uppa* . . . Luck and success have brought a dramatic change in his attitude and behaviour. On the contrary Pareekutti has fallen on bad days. "Pareekutti's curing yard almost shut down. He as not getting any work to speak of. He had no money. His father Abdullah Muthalali came and blamed him for his state of affairs. He said that Pareekutti had given away all his money to a fisherwoman on the seashore. Karuthamma overheard the accusation" (p. 57).

After achieving some success in his profession, Chemban Kunju develops a new concept of living. "Then Chemban Kunju began even more grandiose plans! He must have two boats and nets. He must have land and a house. He must have money in his hands" (p. 57). One day he wants to retire and lead a relaxed life. "And then should one work all one's life? Like Pallikunnath, one must retire and enjoy oneself" (p. 57). He wants his wife to be smart and well preserved like Pappikunju, wife of Kandakoran. He wants to kiss and embrace his wife as Kandakoran does. He wants to have some land and a home and enjoy life like young people. He improves the material condition of his life by buying a few brass pots and pans, even bits of gold and a bedstead. Chemban Kunju is thus drunk with success and money. The other fishermen and fisherwomen, who are on the brink of starvation flock to Chemban Kunju's house to borrow some money from him. For example, Nallapennu sells her brass tumblers to Chakki for a rupee. Laxmi and Kalikunju also go to her for pledging or selling their tidbits. Like women, men are also hard pressed for money. Ramankunju borrows a hundred and fifty rupees from Chemban Kunju by mortgaging his boat to the latter.

While Chemban Kunju's stars are on the ascendant, Pareekutti's are on the descendant. Having lost all his money, he does not know how to manage his day-to-day living. He is advised by his father to close down his courtyard and take up some other work elsewhere. But Pareekutti expresses his inability to take up any other job. That is the reason why he is not prepared for the *chakara* season. Karuthamma feels inwardly anxious about her father's willingness to repay the loan to Pareekutti.

Nowadays Chemban Kunju has been quite lucky, as he is able to collect a large quantity of fish, especially *Chemmeen*. Once Chemban Kunju participates in a rowing competition. But he is defeated in it by a young man called Palani. In spite of the mild defeat at the hands of the young man, Chemban Kunju likes him. He enquires about Palani's family background and learns that he is a forlorn. He thinks that

Palani is a suitable bridegroom for his daughter. He therefore, invites Palani to his home for lunch. When Chakki broaches the subject of marriage, Palani agrees to marry Karuthamma. Although initially Karuthamma hesitates to marry Palani, finally she yields to the parental pressure and consents to marry the forlorn boy. Her parents have not bothered to ascertain Palani's caste. Palani refuses to take any dowry from his parents-in-law. Although Karuthamma is now betrothed to Palani, she loves Pareekutti secretly. "A fishergirl, who loved someone outside her caste, who, however hard she tried to forget him, found herself loving him more" (p. 91). Her mother and neighbours try their best to indoctrinate the philosophy of the community supported by some mythical stories. They draw her attention to the supreme importance of chastity in a woman's life. They tell her, "By their tradition a girl was not entrusted to a man. It was the other way round. A man was entrusted to a woman" (p. 92). The neighbours like Kalikunju and Kunjipennu advise her to save the life of her husband by not allowing her heart to be swayed. They remind her that the daughters of the sea must guard those old traditions. Thus all of them reiterate the highest sanctity and importance attached to feminine chastity by the community. Woman's happiness lies in conforming to the norms of the community. In spite of being indoctrinated with the philosophy of the community, Karuthamma, suffering from the pangs of separation, sneaks out of her hut and meets Pareekutti for the last time. She expresses her secret love for him and says goodbye to him.`

On the day of wedding many problems crop up unexpectedly. Chemban Kunju has made arrangements for a moderate wedding, as he cannot afford to do an elaborate one. The first problem created by Chemban Kunju's neighbours is that the bridegroom has not brought any women in his party. Secondly there is a quarrel between the two parties about the marriage fee. The Headman asks Palani to submit seventy-five rupees as marriage fee. But Palani cannot afford to pay that much. After a lot of higgle-haggling Palani gives seventy-five rupees to the Headman. Meanwhile another unpleasant thing happens. When Pappu, belonging to Palani's party, casts aspersion on the bride's character, Chakki grows apprehensive and falls unconscious repeatedly through the wedding. "The bride was brought to the pandal. The elders pointed out the procedure. The *tali* was tied and the bridal cloth given away. Chemban Kunju took Palani's hands and placed them in Karuthamma's. When he took Karuthamma's hands, Chemban Kunju felt them stiffen slightly. Did she draw back her hand? And it seemed as if she did not hold Palani's hands, as if they merely rested on hers. Like a machine, Karuthamma did mechanically all she was told" (p. 104). The novelist recreates the cultural picture of the wedding in the fishermen's community of Kerala. The lack of knowledge of the caste-identity of the bridegroom creates a further problem to Karuthamma's parents. "When the time came for the feast, there was more trouble. Because of Palani's caste, some women went home without eating. Pappu, who had created all the trouble also left" (p. 104). The wedding takes place through a number of hurdles created by the violation of the normal expectations of the community.

After the wedding is over, a greater problem crops up. Palani wants to take his wife to his place Trikunnapuzha according to their custom. Chemban Kunju asks Palani to wait until Chakki recovers from illness. But Palani insists on taking away his wife. When Karuthamma's opinion is sought, she expresses her unwillingness to go. But when taunted by the mother about her secret love for Pareekutti, she decides to go away with her husband. But Chemban Kunju, who is ignorant about his daughter's love affair, mistakes her readiness to go for her arrogance and disobedience. He grows very angry with his daughter and son-in-law. He behaves in an irrational manner. "Karuthamma prostrated herself before Chemban Kunju and touched his feet. He withdrew his feet and turned away. She lay like that for a while and then got up. Her mother gave her blessings. She advised her to remember everything she had told her. When Palani said goodbye to him, Chemban Kunju didn't speak. Chemban Kunju was not the helpless Chemban

Kunju any more. He wasn't crying. His face was red and swollen. He was transformed into a man of rage" (p. 110). After Karuthamma goes to Palani's village, Chemban Kunju mutters between clenched teeth, "She is not my daughter any longer" (p. 110). Chemban Kunju's behaviour appears to be very impulsive. He should have understood the problems of a newly married daughter and son-in-law instead of worrying about his own family. The sudden transformation of Chemban Kunju from an affectionate father into an angry one is not appreciable at all.

A new phase begins in Karuthamma's life. Now she is the mistress of a house. She improves the bachelor's kitchen into a family kitchen. The men and women of Trikunnapuzha look at her as though she is a mysterious figure nursing a great secret. Some women indulge in gossip about her. She remembers her parents. In spite of her secret love for Pareekutti, she tries to start a new life with her husband. They consummate their love. Karuthamma experiences the ecstasy of love, but yet Karuthamma feels that sex is "something unclean, without morals or decency" (p. 119). She exchanges her confidences with her husband, decides to be an obedient wife and conscious of her responsibilities. Palani is proud of being a son of the sea and offers security to Karuthamma.

Palani is a hard worker and an extravagant man. When Karuthamma warns him against his extravagance, he rationalizes his habit by saying, "A fisherman cannot save. This is because he makes his money at the cost of millions of lives. He makes his money by cheating and catching innocent beings moving freely in the sea" (p. 128). As a few days go by, Palani hears public rumour about Karuthamma's bad character and enquires her about it without suspecting her character. Karuthamma, therefore, promises him that "I - I shall never bring disgrace to your seacoast" (p. 130). Palani feels quite secure due to the wifely promise and attends to his daily work at the sea. But Karuthamma suffers from inner contradictions. In spite of her decision to be an obedient wife of Palani, she cannot forget her lover. She dreams about

Pareekutti and remembers him in her privacy. Whereas the inner feelings of love haunt her secretly, the gossip about the same grows widespread on the seafront. The sweetness of the memory of love is countered by the bitterness of the public gossip about her pre-marital love affair.

After the departure of Karuthamma to her husband's home, many unexpected events happen at her parents' home. Chakki has been bed-ridden since the daughter's marriage. Chemban Kunju refuses to invite his daughter and son-in-law according to the custom. Similarly the son-in-law also refuses to send his wife to her parents' house. Thus both father-in-law and son-in-law are distanced from each other due to their egoism and prestige. As Chakki is seriously ill, Pareekutti meets her out of courtesy. Chakki is very weak and says crying; "I am dying Muthalali" (p. 136). She complains that her husband is not willing to fetch Karuthamma to see her. She promises to return his money as early as possible. She clasps Pareekutti's hands and says, "You are my son, Pareekutti" (p. 137) Her intention is to make Pareekutti have brotherly feelings rather than amorous feelings towards Karuthamma. She makes it explicit, "My son, you must marry a nice girl, have children and prosper in your trade. You must not trouble Karuthamma any longer. She is married. You are now her brother. As my son you must accept her as your sister" (p. 137). Pareekutti is deeply touched by her advice. She requests him further that if Karuthamma cannot come to her (Chakki) before her death, he should inform Karuthamma that she now has a brother. Pareekutti gives his consent rather half-heartedly.

Chemban Kunju has fallen on bad days as his bad-luck has crept in. Once he has an accident on the sea. He feels he has lost his vigour and become a defeated man. Chakki, who is on her deathbed asks Chemban Kunju to "Marry someone else" (p. 140). When Chakki dies, Chemban Kunju is not willing to invite Karuthamma for her mother's funeral. But Pareekutti, who remembers Chakki's request, goes to Trikunnapuzha voluntarily to convey the news of death to Karuthamma. But Karuthamma refuses to open the door and talk with him for fear of a scandal. Pareekutti assures her, "I am your brother . . . Yes, sister. I am your brother" (p. 144). When she opens the door, he breaks the news, "Karuthamma, Chakki is dead" (p. 144). Shocked by the news, Karuthamma cries and wails. By the time the neighbours arrive Pareekutti has gone.

When Karuthamma tells her husband on his return home about the death of her mother and expresses her desire to go to the funeral, Palani refuses to take her there. He finds fault with the violation of the custom of the fishermen's community, "Was that boy sent here by your father? They could not get a fisherman for this in your village?" (p. 145) No amount of Karuthamma's appeal changes his hardness of heart. "She fell at his feet, clasped his feet and cried. He stood there like a statue" (p. 145). Palani is haunted by suspicion about his wife's love affair with Pareekutti and therefore, asks her for clarification. Karuthamma confesses boldly that Pareekutti was her childhood friend but is now her brother. She promises her husband that she would be a good wife. "She gave her word that she would live on that seashore for the rest of her life as became a good fisherwoman" (p. 148).

The scandal of Karuthamma's love affair with Pareekutti has circulated to Trikunnapuzha very fast. When Palani hears it through his friends he feels depressed. Karuthamma also has confessed about her 'friendship' with the Muslim boy. "Even if Palani believed all Karuthamma told him, the story was still a blot on their married life. Palani became morose and depressed" (p. 149). Palani is in a dilemma now. He can neither abandon her nor love her whole-heartedly. His love for her begins to wane gradually. "...He couldn't kiss her with passion any more. He could not embrace her warmly. Her feelings for him strengthened by her tears, she would moan about all sorts of things. She would cling to him, afraid of losing him, not knowing how to regain his confidence. But she felt that her grip on him was slipping. She could only ask him whether he loved her. Perhaps she had forfeited even the right to ask that" (p. 150). Thus both of them suffer for their own reasons. Whereas Palani suffers from suspicion about his wife's fidelity, Karuthamma suffers from a sense of fear of losing him. It because of this fear that she wants to please him specially by hawking fish in the lanes of the village. When the other hawkers feel that Karuthamma has stolen their customers they try to blackmail her by gossiping about her. One of the fisherwomen vents out her jealousy by complaining that "She gets good trade. In all the households the men-folk trade with her. She is such a flirt" (p. 152). The gossip about Karuthamma's so called bad character has reached the ears of Kunjan Valakkaran on whose boat Palani has been working. The superstitious belief of the community in the evil effects of a bad wife is expressed in Valakkaran's suspicion and fear. "Stories about Karuthamma reached his ears too. What a misfortune! The husband of a bad woman was working on his boat. He had no peace of mind until the boat came on shore everyday. Because Palani was on that boat there was danger that it might be smashed into smithereens. The boat might get caught in a current and be dragged into the bottom of the ocean. Anything might happen" (p. 154) Under the effect of such superstitious fear Valakkaran consults his colleagues confidentially and hits upon a plan. The next morning all of them leave the shore before Palani could join them. Palani feels disconcerted by this deliberate act of Valakkaran. When he asks Valakkaran about the reason for his act and tries to defend the goodness of his wife, Valakkaran refers to the public gossip about Palani's wife, which cannot be ignored. Palani feels crestfallen by the answer.

In spite of the public gossip about his wife, Palani forgives his wife, who promises to lead a life of a good fisherwoman. She has been pregnant now. In course of time she gives birth to a baby girl. Karuthamma decides to bring up the baby with great care never allowing her to become another Karuthamma. The birth of a baby gives a new meaning to their life. "The arrival of the baby gave their life a new meaning. Now they both lived for still another human. As far as Palani was concerned, the baby was meant for his perpetual happiness. When he went fishing, the waters of the sea reminded him of the eyes of that little angel. Then he would want to return home" (p. 165). Taking Valakkaran's insult of him as a challenge Palani decides to be 'a son of the sea,' buys a boat and a net and continues his daily adventure on the sea. When Karuthamma wants to go to Nirkunnam to see her younger sister Panchami, Palani taunts her that she is eager to see Pareekutti. Hence Karuthamma drops the idea of going to Nirkunnam. The shadow of her past love still darkens her life.

Meanwhile drastic changes have happened in Chemban Kunju's life at Nirkunnam. After the death of his wife, he felt as though he 'had lost his right arm" (p. 168). By now he had become a tired man. Compelled by the domestic necessity as well as by Achakunju's suggestion, Chemban Kunju marries another woman namely Pappikunju, the widow of Pallikunnath Kandakoran Valakkaran. Though Pappikunju has lost her earlier beauty and glamour, she is still an attractive woman. Unfortunately she has brought a liability with her i.e. her son Gangadharan by her former marriage. The arrival of the stepmother creates an emotional problem for Panchami. She dislikes her stepmother. Although Chemban Kunju had admired Pappikunju in the past as the wife of another man, now he cannot love her deeply. She has lost her colour and radiance. Thus their coming together happens to be rather mechanical. ". . . There was no warmth in their kisses. Their embraces were not ardent . . . The laughter was a little forced in that house. The fun was not spontaneous" (p. 171). Chemban Kunju remembers the late Chakki and realizes her importance retrospectively. He also senses the clash of personalities at home. For example Panchami hates her stepmother Pappikunju and her son Gangadharan. She mocks at Pappikunju and is beaten by her father for that. This event leads to a quarrel between Nallapennu, the neighbour and Pappikunju. Nallapennu highlights the mistakes of both

Chemban Kunju and Pappikunju. Pappikunju, who is humiliated as never before in her life, indulges in self-pity and desperately taunts about Karuthamma's so called immoral behaviour acting as a model for Panchami, "She is the same. Like her elder sister, she, too, will find a boy like Pareekutti and gad about the seafront" (p. 176). Chemban Kunju has lost his eldest daughter, but he does not want to lose his younger daughter also. So far he did not know anything about Karuthamma's love affair, as Chakki had managed to keep it a secret. But Pappikunju's public reference to Pareekutti gives Chemban Kunju a belated knowledge of his eldest daughter's secret. "Had Karuthamma loved a Muslim boy? Suddenly the story was clear to Chemban Kunju. He now understands Karuthamma's anxiety to return Pareekutti's money! She - she - was Chakki a partner to it too? That was all he wanted to know now" (p. 176). He grows mad with anger, drags Panchami away from Nallapennu's beats her and asks her, "Say you won't go with a Moslem!" (p. 177) Panchami, afraid of the thrashing promises, "No, I won't go with a Moslem, Father" (p. 177). In his anger Chemban Kunju goes to the grave of Chakki at night and starts digging the place. "Perhaps he wanted to ask her himself" (p. 177).

Chemban Kunju has fallen on bad days now. He is a beaten man. Both the boats and nets of his are so damaged that they cannot be used for fishing. As Chemban Kunju has no money he worries about it deeply. Pappikunju suggests to her husband to borrow some money from Ouseph. Accordingly Chemban Kunju borrows Rs. 795 from Ouseph by mortgaging his boats and nets to him. He keeps the money in the safe. In the meantime Pappikunju has her private problem to solve. Her son from the previous marriage, Gangadharan has not been getting on well with the stepfather and stepsister. He, therefore, wants to go away from there to take care of himself. He asks his mother for some money. But Pappikunju does not have any money with her. She, therefore, steals Rs. 200 from her husband's safe and gives it to Gangadharan and sends him away. But Panchami, who has noticed the theft, carries tales to her father. Exasperated by this piece of information, Chemban Kunju drives Pappikunju out of his house. Pappikunju wanders helplessly on the seashore. When this matter is brought to the notice of the Headman, he arrives at Chemban Kunju's house and charges him of irregular activities and ill treatment of his wife. But Chemban Kunju defies and insults the headman and the community by lying that Pappikunju is not his wife but only a housekeeper. Chemban Kunju has become desperate because of all the unpleasant events that have happened in his life. Now he is sure of losing his boats and nets to Ouseph. Besides, his retrospective knowledge of Pareekutti's love affair with Karuthamma has driven him mad with anger. When he happens to meet Pareekutti face to face, he asks him, "How much do I owe you?" He shouts at Pareekutti, "You gave the money with an eye on my daughter, didn't you? Do you realize the harm you have done . . . You don't realize it. How would you realize it? You are the devil himself . . . You broke up a family. Ruined it. You have ruined my life too. Do you realize how many people you have ruined? My Karuthamma, who ran about this beach like a carefree bird – you ruined her" (pp. 192-3). Pareekutti cannot deny the charges. Chemban Kunju returns rs.595/- to Pareekutti. Pareekutti accepts the money rather mechanically, as he has no courage to refuse to accept it. Then suddenly hears a terrible laughter ofChemban Kunju, which is like the laughter of death.

In the meantime Panchami has absconded from home and gone to Karuthamma's at Trikunnapuzha. Palani is not happy to see Panchami and remember the unpleasant events of the past – like his encounter with his father-in-law. He goes to the sea. In his absence both the sisters exchange news about their households. Panchami tells her about mother's death, father's second marriage with Pappikunju, Pappikunju's slandering about Karuthamma's love affair with the Muslim boy, father's insanity etc. Then Panchami casually refers to Pareekutti's plight, "He has nothing left. He is starving.. And he wanders about on the shore. One would think he is mad. Such a shame" (p. 200). Panchami's reference to Pareekutti awakens her latent memory about him. She, therefore, asks Panchami, "Does he see you sometimes?" and "Would he then ask for news of me?" (p. 200) When the two sisters are talking privately about several things, including Pareekutti, Palani happens to have returned home and overheard their talk. His sexual jealousy is whipped up in him. He, therefore, enters the house and taunts them. "And suddenly they heard a voice which seemed to come from nowhere, a voice distorted with pain and anger and contempt. 'Oh, No. Panchami, he would ask for news of Karuthamma.' Palani stood before them. Panchami and Karuthamma jumped up. Karuthamma's secret was out" (p. 200). Palani vents out his sexual jealousy and anger especially because he has suffered in his life on account of public gossip about his wife's pre-marital love affair.

The repeated reminders of her love affair with Pareekutti drive her desperate and whip up her sense of identity. So far she has tried to conform to the ideals of the patriarchal society of fishermen and rectify her bygone mistake. But now she grows desperately courageous. "Karuthamma suddenly had a new awareness of life. All her values changed with a new indefinable logic. Until now she had been afraid of life. She was afraid of everybody and everything. She had no will of her own. And that was because she wanted to cling to life. When her secret was out, there was nothing left to hide nothing to be afraid of. The urge for security disappeared. And she was not alone in her insecurity. She had Panchami with her" (p. 201). When her husband asks her, "Did you love him?" she answers boldly; "Yes I loved him" (p. 202). Palani is disarmed by her frank confession and does not know what to do about it. The next morning he goes to the sea as usual. Karuthamma and Panchami console each other.

Karuthamma's memory of Pareekutti being awakened, she begins to brood about him. Obviously, she has been violating the norms of the fishermen's community. Far from being a mentally chaste wife, she has become an adulteress thereby endangering the life of her husband on the sea. "Her husband had gone out to sea alone. He was fishing on the deep sea. At that time, like the first fisherman of them all, she should be praying for him. Instead she was thinking of Pareekutti" (p. 205). Karuthamma has no regrets about her love for the Muslim boy. Her desire to meet Pareekutti grows intense and irresistible. Perhaps Pareekutti also has understood her heart telepathically. When she is obsessed with his memory at night, Pareekutti comes to his place as if miraculously and knocks at her door. Karuthamma opens the door and sees Pareekutti there actually. Far from being shy, guilty and hesitant, she meets him boldly and confidentially. "She had met him before alone in the darkness of night. If she would give a man whose life she had crushed at least a moment's happiness, shouldn't she grant it? She stood face to face looking at each other. The man that she had ruined stood before her. She knew for certain that he would love her forever. He would always understand her and forgive her. She could do anything to him. He would put up with anything from her. In those few seconds Karuthamma forgot all the sorrows of her life. She felt she had not been vanquished. She had the strength few had. She was under the protection of a strong man, life was secure. Palani would see to it that the world outside wouldn't dare touch her or hurt her. And she also had something else which gave her spirit sustenance. A man loved her as no man had loved a woman. Between these two, her life was full. Now the man who loved her stood in front of her. She entered his extended arms and her body became one with his. Their faces met" (p. 207). Pareekutti, who had promised Chakki that he was the brother of her daughter, has clean forgotten that. Now both of them experience the ecstasy of love. He strokes all over her body including her breasts where he used to stare. Karuthamma enters the semiconscious state of ecstasy. When Pareekutti asks her, "What am I to you?" she answers,

"Everything. My pot of gold" (p. 208). They stare at each other, whisper into each other's eyes and remain locked in embrace. Their final union testifies to the triumph of love over matrimonial bond; of elemental passion over conformity to patriarchal discipline; of Nature over Culture. Both the lovers experience almost the mystical ecstasy of love and remain oblivious of the mundane world around them. Just as Pareekutti has broken the promise that he had made to Chakki, Karuthamma has broken her promise to her husband of being a devoted and pure wife. Now both of them have thrown their promises to winds. The novelist has shown the extraordinary power of love in the man-woman relationship.

Karuthamma's violation of the law of sexual and emotional purity enjoined by the fishermen's community follows the logic of sin and retribution embodied in the myth of the sea-goddess Katalamma. According to the myth, the sea-goddess punishes the man whose wife does not remain loyal to him. The safety of man on the sea lies in the hands of his wife. The community's faith in the myth of Katalamma starts coming true. As Palani goes into the sea, his boat is surrounded by a few monsters. After some time of exploration Palani baits a really big shark and finds himself in a dilemma. He can neither pull the line nor allow it to drag his boat. As darkness has descended on the earth, he cannot find his direction. He tries hard to find his bearing by the stars. The shark has been pulling his boat with an unimaginable speed. Palani shouts, "Stop, stop there. Stop there before you drag me to the palace of the sea-goddess" (p. 209). By this time the shark dies, but unfortunately Palani's boat is caught in a whirlpool. All around him is a circular mountain of water. "The palace of the goddess of the sea was at the bottom of the deep sea. There the sea-goddess was enshrined. Palani had heard descriptions of that palace. He had to go there through a whirlpool, a whirlpool which made the whole sea churn around in circles, knocking at the gates of the sea-goddess' abode" (p. 209). Palani faces a multiple danger. Caught in the whirlpool in the overwhelming darkness, he has to brave the lightning, thunder, rain and storm simultaneously. The sea-goddess appears to be terribly angry with the poor fisherman. Finally Palani's boat capsizes. At that dangerous moment he shouts the name of Karuthamma. "Why did he cry out for Karuthamma? The guardian angel of the fisherman at sea is his wife at home. He was begging her to pray for his safety" (p. 211). But alas! His faith in her is falsified. Far from praying for the safety of her husband, Karuthamma is experiencing the ecstasy of love with her lover in the moonlight. Hence Palani is doomed completely. The fury of the storm increases. The storm and the thunder and the lightning join together in the destruction. The whole sea becomes a kind of cave. Finally the boat is caught in a whirlpool and sinks like a stone. Palani meets his watery death. The fisherman's Arundhati star, which is a symbol of chastity, lacks in lustre, thereby symbolizing Karuthamma's lack of chastity. The next day Panchami waits for Palani and Karuthamma on the seashore. The baby in her arms cries bitterly for her parents. But neither of them returns. "Two days later the bodies of a man and woman locked in embrace were washed on the shore. They were the bodies of Pareekutti and Karuthamma. And at the Cheriyazhikkil seafront a dead shark that had been baited was also cast on the shore" (p. 212). Katalamma, the sea-goddess has punished the violators of her law properly. She has punished Palani for his wife's betrayal of his faith. Likewise, she has punished the lovers like Karuthamma and Pareekutti also with death. Thus there is a balance between sin and retribution. The novelist suggests through this story how chastity is held in highest esteem by the fishermen's community and how it is corroborated by the natural events mythologized by the provincial community of Kerala. The novelist creates a very authentic picture of the ethnic society with their own beliefs, superstitions, manners, code of conduct and subcaste system. *Chemmeen* is undoubtedly a classic of modern India.

Works Cited

Pillai, T. Sivasankara, *Chemmeen*, Eighth Reprint, tr. Narayana Menon.

Bombay: Jaico Publishing House. (All the page numbers shown in the brackets refer to this edition.)

Notes

1. R.E. Asher, "Three Novelists of Kerala," T.W.Clark, (ed.) *The Novel in India: Its Birth and Development*, London: Allan & Unwin, 1970, p. 224.
2. Sujit Mukherjee, *Translation as Discovery*. Hyderabad: Orient Longman, 1994, p. 134.

22

Priscilla Hart's Search for Identities in *Riot*

Amrendra Sharma

> I do not so much care about what the woman *feels*. . . . I only care about what the woman *is* – what she IS – inhumanly, physiologically, materially . . .
>
> (In Aldous Huxley {ed} 1932, p. 198)

This article tries to access and dig into Priscilla Hart's character (the protagonist of *Riot* by Shashi Tharoor) from the perspective of existentialism and feminism. In other words, this paper tries to do an in-depth study of Priscilla Hart's doings and thinking with reference to the beliefs of existentialists and also feminists. The novel is full of instances and conversations which seem to mark her belief in these theories to a fairly significant degree. Nonetheless, she is different from several major woman characters of other novels in the sense that whereas other woman character has been found fighting for the self only, Priscilla Hart fights for masses too especially for those women and even men who suffer a lot because of their ignorance or compulsions of financial instability or a set of prevalent social beliefs. The decision to explore her character from this viewpoint has been taken as no critics or reviewers seem to have studied her extensively from these perspectives. Nobel Laureate Elie Wiesel (2001) hails Shashi Tharoor as 'a major voice in contemporary literature.' He has been appreciated for the freshness of ideas, stylistic novelties, and unrestrained experimentation in narrative technique in *Riot*. Besides, he has also been commended highly to bring in the rhetoric of different types of conflicts and also his great sense of nationalism. Nonetheless, it is somewhat surprising that critics or reviewers have not looked at Priscilla Hart's character from the perspective of her constant battle for gaining her identity as well as helping lots of other women who have not got any clear identities of their own even towards the end of 20th century. Anita Nair in one of the interviews with Bindu Menon (2001) affirms:

> There is a lot of strength in women that doesn't come out naturally, it has to be forced out of them – it could be circumstances or a change in lifestyle.

Here we may bring in some basic tenets of existentialism. Tanweer Akram (nd, 1) feels that existentialism highlights the risk, the voidness of human reality and admits that the human being is thrown into the world in which pain, frustration, sickness, contempt, malice and death dominates. The fundamental idea of this school of thought is the study of *being*. It stresses the fact that a human being has no essence if s/he does not think/work for her/his existence. S/He has liberty to choose and decide and, therefore, to make or mar herself/himself. In fact, if s/he allows herself/himself to be carried away by the dictates and necessity of the society, s/he is bound to suffer endlessly. Herein lies the difference between a *thing* and a *being*. Things are only what they are. But the human being is what s/he can be. S/He can add flavour and essence to her/his life in due course of time. The human being is free to chase and drive her/his dreams home. In addition, existentialists believe that a human being is free to do whatever he pleases. Here Akram (nd, 5) slightly disagrees with them as a human being's freedom is curtailed not only by the objective reality s/he encounters, but also by her/his own limitations. Taking this view as a crucial point, let us attempt to find if Priscilla Hart lives a totally authentic life pursuing her dreams and ambitions. Further, it may also be investigated if she strongly raises her voice for women's autonomy, liberty and rights and freedom as normally a libertarian (individualist) feminist does or as a radical feminist she often hammers for a social change by making them free from their previously determined narrow gender roles. It might also be interesting to discover if Priscilla Hart as a cultural feminist suggests to embrace women's ways in spite of their having biological and psychological differences from men.

Here it may not be out of place to define the beliefs and roles of a cultural, radical and libertarian (individualist) feminist as formulated by Kathy Henry (2007). Cultural feminists accept the biological and psychological differences between sexes, however they feel that the differences can be bridged to a great extent by embracing women's natural ways i.e. their ways of living and doing things. Libertarian (individualist) feminists promote women's rights, autonomy, liberty, interests and issues and therefore, naturally campaign on issues such as reproductive rights, violence within domestic partnership, discrimination and sexual violence. A radical feminist attempts to challenge patriarchy, stereotyping, sexual objectification and oppression. In fact, it is difficult to consider them as completely separate entities because at times they have been found to overlap too. To elaborate, some issues, like sexual violence are of common interest for both libertarian and radical feminists.

Priscilla is a 24-year-old American volunteer working for an NGO, 'Help-Us'. She is involved in developing awareness among women about population control.

She has come to India because of her father's job when she is only fifteen and has tasted the various realities of India, like the poor and abject condition of the lower class, the bazaars, the cinemas, the mosques and the temples. She has engaged herself in selfless services, such as reading for blind children and helping them living in orphanages.

She returns to India after nine years and starts working on a population control programme in Zalilgarh, a district in UP. She gets moved with the condition of Zalilgarh with broken and dusty roads, cow dung on side walks and rusted tin shades, walls full of betel leaves stains and poor people clad in dirty dhotis. All these make her task difficult as she is going to work in the midst of people who are not enlightened in a big way. She tries to wake up those ladies who have not woken up or who do not want to wake up on their own. She does not find anything changing as women are still so submissive that they cannot raise a question even for their welfare rather they submit to the demand of their menfolk and accept any number of pregnancies happily. In her scrapbook (on 5 December 1989), Priscilla, as a radical and individualist feminist, writes in a verse form:

> Here I have come to do a good. It's true:
> So simple a task in so complex a land.
> I wheel my bicycle into their habits,
> Tell them what's right, what can be done,
> And how to do it. They listen to me,
> So ignorant, so knowing, . . .
> They go back to their little huts,
> Roll out the chapattis for dinner, . . .
> Serve their men first, eat what is left.
> . . . and then submit unprotected
> To the heaving thrusts of their protectors,
> Abusers, masters. One more baby comes,
> To wallow in misery with the rest. (p. 15-16)

The task that she has undertaken is truly a difficult one. Rather than getting depressed, this idealistic and determined lady prays to God to give her strength and wisdom to change and make a difference to these poor and ignorant women. Her task is not so easy because religion, age-old traditions and the male's ego intervene in achieving her objective.

Further, she also accepts that these womenfolk are so talented, so knowing, yet so weak to stand up and fight against the prison house of their tradition and society in limiting their family and thus providing their children a quality life and preserving their health too. She tries to win their confidence by persuading them to stop undesirable children but she has to pay a price for this by suffering the wrath of Fatima Bi's husband who calls her a foreigner and threatens to kill her as she is thought to be responsible for the abortion of Fatima Bi's eighth child. She feels confused as to why they are after her life when she is trying to uplift their condition by showing the way of living with dignity and happiness. This comes up as a great conflict in any developing nation where normally one is not ready to take into account another's perspective, where one does not wants to change, where one does not wish to stand and ask questions regarding his/her better future. This could be perceived as a socio-cultural clash in constructing and performing individualistic identity.

As a radical feminist she questions the authenticity of patriarchal society where a woman still suffers domestic violence in spite of sacrificing a lot for her family:

> She (Fatima Bi) lives with her husband and seven kids in a two-room flat, cooks in the corner of one of the rooms on an open stove, . . . washes their clothes at a public tap, and suffers the demands and the blows of her husband, to judge by a visibly bruised cheek.
>
> Besides, still in this modern age, Ali, Fatima Bi's husband, keeps on shouting, "I decide how my wife conducts her life!" (p. 160). Nevertheless, Priscilla firmly believes, "it was his wife's right to have as much information as she needed to decide how to conduct her life" (p. 160).

Priscilla does not want to lose any chance in campaigning on issues of universal interests, like women's right to autonomy, pregnancy and education:

> I want to change the lives of these women, the choices they believe they have. I want to see them one day . . . standing around the well discussing their own lives and hopes and dreams . . . . I want to hear them not say, "My husband, he wants lots of children." But rather, "I will decide when I am ready for a child." I want them instead of planning to arrange their teenage daughter's marriage, to insiston sending her to high school. I want all this for them and that's why I am here (p. 170).

Related to the above-mentioned issues are issues of reproductive rights and a right to sound health. Priscilla very boldly tries to bring these rights home in Zalilgarh which is still a sleeping town unaware of any new thinking:

> I see myself as trying to make women aware of their reproductive rights, not just to control population but to give them a sense of their rights as a whole, their rights as women. Being forced to have babies is just one form of oppression, of subjugation by men. . . . I want to help these women understand that control of their bodies is a rights issue, it's health issue and if they can improve their health and assert their rights, they will have a real future, and they will give their daughters a real future. (p. 171)

The American version of the novel has been subtitled "A Love Story" as this is really a sensual, stormy, ill fated romance between Priscilla Hart, the American family planning counselor and V Lakshman (nicknamed Lucky), an older married government official posted as the District Magistrate. The two different titles of the same novel seem to echo a conflict between two diverse approaches in constructing and performing social identities of men and women in terms of their inter-personal relationship. Shashi Tharoor also expresses somewhat identical views in *The Hindu* on 16 September 2001:

> American readers looking for a love story will find

> a novel about the construction of identity, the nature of truth and the ownership of history; Indian readers expecting a novel about the dangers of communalism will discover a tale of another kind of passion.

In fact, the novel is superbly rich with a lot of magical descriptions of cross-cultural love and really deserves to earn Riot its subtitle as a love story, though a tragic one. This tragic love story makes Priscilla emerge as a robust, individualist feminist. Lakshman seems stuck in a loveless marriage though he is deeply attached to his daughter. Naturally, in spite of getting true love and a very high degree of physical satisfaction, he vacillates between sacrificing his career and family for an American girl. She considers even her first encounter with him a very romantic one:

> . . . there was something about his voice that reached out and drew me in, something that was both inviting and yet reassuring. It was a voice like a warm embrace, a voice that was seductive. (p. 19)

Though she is aware of the fact that he is already married and has a daughter, she falls in love with him and very soon starts enjoying all the moments spent with him. The novel is replete with lots of very detailed sensual encounters which Lakshman is also very fond of. He develops his interest to the extent of deserting his wife and leaving for the USA with Priscilla but the age-old tradition and his love for his daughter, for his country and for his job stop him from taking an extreme step of stepping out of marriage and start a completely new relationship publicly. Priscilla finds it difficult to accept Lakshman's decision in favour of his family and social convenience ignoring her deep love for and commitment to him and naturally as an libertarian (individualist) feminist she bursts out stressing the legitimacy of emotional love over physical love:

> I love you with all my heart and soul, but I don't want a relationship with a man who doesn't feel the same way as I do. I want a man who loves me an .

> a relationship where I can rely on the fact that he loves me. Not my body, not my embrace, ME. (p. 207)
>
> You're so good at understanding everyone else's claims on you - your family's, your daughter's, your job's. Do I have a claim on you, Lucky? Am a just a convenient outlet for your passion, your escape from humdrum reality? (p. 207)

Priscilla undertakes several existential issues, like the conflict between the existential need and social expectations. Lakshman, though deeply in love with Priscilla Hart, refuses to go with her as he finds it difficult to ignore his social and ethical values inculcated in him from his early childhood. Conversely, for Priscilla, her feeling of love is her whole existence. Naturally, she feels cheated and gives vent to her anger very strongly:

> I have given up the carefully circumscribed order of my life, with its assumptions, its compromises, its predictabilities. I've given up the sense a Brahmin strives all his life to attain, the sense of being anchored to the world. Loving you, I'm adrift. Everything around me is turbulence. I don't know whether I'll sail to a new and sunny paradise with you or crash foundering on the rocks. (p. 216)

Perhaps falling in love is a luxury for Lakshman, whereas Priscilla considers it as risking her whole life:

> You haven't taken a risk in this relationship. At all. But I have. It was my risk to take, to fall in love with a married man, and I did. I am crying as I write this. But I don't want you to feel sorry for me. I want your love, not your pity. (207)
>
> A woman who's available at your convenience, two evenings a week, you don't have to give up anything. Your work, your social life, your family, your official commitments. You have it all, including me.(pp. 214-15)

Here Priscilla appears to be negotiating for a reconstruction and performance of a new identity of Lakshman which needs to be fair and just in his mutual relationship with her even if it is at odds with his own socio-cultural milieu.

We also witness her helplessness in not approaching Lakshman whenever she feels like approaching him as he is a senior civil servant and therefore cannot express even her feelings as per her convenience:

> Do you know what it's like to have a man you can't speak to when you need him? To feel the ache of needing you and knowing you're beyond reach? To not be able to acknowledge you in public, not to go out openly together, not to be able to see you across a crowded room and know that we belong together. (p. 216)

To an existentialist, she may appear to be a weak character, as she lives in a predetermined world; she is not free to realize her goals, and to translate her dreams into realities. Existentialists observe that a human being is free to do whatever he pleases. But this is not true always. A human being, to a large extent, is the outcome of his/her own socio-cultural ethos. Her/His being in the world is something s/he had no choice or little choice over. In the case of Priscilla there are situations where she does not have any control – for instance, she falls in love with a senior and married bureaucrat as she has been interacting with him regularly on various issues related to her project in India.

If we take the other perspective of the story, Priscilla wants the man in spite of all odds, such as in spite of his married status and being a proud father of a daughter. All these details simply do not carry any meaning for her and she utters the following to Lakshman: 'I don't care about your background . . . I love you' (p. 89). In fact, several topics that are normally taken as taboos, like extramarital affairs etc in Indian culture, do not even cause Priscilla to raise her eyebrow. To illustrate, she perceives sex as a means of expressing love to the man she loves. So she is totally unfazed by the fact that she has already enjoyed several dates and sexual encounters with Lakshman.

Further, Priscilla questions the very foundation of the traditional Indian marriage system where the elders of the family map out and arrange the marriage of their grown-up adult children. She is unable to swallow this marriage as the lifetime commitment between a boy and a girl. She is more shocked to accept this kind of marriage in the case of Lakshman who is highly educated and quite liberal in his philosophy of life. Even Lakshman is not very happy with this kind of marriage, as he does not find an intellectual compatibility with his wife. He finds a great level of compatibility with Priscilla but he does not feel bold enough to come out of the niche of traditional marriage and declare to the whole world that she is a better, more fulfilling and satisfying match for him. In this situation, she finds herself just an instrument to keep him in good humour and mood without getting any mileage in his life. At times she feels pity on him and labels him as 'Mr Right in the wrong place at the wrong time' (p. 69). This highly significant comment reflects how the construction of social identities in inter-personal relationship is at odds in Indian and Western cultures. Naturally, he is helpless to challenge the marriage imposed upon him by society and this leads to the estrangement in their relationship, though she, as a radical feminist, highlights even a man's predicament in Indian setting:

> . . . I saw so much Lucky, a good man in bad marriage, someone capable of love who had no opportunity to love until I came along, a man who had not seen his own happiness fully until he met me. With me I think he realized for the first time that he hadn't truly known love in his life and that he could find happiness, loving and being loved happiness, of course, at a price. A price that in the end he was not prepared – with his upbringing, his sense of his

> responsibilities, his inability to escape from Indian society. (p. 241)

This also brings to the surface some of the so-called social taboos, like sex for discussion in a very bold way as sex also plays a vital role in bringing this civil servant closer to the foreign researcher. Geetha, Lakshman's wife, has a different attitude towards sex. She just takes it as a routine chore where she does not want to initiate or welcome it in any way; she just wants to remain a passive partner. Patil (2007, p. 83) also feels she (Geetha) is born to endure it rather than enjoy it. On the other hand, Priscilla enjoys every moment of it as sex is a great festivity and celebration for her. Therefore to achieve a heightened sense of pleasure, she initiates it, welcomes it and looks forward to every other step with a great expectation and fulfilment. Priscilla's these viewpoints about sex bring Lakshman closer to her but ultimately his social face wins over his personal and existential faces and he decides to end the relationship. All these details point to the fact that Indian characters have not been able to construct such identities which could give a front seat to the emotional aspect of inter-personal relationship rather than to a social institution, like marriage. Priscilla cannot swallow his decision to stick to the same loveless marriage:

> Here I am, on Independence Day, wanting to give up my independence for him, knowing he has to win his own independence first. I can't believe he's even hesitating to leave loveless marriage he hates for the woman he says he loves. (p. 199)

Priscilla is always lost because of his double standards and feels that perhaps it is a part of Indian culture. She finds even Holy Scripture supporting her point and sounds like a great radical feminist:

> Learned something interesting about the Hindu god, Rama the one all fuss is about these days. Seems that when he brought his wife back from Lanka and became king, the gossips in the kingdom were

> whispering that after so many months in Ravana's captivity, she could not possibly be chaste anymore. So to stop the tongues wagging, he subjugated her to *agni-pariksha,* a public ordeal by fire, to prove her innocent. She walked through unscathed. A certified pure woman. (p. 63)

She further continues:

> That stopped the gossip for a while, but before long the old rumours surfaced again. It was beginning to affect Rama's credibility as king. So, he spoke to her about it. What could she do? She willed the earth to open up, literally and swallowed her. That was the end of the gossip. Rama lost the woman he had warred to win back, but he ruled on as a wise and beloved king. . . . What the hell does this say about India? Appearances are more potent than truths. Loyalty is all one way from the woman to the man. And when society stacks up all the odds against a woman, she'd better not count on the man's support. She has no way out than to end her own life. (p. 63)

Thus, she is full of regret for having an affair with the civil servant: 'And I am in love with an Indian. I must be crazy.' (p. 63). Naturally, these observations speak volumes about women's status in India even towards the end of 20th century.

Related to the dichotomy of standards in Indian society is the dichotomy between the scientific facts and public opinion which is the result of the compulsions of socio-cultural ideologies. She is shocked to find that even now ordinary people believe that a lady is responsible for the birth of a girl or a boy not the gentleman. Besides, on occasions, her value is decided by the fact if she has been able to deliver a male child in the family. Priscilla brings forward Sundari's case. Sundari is rebuked often by her mother-in-law for not delivering a male child. Implicitly, a girl child is a curse and a boy is considered, more often, a boon. Sundari, who is brought to hospital with 75 per cent burns and in her feeble voice, narrates the circumstances leading to the severe burns. She could not bring the expected dowry from her parents. Besides, she is accused of carrying a female child in her womb. So the result is that her own husband and mother-in-law set her on fire. Through Sundari, Tharoor experiences the trauma and pangs of the evil of dowry. Kadambri calls it our major concern:

> That is the real issue, for women in India. Not population control, but violence against women, in our own homes. (p. 249)

Patil (2007, p. 100) appears justified in saying that his (Tharoor's) writing records a seismograph of pressures and in summing up, it may be observed that Priscilla Hart tries to assert as an existentialist and analyse social constructions of gender and sexuality and highlight gender inequality, gender politics, and power relations in great length. To achieve her objectives, she has been found to campaign on issues such as reproductive rights, domestic violence, discrimination, stereotyping and oppression of various types and degrees. Further, she often seems to cross-boundaries based on social class, culture and religion. So, supposedly, she appears a very robust feminist changing her tones between a radical and individualist (libertarian) feminist depending on the issues and situations. Finally, what sounds great about her feminism is her constantly stressing the fact that these deprived and less-privileged women have the right to enough information to make informed choices about their social and personal lives which could be seen as her plea for Indian women and also men to construct and perform new identities in new lights which are more democratic and fairer.

Works Cited

Akram, Tanweer (nd), "The Philosophy of Existentialism", Online. http://www.Columbia.edu/~ta63/exist.htm. p.1. Accessed on 19 November 2002.

Henry, Kathy, 2007, "What is Feminism", online. http://www.yoursdaily.com. p. 2. Accessed on 9 September 2008.

Huxley, Aldous (ed) (1932), *The Letters of D H Lawrence*, London: Heinemann. p 198.

Menon, Bindu. (2001), "Ladies Coupe was harder to Write: An Interview," Online. http://www.anitanair.net/pages/articles-lc-ht.htm. p. 1. Accessed on 21 October 2006.

Patil, Geeta, M. (2007), *Shashi Tharoor: Hs Vision and Art*, New Delhi: Creative Books.

Tharoor, Shashi. (2001) "The Shashi Tharoor Column : A departure fictionally", *The Hindu*, Sunday 6, September 2001. On line. http://wwwhinduonnet.com/thehindu/2001/09/16/stories/13160675.html . Acceessed on 19.11.2007.

Wiesel, Elie. (2001) 'Shashi Tharoor.' Online. http://www.emalayali.com/a6news.htm Accessed on 19.11.2007

The writer is indebted to Dr V.S. Thakur, Assistant Professor of English, Dhofar University, Salalah, Oman for his valuable suggestions in developing this article.

Contributors

Shyam Bihari Tiwar: Retired Reader and Head, Department of English, B.S. College, Lohardaga, Ranchi University (Jharkhand).

Amandeep Rana: Lecturer, P.G. Department of English, JC DAV College Dasuya Distt. Hoshiarpur, Punjab.

Prabhat Kumar Thakur: Lecturer in Engish, Ram Jaipal College, Chopra-841301.

Namrata Rathore Mahanta: Lecturer in English, Mahila Mahavidyalaya Banaras Hindu University Varansi.

Sadhana Chaturvedi: Reader, Dept. of English, D.A.V. College, Kanpur.

Veena Shukla: Lecturer, Dept. of English, Firoz Gandhi College, Rai Bareily.

P. K. Singh:- Reader, Dept. of English, Sakaldiha, P.G. College, Sakaldiha, Chandauli (U.P.).

Devesh Chand:-Research Scholar, Purvanchal University. U.P.

Tribhuwan Kumar: Research Scholar, Patna University.

Smita Ajgaonkar-Nayak: Dept. of English, Shivaji University, Kolhapur Maharastra.

Alka Saxena: Reader, Dept. of English D.A.V. College, Kanpur.

Punita Jha: Head, Dept. of English M.R.M. College, Darbhanga.

Arjun Kumar: Lecturer in English, Patna College, Patna.

Rajendrakumar B. Chaugule: Dept. of English, Kankavli College, Kankavli. Dist- Sindhudurg.

Prerana Sinha: New Delhi

C. P. Sharma: Reader, Dept. of English, B.R. Ambedkar College, University of Delhi.

Sadhya Saxena: Lecturer, Dept. of English, R.A.L. Govt. Girls P.G. College, Bareilly (U.P.)

Sudhir Kumar Arora: Dept. of English, Maharaja Harishchandra P. G. College, Moradabad (UP).

V. Sunitha: Assistant Professor, English, Sreenivasa Institute of Technology and Management Studies, Chittoor, Andhra Pradesh.

Basavaraj Naikar: Professor & Chairman, Department of English, Karnatak University, Dharwad.

Amrendra Sharma: Asst. Prof. of Linguistics, Dhofar University, Salalah, Oman.

Suchi Agrawal, Dept. of English Amity Noida (U.P.).

Index